IN THE BEGINNING
Secretary-General Trygve Lie and the
Establishment of the United Nations

Ellen J. Ravndal

First published in Great Britain in 2024 by

Bristol University Press
University of Bristol
1-9 Old Park Hill
Bristol
BS2 8BB
UK
t: +44 (0)117 374 6645
e: bup-info@bristol.ac.uk

Details of international sales and distribution partners are available at bristoluniversitypress.co.uk

© Bristol University Press 2024

British Library Cataloguing in Publication Data
A catalogue record for this book is available from the British Library

ISBN 978-1-5292-1043-9 hardcover
ISBN 978-1-5292-1179-5 paperback
ISBN 978-1-5292-1045-3 ePub
ISBN 978-1-5292-1044-6 ePdf

The right of Ellen J. Ravndal to be identified as author of this work has been asserted by her in accordance with the Copyright, Designs and Patents Act 1988.

All rights reserved: no part of this publication may be reproduced, stored in a retrieval system, or transmitted in any form or by any means, electronic, mechanical, photocopying, recording, or otherwise without the prior permission of Bristol University Press.

Every reasonable effort has been made to obtain permission to reproduce copyrighted material. If, however, anyone knows of an oversight, please contact the publisher.

The statements and opinions contained within this publication are solely those of the author and not of the University of Bristol or Bristol University Press. The University of Bristol and Bristol University Press disclaim responsibility for any injury to persons or property resulting from any material published in this publication.

Bristol University Press works to counter discrimination on grounds of gender, race, disability, age and sexuality.

Cover design: Hayes Design and Advertising
Front cover image: UN Photo/Albert Fox

For my parents

Contents

List of Photographs   vi
List of Abbreviations   vii
Acknowledgements   ix

Introduction   1

1   Setting the Stage: The Creation of the UN and Expectations for the Role of the UN Secretary-General   11
2   Establishing Precedents: The Iranian Crisis, UN Membership and the Greek Civil War, 1946   29
3   Urging Forceful Action: 'The Palestine Problem' and Management of Regional Conflicts, 1947–49   48
4   Building Bridges: The Cold War from Berlin to Korea, 1947–50   70
5   Advocating Global Interests: Trygve Lie's Peace Plan, 1950   88
6   Administering the International: The International Civil Service and the UN Secretariat, 1946–53   106

Conclusion   131

Appendix: UN Charter, Chapter XV: The Secretariat   143
Notes   145
References   171
Index   187

List of Photographs

1	Trygve Lie addresses the UN General Assembly after his election on 2 February 1946. Credit: UN Photo/Marcel Bolomey	65
2	On 25 March 1946 the Security Council convenes for its first meeting on US soil in the former gymnasium of Hunter College in New York on 25 March 1946. Credit: UN Photo	65
3	On 25 March 1947, Lie received a check from John D. Rockefeller III for the purchase of the site in New York where the UN permanent headquarters would be constructed. Credit: UN Photo	66
4	UN truce observers with children in Palestine, 1948. Credit: UN Photo	66
5	Ralph Bunche meets with Trygve Lie in New York in April 1949 after successfully concluding armistice talks between Israel and Egypt, Lebanon, and Transjordan. Credit: UN Photo/MB	67
6	Trygve Lie reads letters from the public in preparation for a radio broadcast in June 1950. Credit: UN Photo/MB	67
7	Trygve Lie's term in office is extended by the General Assembly on 1 November 1950. Credit: UN Photo	68
8	Trygve Lie being filmed by a UN film crew on 30 June 1951. Credit: UN Photo/MB	68
9	Trygve Lie demonstrates the earphones in one of the booths of the United Nations conference room to his grandson in March 1950. Credit: UN Photo	69
10	Trygve Lie welcomes his successor, Dag Hammarskjöld, on 9 April 1953. Credit: UN Photo	69

List of Abbreviations

ACC	UN Administrative Committee on Coordination
CCC	Andrew W. Cordier Collection, Columbia University
CCOHC	Columbia Center for Oral History Collection
ECOSOC	United Nations Economic and Social Council
FBI	US Federal Bureau of Investigation
FRUS	*Foreign Relations of the United States*
GAOR	*General Assembly Official Records*
IGO	intergovernmental organization
ILO	International Labour Organization
ITU	International Telecommunications Union
NAN	National Archives of Norway, Oslo
NARA	United States National Archive and Records Administration, College Park, Maryland
NATO	North Atlantic Treaty Organization
NLN	National Library of Norway, Oslo
P5	The five permanent members of the Security Council
PRC	People's Republic of China
R2P	'Responsibility to protect'
SCOR	*Security Council Official Records*
SRSGs	Special Representatives of the Secretary-General
TPL	Harry S. Truman Presidential Library, Independence, Missouri
UCB	The Brian Urquhart Collection of material on Ralph Bunche, UCLA
UKNA	United Kingdom National Archives, Kew Gardens, London
UN	United Nations
UNA	United Nations Archives and Records Management Section, New York
UNCIO	*Documents of the United Nations Conference of International Organization*
UNDHL	United Nations Dag Hammarskjöld Library, New York

UNEF	United Nations Emergency Force
UNISPAL	United Nations Information System on the Question of Palestine
UNSCOP	United Nations Special Committee on Palestine
UNTSO	United Nations Truce Supervision Organization
US	United States of America

Acknowledgements

This has been a long project and I am deeply grateful to everyone who has helped me, directly or indirectly, along the way. This book started out as my DPhil thesis at the University of Oxford. My supervisor Noa Schonmann has been a steadfast supporter from the start of the project. She helped to sharpen the argument and analysis, and also forced me to think critically about what the evidence could support. Kalypso Nicolaïdis kindly agreed to come on board as a second supervisor during my last year in Oxford. She provided invaluable advice on how to combine historical research with writing a thesis within the discipline of International Relations (IR), and forced me to think about the broader claims and implications of my research. Oxford provided an academically stimulating environment for the thesis, and I benefitted greatly from conversations with several other faculty members and fellow IR doctoral students. Thanks in particular to Louise Fawcett who served as the thesis' assessor at two internal evaluations and as an examiner at the end. Her perceptive questions and criticism helped shape the thesis and improve the project. Edward Newman provided invaluable criticism and advice when he served as the thesis' external examiner.

"Find your group and take the circus on the road," Noa told me when I attended my first international conference. I'm grateful to the group of scholars I've gotten to know over the years who share my interest in the UN secretary-general and questions of individuals and leadership in international organizations. Together we've attended panels at various conferences over the years, primarily at the Academic Council on the United Nations System (ACUNS) and the International Studies Association (ISA) annual conferences. Thanks to Ingvild Bode, Manuel Fröhlich, Kirsten Haack, Tana Johnson, Margaret Karns, Kent Kille, Alynna Lyon, and Bob Reinalda for your advice and feedback on my work and many interesting conversations.

After leaving Oxford, I was fortunate to join first the Department of Political Science at Lund University and then the Department of International Relations at the Australian National University (ANU), before I started my current position at the University of Stavanger. All three departments proved to be friendly and supportive environments where I was allowed freedom to develop my research interests. My colleagues at the ANU, in particular, deserve credit for pushing me to finally turn the thesis into a book. My heartfelt thanks to Mathew Davies and Wesley Widmaier who commented on the proposal, and Luke Glanville who provided comments and also helped me decide on the book's title.

I'm also indebted to Stephen Wenham at Bristol University Press for believing in the project and for being a very patient editor. Thanks also to the reviewers who helped to improve the manuscript during the review process.

During my time in Oxford, this project benefitted immensely from formal and informal conversations with my fellow IR doctoral students. It was also a stroke of good luck that I started at Oxford at the same time as Kate Millar, Julia Costa Lopez, James Hollway, and Mike Sampson. Maria Tanyag and Abidah Setyowati also started out as colleagues but became dear friends. I hope we'll soon be able to meet again, once this pandemic ends ...

Throughout the long process of research, writing, and revisions, searching for jobs, and moving to the other side of the world and then back again, my family has been a constant source of support and encouragement. As the book was nearing its end, Simon and his family very generously welcomed me in and reminded me that life is about so much more than work, writing, and deadlines. This book is dedicated to my parents, who have been there for me in every way that matters from the beginning.

Copyright acknowledgement

Parts of Chapter 3 were previously published as Ellen J. Ravndal (2016) '"The First Major Test": The UN Secretary-General and the Palestine Problem, 1947–9', *International History Review*, 38(1): 196–213 and are reproduced here by permission of Taylor and Francis.

Introduction

The founding moment of an intergovernmental organization (IGO) often concludes with a grand, symbolically significant ceremony where representatives of the founding member states sign the treaty one after the other. But what happens when this high-level event concludes? Once the cameras have turned off and the politicians head home, the task of setting up the new organization falls to its secretariat. In the beginning of an organization's life, its executive head and the first staff members can exert considerable influence on the future shape of the organization. During these first few years, when rules and expectations are fluid and new situations without former precedent, it is left to them to interpret what the founding treaty means and to determine how its goals can be put into practice. This book examines one prominent example of how IGO founding treaties move from paper to practice – the establishment of the United Nations (UN) during the tenure of its first secretary-general, Trygve Lie (1946–53).

The UN today occupies an important position in international affairs as the central arena for states to come together to try to solve global problems. The secretary-general plays a key part in these processes. Although the UN Charter merely describes the secretary-general as the 'chief *administrative* officer of the Organization',[1] today she[2] is widely regarded as the UN's chief diplomatic and *political* officer. Former secretary-general Kofi Annan wrote that 'for better or worse, the role of the Secretary-General has come to be seen as primarily political',[3] while the UN website describes the secretary-general as 'equal parts diplomat and advocate, civil servant and CEO'.[4] The secretary-general today plays important roles in the UN apparatus for peace and security. She can serve as a mediator and provide 'good offices' or act as a 'channel of communications' to help solve conflicts between states.[5] The secretary-general also performs important functions for the UN as an investigator who can establish fact-finding commissions and write reports, on her own initiative or at the request of the member states.[6]

Furthermore, the secretary-general occupies an important public role as an 'advocate' or 'norm entrepreneur' for global issues.[7] She may use her 'bully pulpit' to seek to push states to action,[8] and will also try to mobilize the world's peoples in defence of the UN and to put pressure on states. Trygve Lie described this part of the secretary-general's role as that of 'a spokesman for the world interest',[9] while the UN website claims she is 'a symbol of United Nations ideals and a spokesperson for the interests of the world's peoples, in particular the poor and vulnerable among them'.[10] Later observers have also noted her role as 'a living symbol and embodiment of the United Nations',[11] who 'alone symbolizes and speaks for the entire international community as represented by the UN'.[12] The 2016 election campaign saw widespread acceptance of this understanding of the secretary-general's importance as different groups put forward competing claims for 'representation' by the secretary-general.[13] Overall, the secretary-general can be described as a 'guardian' of the UN Charter, because 'more than anyone else, the UNSG represents the UN overall, and stands for the institution in the mind of observers'.[14]

Thus, the secretary-general today is widely recognized as the UN's chief diplomatic and political officer, and yet the UN Charter describes her merely as the 'chief administrative officer'. Overall, the Charter is circumspect regarding both the secretary-general and her Secretariat, awarding them only five articles and just over 300 words out of 111 articles and nearly 9,000 words in total.[15] What is now understood as the political power of the secretary-general derives primarily from article 99, which simply states that the secretary-general has the right to 'bring to the attention of the Security Council any matter which in his opinion may threaten the maintenance of international peace and security'.[16] Despite the inclusion of article 99, the general expectation among government representatives, UN officials, and independent observers in early 1946 was that the secretary-general would adhere to an administrative role. Most observers believed that article 99 would seldom be used,[17] a belief which proved prescient, as in the past 75 years, it has been formally invoked only twice.[18] As Leo Pasvolsky, a central figure in the Charter drafting process at the US State Department, explained to a meeting of the American delegation to the General Assembly in January 1946: 'this provision of the Charter was only for convenience in bringing situations involving non-members to the attention of the Council and … too much importance should not be attached to it'.[19] Similarly, at the San Francisco conference in 1945, several delegates explicitly articulated their conviction that 'the Secretary General is to be chief administrative officer, not a political representative'.[20] How did the office develop from such seemingly insignificant beginnings into the highly visible and deeply political role it occupies today?

This book's central argument is that the foundations for an expanded UN secretary-general role were laid during the initial period of UN history, and that Trygve Lie's contribution to this development was greater than has later been acknowledged. The interplay of crisis decision-making, institutional constraints, and the individuals involved in the beginning of the UN's existence thus built the foundations for the UN organization we know today.

The argument and contributions

This book makes five main contributions to contemporary academic and policy debates. First, the book's central story challenges existing narratives about the development of the role of the UN secretary-general. Accounts of the UN secretary-general tend to emphasize the contribution of Dag Hammarskjöld, the UN's second secretary-general (1953–61). Sir Brian Urquhart, who worked in the UN Secretariat from 1945 to 1986, described Hammarskjöld as 'undeniably the most remarkable of the Secretaries-General so far appointed'.[21] Kofi Annan, the UN's seventh secretary-general (1997–2006) praised Hammarskjöld as the model secretary-general, and said in a 2001 lecture that 'there can be no better rule of thumb for a Secretary-General, as he approaches each new challenge or crisis, than to ask himself, "how would Hammarskjöld have handled this?"'[22] Indeed, compared with the other nine secretaries-general to date, Hammarskjöld has inspired the largest number of scholarly publications dedicated to his life, tenure, and contributions to the development of the UN and the role of the secretary-general.[23] This book offers a different story as it explores the many precedents established for the role of the UN secretary-general during the tenure of Trygve Lie in the earliest years of the UN's existence. Lie's contribution to the development of the secretary-general's political role and the UN institution has been largely overlooked by later scholarship.[24] Hammarskjöld was undoubtedly an important secretary-general, but his actions built on and expanded foundations Lie had first established. The book argues that insufficient attention has been devoted to this early crucial period of UN history, and that one consequence if we do is that we need to modify our account of the development of the UN secretary-general's role.

Second, the book contributes to debates about the role of individuals in world politics, particularly to the growing literature on executive heads and leadership in international organizations and global governance.[25] This literature also relates to ongoing debates about the sources and extent of the autonomous role of international secretariats in general. The UN secretary-general is one of the most frequently studied examples of executive head leadership,[26] while a few studies have also focused on other IGOs,[27] but as argued earlier, the tenure of Trygve Lie has hitherto gone largely unexamined in this literature. A much larger literature has focused on the general question of why and how international secretariats gain autonomy, analysing the question both from a constructivist approach and with a principal-agent framework.[28] This book explores in detail the process whereby Lie was able to take advantage of institutional flexibility and ambiguity to expand the mandate of the office of UN secretary-general. Informed by a conceptual framework from sociological institutionalism, to be discussed later, the book argues that this expansion was made possible by how the UN had been established, and the autonomy this institutional setting afforded the role of the UN secretary-general. The book thus builds on and expands a theoretically informed argument which bridges institutional and personality factors in explaining the expansion of the UN secretary-general's role. Personalities matter in the early life of an organization – as the example of Trygve Lie shows – but only because the institutional set-up gives them importance.

Third, the book contributes to scholarship on the establishment of IGOs and institutional history. In recent years there has been renewed interest in the 'life cycle' of IGOs, with focus both on their establishment, operations, and, in some cases, death. Institutional design is considered a crucial process with lasting consequences, because once an organization exists it becomes difficult to change.[29] Scholars have analysed, for example, how staff of IGO secretariats can exert an influence on the process of designing new IGOs.[30] Yet the majority of this literature tends to examine the process leading up to the agreement for a new IGO, without taking into account what happens once the organization starts operating. Another branch of scholarship focuses on more mature organizations in contemporary global governance, and examines, for example, the role IGO staff play in implementing policy decisions,[31] or how IGO staff have succeeded in expanding organizations' mandates to include funding for climate change programmes.[32] Several scholars have also considered the patterns and explanations for why some IGOs 'die' while others go on to continue life as 'zombies'.[33] This book contributes a new perspective to these debates by analysing the role of IGO staff, particularly its executive head, in establishing the organization itself. Once the founding conference is over, it is left to the first executive head and the secretariat staff to transform treaties from paper to practice. This book examines the example of how Trygve Lie, the first UN secretary-general, sought to carve out a central role for the UN in world politics, and for the secretary-general within it.

Fourth, the book sheds new light on the early history and development of the UN. For a long time, historians largely neglected the topic of IGOs. Thus, as late as 2003, historian Margaret MacMillan could write that 'only a handful of eccentric historians still bother to study the League of Nations. Its archives, with their wealth of materials, are largely unvisited.'[34] Since then, the situation has changed, and today studies of IGOs both as actors and forums are a growing field of scholarship.[35] Particular attention has been paid to the role of the League of Nations and its transition to the UN system.[36] Others have focused on the link of IGOs to internationalism,[37] gender,[38] empire and imperialism,[39] or decolonization.[40] Scholars have studied the origins of the UN during WW2,[41] and a particular subfield focuses on the planning and preparation by the great powers, particularly the US.[42] There are also some accounts of the early history of the UN, although except for the excellent book by Ilya Gaiduk,[43] most of these books are now several decades old and were written without access to archival material. In providing a theoretically informed account of the development of the UN institution and the role of the secretary-general during Lie's tenure, based on extensive archival material, this book therefore offers a new perspective on this crucial period of UN history as the organization began its operations.

Finally, the book's focus on early UN history has implications for policy debates about the UN today. In examining the initial creation of the organization, the book explores how the text of the UN Charter was given life. It reveals how some parts of the Charter were abandoned, while new practices emerged to deal with unanticipated situations. Knowledge about how we got to where we are today is relevant for thinking about what is possible today and in the future. The UN today faces increasing demands for reform. Knowing how the UN has changed and responded to new situations in the past, can help us understand how it might change in the future. In its own way, therefore, the book is also a contribution to debates about UN reform.

Theoretical approach and sources

This book relies on a conceptual approach based on sociological or normative institutionalism, which I have also explained elsewhere.[44] The approach allows us to view the secretary-general as occupying a special symbolic role within the UN organization as a 'guardian' of the UN Charter.[45] This position helps explain both why the secretary-general has authority to engage in a wide range of activities beyond the limited description of the UN Charter, why individual holders of the office have autonomy and may 'push' to take the initiative and expand their role, and why the secretary-general's role has expanded over time as she has been 'pulled in' to fill a vacuum left by inaction by other UN organs.

Sociological or normative institutionalism argues that an *institution* 'comprise regulative, normative, and cultural-cognitive elements that, together with associated activities and resources, provide stability and meaning to social life',[46] while a *role* consists of 'conceptions of appropriate goals and activities for particular individuals or specified social positions'.[47] As social constructions, institutions only exist through the performance of actors in these roles. Although a role defines appropriate action, this is not a deterministic model. Actors possess autonomy in the act of interpreting which roles apply to a given situation and what those roles recommend as appropriate.[48] A further element of uncertainty arises because actors may be empowered or constrained by their access to resources, which can also be assigned by the institution. Reproduction of an institution is therefore never perfect: 'social change, no less than social stasis, can be generated by the enactment of structures in social life'.[49] The secretary-general operates within the rules of the UN institution, but those rules may change, and the secretary-general is one of the actors shaping them.

All actors within the UN, from the visiting dignitaries and permanent representatives of states to the translators and security guards, occupy roles defined by the institution. Together, they *are* the UN, and the institution would not exist without their actions and beliefs. In this sense, all roles represent the institution that defines them. Yet not all roles are equal. Some roles more than any other symbolically represent the institution overall. These roles are important in society as representing the integration of all parts into a meaningful whole, and they therefore hold special importance in legitimating those institutions to members of society.[50] The secretary-general occupies such a symbolically important role within the UN. More than anyone else within the UN system, the secretary-general represents the UN overall. She is 'a living symbol and embodiment of the United Nations',[51] who 'alone symbolizes and speaks for the entire international community'.[52] Trygve Lie called the secretary-general 'a spokesman for the world interest',[53] while Kurt Waldheim used the phrase 'spokesman for humanity'.[54] Thus, the secretary-general can be described as a 'guardian' of the UN Charter.

This role comes with a heavy responsibility. Article 7 of the UN Charter designated the Secretariat, and with it, the secretary-general, as one of the principal organs of the UN. With this, the Charter assigned the secretary-general a shared responsibility for the fulfilment of the UN's purposes and principles with the Security Council, the General Assembly, and other UN organs. Yet because of her special position as representing the UN overall, whenever there is a job that 'someone' needs to do, and the other organs are unable or unwilling to act, that 'someone' often ends up being the secretary-general. Kofi Annan used to joke that the commonly used acronym 'SG' actually stood for 'scapegoat'.[55] This 'vacuum effect', or institutional pull, is one mechanism that can help explain why the secretary-general's role over the years has expanded to include a number of political functions.

In addition to a vacuum effect that 'pulls' the role to assume more autonomy or assigns a broader array of tasks to the role, individual secretaries-general may also 'push' to expand their role. As explained earlier, although a role defines appropriate action, different actors still possess a degree of autonomy in interpreting which roles apply to a given situation and what those roles recommend as appropriate. This autonomy means that two different incumbents of the same role facing the same situation may still act differently. An activist secretary-general may choose to push for expansion, where a more modest individual sees her duty in resisting pressure from states or other UN organs to expand the role. Yet all secretaries-general, regardless of their personality and prior experiences, will be socialized into the role. When occupying the office of UN secretary-general, they act as the secretary-general and not in their personal capacity. Expectations from member states, Secretariat staff, and the public, and the weight of history, will therefore influence their actions. Thus they will often end up acting in similar ways because of the expectations of their position despite their different backgrounds and personalities.

Through both of these mechanisms, institutional pull and individual push, the secretary-general's role may change, yet the direction and nature of that change will depend on the circumstances and the inclination of the person holding the office at critical junctures. Not all innovation will create lasting precedents. Whether or not a new activity translates into a permanent expansion of the secretary-general's role depends on the reaction of other actors within the UN. If a sufficient number of government representatives, UN staff, journalists, and experts accept the activity and the new procedural norms underlying it, it becomes entrenched in the institution.[56] Once accepted, such precedents are difficult to undo. To understand how and why the role has expanded we need to examine the tenures of individual secretaries-general. This book undertakes such a detailed examination of the tenure of Trygve Lie who held office at the beginning of the UN's existence.

As discussed earlier, Lie's contribution to the development of the UN secretary-general's role, and UN history more broadly, has gone largely unexamined in scholarship so far. This necessitates going to the primary sources. This book is based on multi-archival and multi-language research from archives across several countries and institutions, and it therefore makes a contribution to existing scholarship by bringing these sources, including largely neglected Norwegian-language primary sources, into the debate.

The primary source of material for the book is the archives directly related to Lie's tenure as UN secretary-general. Lie's personal papers, including documents from his work at the UN, are held at the National Archives of Norway (*Riksarkivet*) in Oslo (NAN). Another collection of Lie's letters is available in the National Library of Norway (*Nasjonalbiblioteket*), also in Oslo (NLN). Many of these letters and documents are in Norwegian, and have been translated into English by the author, as indicated in the relevant notes. The papers of Andrew Cordier, executive assistant to Lie, at Columbia University (CCC) also contain many of the secretary-general's files. These sources, as any source, are potentially biased. In the course of research, it became clear that the archival collections in Oslo contain only a selection of Lie's papers, those he himself selected in the process of writing his memoirs and going through his personal files in later years. Given this selective inclusion, it may be speculated that the content of Lie's papers, like his memoirs, may render an overly positive view of the UN and of his own work within the organization. To compensate for these biases, Lie's papers and memoirs have been triangulated with other sources, to support the narrative with evidence from other archives and secondary literature.

The book also builds on material from UN archives, including the United Nations Archives and Records Management Section (UNA) in New York, the United Nations Dag Hammarskjöld Library (UNDHL), and online sources. Furthermore, the analysis has been supplemented with documents from state archives related to these events, primarily the collections of the National Archives of the United Kingdom in London (UKNA) and the United States National Archives and Records Administration outside Washington DC (NARA), as well as the published collections of American documents in the *Foreign Documents of the United States* (FRUS) series.

Book outline

Chapter 1 examines the founding of the UN and earlier precedents for the office of UN secretary-general from the League of Nations and the International Labour Organization. The chapter establishes that although the text in the UN Charter is sparse, ambiguity and autonomy were incorporated in the text primarily through the inclusion of article 99. Furthermore, the drafting process as well as the election of the first secretary-general, revealed competing ideas about what the secretary-general should be, and some of these ideas pointed to a more political conception of the secretary-general's role. The office was political by design, but it remained unclear precisely what such a political role would mean in practice. Thus the first holder of the office would have room for manoeuvre in exploring the role and seeking to push for a more expansive role conception.

Chapter 2 examines the 'first crisis' the UN and its newly appointed secretary-general faced: the Iranian crisis of 1946. In January 1946 the Iranian government asked the Security Council for assistance when the Soviet Union proved slow to withdraw its troops from Iranian territory after the end of WW2. Over the next few months, the Security Council discussed the question against the protests of the Soviet Union. Frequently seen as the first crisis of the coming Cold War, the episode also had lasting consequences for the role of the UN secretary-general. In April 1946 when Iran and the Soviet Union reached an agreement, and the Iranian government subsequently asked the Security Council to remove the issue from its agenda, Trygve Lie decided to enter the fray and offer his opinion on the best way to proceed. Nothing in the existing rules explicitly permitted the UN secretary-general to take part in Security Council discussions, and the intervention therefore 'fell like a bombshell'.[57] Although the Security Council in this instance decided to disregard the secretary-general's advice on the substantive matter of the Iranian crisis, the intervention led to a renegotiation of the Security

Council's rules of procedure to recognize the secretary-general's right to participate in Council discussions. This represented the first expansion of the secretary-general's role.

Whereas the Iranian crisis was the first, Lie himself saw Palestine as the first *major* test for the UN organization, and this episode is the focus of Chapter 3. Another year into his tenure, the secretary-general was more confident in his role and determined to ensure that the UN member states would follow his advice. From the moment the United Kingdom asked the UN to help determine the future of the Palestine mandate – where the Jewish population sought to establish an independent Jewish state against the wishes of the local Arab population (and regional Arab governments) – UN secretary-general Lie sought to guide the UN towards his preferred solution: the creation of an independent Jewish state, and avoidance of large-scale warfare. In the process, Lie further expanded the scope of the secretary-general's role. Although UN member states did not necessarily follow the secretary-general's advice, they accepted that he was allowed to give such advice, and that he had the right to push and prod behind the scenes to urge member states to act. Furthermore, Lie added a more public aspect to the secretary-general's role during this period, as he used speeches and press conferences to seek the support of the public and to add pressure on state governments to act.

Chapter 4 examines secretary-general Lie's views of the Cold War and his attempts to use the UN as a forum to overcome tensions between the two sides in the emerging global conflict. During the first few years, Lie sought to build bridges between East and West, and to ensure a central position for the UN in world affairs. In reaction to the American announcement of the Truman Doctrine and the Marshall Plan in 1947, Lie sought (without success) to involve UN organizations and to channel American aid through the UN system. During the Berlin Blockade of 1948–49, the secretary-general sought, again, to use the UN as a mediator between the two sides to avoid major conflict. He offered to send members of his own staff to the US and the Soviet Union to work out a proposal for solving the underlying conflict behind the blockade. As the years passed, Lie gradually came to distrust the Soviet Union. At the outbreak of the Korean War, he therefore abandoned all attempts to build bridges, and instead openly opposed the North Korean invasion. Lie took the unprecedented step of speaking first at the Security Council meeting on 25 June 1950, urging the UN membership to come to the aid of South Korea. Although legal scholars agree this did not constitute invoking article 99, this should not detract from the fact that it represented another leap in the expansion of the UN secretary-general's role.

Chapter 5 continues the narrative of bridge-building and examines secretary-general Lie's most high-profile intervention for peace; a 1950 proposal for a peace plan to end the Cold War. Although the plan itself largely called for renewed focus on existing UN programmes or further progress on already established priorities, the overall plan and its presentation is a key early example of the UN secretary-general's role as an advocate for global issues, or what has later become known as being a 'norm entrepreneur'. Secretary-general Lie employed all the tools at his disposal to promote his peace plan: public speeches, distributing a memorandum to the member states, and embarking on a widely publicized 'peace tour' to appeal directly to world leaders and public opinion to support his plan. Ultimately, Lie's peace plan, like so many of his earlier initiatives, must be classified largely as a failure. Less than a month after Lie's return to New York from his tour, the Korean War broke out, putting an end both to Lie's attempts to build bridges between East and West (Chapter 4) and the peace plan. Yet although the plan itself did not succeed in ending the Cold War, the episode further served to solidify the procedural norms underlying an expanded UN secretary-general role.

Chapter 6 turns away from explicitly political affairs and the repeating cycles of high-level crises, to examine instead the establishment of the UN Secretariat and the administrative apparatus and norms of the UN. Lie chose to focus most of his attention and energy on the political role of the UN secretary-general and the questions of peace and security discussed by the Security Council. Yet to understand the process by which the UN Charter was transformed from paper to practice, the establishment of the UN Secretariat is also of crucial importance. The concept of an International Civil Service (ICS) was first developed at the founding of the League of Nations, before being adopted and adapted in the UN system. This is another area where Lie is frequently seen to have failed – if not outright to have betrayed the organization – as he allowed the Federal Bureau of Investigation (FBI) onto UN premises to fingerprint and interview American staff members in response to the McCarthy process, seemingly in breach of the principle of the International Civil Service's independence. The final chapter also discusses the process of establishing UN headquarters, where Lie played a central role in ensuring the UN settled permanently in New York.

Drawing together the main findings from each chapter, the conclusion summarizes the main argument of how the interplay of crisis decision-making, institutional constraints, and the individuals involved in the earliest years of the UN's existence built the foundations for the UN organizations we know today. Trygve Lie's contribution to this process was greater than has later been acknowledged in scholarship, as his persistent actions created precedents for a public and political role for the UN secretary-general. The conclusion also briefly discusses the tenures of Lie's eight successors in the role as secretary-general, and highlights how their tenures support the book's overall argument about the importance of institutional factors in the development of the secretary-general's role.

1

Setting the Stage: The Creation of the UN and Expectations for the Role of the UN Secretary-General

> The Secretary-General, more than anyone else, will stand for the United Nations as a whole. In the eyes of the world, no less than in the eyes of his own staff, he must embody the principles and ideals of the Charter to which the Organization seeks to give effect.[1]
>
> Report of the Preparatory Commission of the United Nations (December 1945)

Introduction

On 2 February 1946 Trygve Lie, up until then the foreign minister of Norway, was sworn in as the first secretary-general of the UN. He took on the role of secretary-general in a brand-new organization. The UN Charter had been signed just seven months earlier in San Francisco on 26 June 1945, and the first General Assembly opened in London on 10 January 1946. As the first secretary-general, to some extent Lie had to make up his own role as he went along. But he was not completely free to do whatever he desired. This chapter examines what expectations for the role of the UN secretary-general existed before Lie took office. The following chapters will then examine what Lie did with these expectations and how the role developed beyond the baseline from 1946.

In canvassing early government and public expectations of the role of the UN secretary-general, the first point of reference is the minimalist description as the 'chief administrative officer of the Organization' in article 97 of the UN Charter.[2] This would indicate that the secretary-general was expected to play a primarily administrative role. Brian Urquhart, who worked in the

Secretariat from the start and later published extensively on the office of the secretary-general, confirmed this when he wrote that

> the general concept of the position and functions of the Secretary-General in 1946 bear little relation to the office's responsibilities today. There [was] then ... a highly restrictive and conservative view of the functions, let alone the independence, of the world's top international civil servant. He was considered, especially by the Europeans, to be an almost exclusively administrative official, and efforts by Lie to assist in political matters were often resented or ignored.[3]

At the same time, most of the generalist literature on the UN secretary-general, as well as the literature on the founding of the UN, finds that the office of UN secretary-general was somehow 'different' from its League of Nations predecessor in that it was more 'political'.[4] This observation emanates from the Charter's terse and vague article 99 that opened some space for political initiatives in giving the secretary-general the right to 'bring to the attention of the Security Council any matter which in his opinion may threaten the maintenance of international peace and security'.[5] Russell in her book from 1958, which is still the most detailed account of the drafting of the UN Charter, wrote that the UN secretary-general was given 'a more important political role than his predecessors in the League'.[6] Schlesinger also briefly stated that including the secretary-general as one of the principal organs of the UN was to 'elevat[e] this post above the clerical/administrative status given it by the League of Nations'.[7]

This chapter re-examines the expectations of the UN secretary-general's role prevalent in 1946. It finds that the assumption that the secretary-general was perceived as a principally administrative office doesn't fully hold up against the historical evidence. Neither is the story as simple as saying that the UN secretary-general was 'more political' than the League secretary-general. This chapter argues that the office of UN secretary-general was political by design, and that both government officials and media observers expected that the secretary-general would play an autonomous and political role. Three main observations support this argument. First of all, the League of Nations secretary-general, the most readily available model for the office, had in fact already played a limited political role. The general expectation in 1946 was that the UN secretary-general would build on what the League secretary-general had done, and expand the political scope of the office even further. The second observation supporting the claim that the UN secretary-general should play a political role is that he was given a specific political task in article 99 of the UN Charter. Lastly, the founders of the UN, in considering candidates for the post, were looking for a 'statesman', and the person they ended up choosing, Trygve Lie, was a politician. Even if they had chosen one of the ambassadors or civil servants on the shortlist, the expectation of the secretary-general as a 'statesman' would indicate that he was not expected merely to be an ornamental figurehead or an administrative officer.

The expectation that the secretary-general was to be political was not a unanimous consensus. There were those who saw the office as primarily administrative; and even those who wanted a political secretary-general were unclear on what exactly this would entail. The founders of the UN thus opened the door for the secretary-general to play a political role, without thinking through what this role might look like in practice. The office was therefore inherently flexible, and the way had been opened for the role to expand further, perhaps going beyond what anyone in 1946 had thought possible or desirable.

This chapter is divided into four parts, arranged chronologically. The first looks at the precedents set for the office by the League of Nations secretary-general, as well as the alternative model of the International Labour Organization (ILO) director. The second part examines thinking about the secretary-general in the first American drafts for the UN Charter and during the proceedings at the Dumbarton Oaks conference in 1944. The third part brings the story of wartime planning forward to the San Francisco conference of 1945, and also discusses the report of the Preparatory Commission. Lastly, the fourth section examines the process of electing the first UN secretary-general, and establishes what characteristics the states' representatives were looking for in candidates for the office. All in all, the chapter concludes, the expectations for the office in early 1946 were vague and unclear, but this left considerable flexibility which would allow the office to expand once Lie took office and started to add practice and initiative to the institutional foundations of the role.

Earlier models: the League of Nations and International Labour Organization

One reason I argue that the UN secretary-general was expected to be political from the start was that his predecessor in the League of Nations had also played a political role, albeit limited. In fact, consensus among the UN's founders was that the League secretaries-general had not been political enough, and it was therefore decided to give the UN secretary-general broader political powers. When the states decided to expand the powers of the UN secretary-general they may have had in mind the alternative example provided by the ILO director. This section discusses these two models.

The planners of the new post-war organization used the League of Nations as their primary point of reference. The US State Department, for example, included analysis of relevant Covenant articles in its working papers, and discussed the League's experience as 'test cases' for the new organization.[8] Similarities in the formal design of the two organizations, as much as points of departure, are therefore highly telling of the intentions of the drafters of the UN Charter. The League was set up by the Paris Peace conference in 1919, and the first secretary-general of the organization was to be Sir Eric Drummond, a civil servant from the British Foreign Office. Drummond has been widely praised for the administrative job he did as secretary-general. His most famous contribution was the development of the concept of the 'international civil service'; that is, that League staff were to be recruited among the most qualified individuals, not upon the recommendation of national governments, and they would therefore owe their primary allegiance to the international organization.[9] This concept was taken up and formalized in the UN Charter.[10] But Drummond's political initiatives are less known.

Scholars today generally portray Drummond as a quiet civil servant who 'famously refused to speak to the press at all'[11] and 'intentionally minimized his public role'.[12] He had 'concentrated on indirect influence while leaving undeveloped the powers which might have given him a more leading public role'.[13] The League Covenant had not granted any explicit political powers to the secretary-general. He was to be 'appointed by the Council with the approval of the majority of the Assembly', and to 'act in that capacity at all meetings of the Assembly and of the Council'.[14] In the event of 'war or threat of war ... the Secretary-General shall on the request of any Member of the League forthwith summon a meeting of the Council'.[15] The secretary-general had thus been given a part in the League's apparatus for dealing with issues of peace and security, but he had not been given a right of independent initiative, rather his job was an administrative one of calling meetings at the request of member states.

In practice, however, the League secretaries-general wielded some, limited, political influence behind the scenes. They took part in mediation between states, and helped resolve potential conflicts.[16] In the dispute between Sweden and Finland over the Åland islands in 1919–21, or the Greek-Bulgarian border skirmish in 1925, Drummond acted as a mediator and a channel of communications between parties to the conflict.[17] Joseph Avenol, the second holder of the office, also tried to negotiate on several occasions, and in 1936 he travelled to Rome to induce Mussolini to rejoin the League.[18] Yet, neither Drummond nor Avenol developed the political powers of the office to its full potential.[19] Furthermore, Avenol's activities had left him with a near scandalous reputation that could serve as a cautionary tale of the perils of giving the secretary-general too much autonomy in the political field. In particular, his appeasement towards Nazi Germany and Fascist Italy is seen as a 'betrayal' of the principles and values of the organization he had been entrusted to lead.[20] Nevertheless, the League secretaries-general did not offer a merely administrative model for the office of UN secretary-general.

And the founders of the UN recognized that these political powers were there, and sought to formalize, institutionalize, and enhance them in the UN Charter.[21]

In addition to the recognition that the League secretary-general had held too little political power, another reason why the founders sought to expand the political role of the UN secretary-general may have been the example of stronger executive leadership found in the director of the ILO.[22] The ILO, like the League of Nations, was established by the Paris Peace conference, but it had a different structure to the League. It operated on a tripartite model where representatives of government, employers, and workers from each country all participated in ILO conferences.[23] This may have helped open the way for the director and his staff to take an active role in proceedings because there were already other non-state actors on the scene. Furthermore, the ILO dealt with social and economic matters, not issues of peace and security, or 'high politics', and this represents another factor that may have facilitated a more active secretariat role. These differences, however, should not lead us to overlook the model of the ILO completely. Indeed, Britain mentioned the principle of election to the governing body of the ILO as a relevant example for the council of the new UN organization, despite this being a non-political organization, in its pre-Dumbarton Oaks draft.[24]

The first director of the ILO was Albert Thomas, a French Socialist politician. Thomas had his own vision of the ILO and its work, and the role he would have to play in its proceedings for this vision to come about. He saw the ILO as an organization of peoples, not of states, but he was also conscious of the many conflicts and disagreements existing between states – as well as between workers and employers within states – in the period. For this reason, he decided that policy proposals would have to come from the ILO secretariat, so that they would be seen as impartial and 'untainted', otherwise the organization would never reach any decisions. 'Thus the Director had secured a position not very different from that of a Minister making and defending his proposals before a representative body.'[25] He largely delegated administrative tasks to a deputy, choosing to focus instead on the policy of the organization.[26] And Thomas' approach did succeed, as he 'turned the International Labor Organization almost overnight into a powerful voice for the protection of workers' rights within a safely capitalist framework'.[27] The inclusion in article 98 of the duty of the UN secretary-general to provide an annual report to the General Assembly may have been written into the Charter because the UN founders sought to have the secretary-general play a greater part in the proceedings of the Assembly, and thus to have the UN function closer to the ILO model.

Records from wartime discussions in both Britain and the US show that the UN founders actively considered and evaluated the League and ILO examples in setting up the new UN organization. One of their conclusions was the desire to give the secretary-general a more political role in the new organization, to counteract the perceived weaknesses of the League.[28] But as the next sections will discuss, they failed to consider what this role would look like in practice.

Wartime planning

The UN Charter was largely drafted by the US State Department, while British officials had some influence. The Soviet Union and China were to play much smaller roles in the process, although they did take part in the Dumbarton Oaks conference. Unlike Britain, China, and the Soviet Union, which had all been members of the League of Nations, the US appears not to have been fully aware of the political importance of the office of the secretary-general.[29] This may have contributed to the confusion that was to surround the role of the UN secretary-general throughout the planning process, and thus to the inherent flexibility of the office.

During the internal American drafting process confusion and changes would lead to a concept of the secretary-general in the UN Charter that was less explicitly political than it had been in the earlier American plans. In the summer of 1943, staff in the US State Department produced the first drafts for a new international organization. These plans included provisions for a 'general secretary' or 'director general' who would be the non-voting chairman of the (Security) Council, and who would also 'in the event of a threat to, or breach of, the peace between nations ... after consultation with the Members of the Council ... request the parties involved to desist from any action which might prejudice a peaceful settlement'.[30] The director-general 'would give added weight to Council decisions as representing the general interests of all the United Nations'.[31] These provisions are not dissimilar to article 99 of the UN Charter, in that they give the secretary-general a voice in the Council and a share of the responsibility for the maintenance of international peace and security. Surprisingly, however, this is not where article 99 originated, because this idea disappeared from later American drafts.

These first plans were never really discussed above staff level,[32] and the memorandum given to the president in December 1943 merely said that 'the various component organs and agencies of the organization should have appropriate administrative staffs'.[33] It was US President Franklin D. Roosevelt who brought up in subsequent discussions an idea for 'a head for the entire institution' that he wanted incorporated into the plan. What exactly Roosevelt had in mind is not entirely clear, but he seems to have used the term 'moderator', and been thinking 'of an individual with the full prestige of the organization behind him who could, as Council chairman, exert great diplomatic influence in "moderating" differences especially between the great powers'.³⁴ Over the next few months, the staff tried to incorporate this concept in their existing plans with the result that they introduced the role of 'president' in addition to the 'director-general' from earlier drafts. The president, 'a person of widely recognized eminence', was to be the non-voting chairman of the Council, and

> in the event that a threat to the peace or breach of the peace occurs at a time when the executive council is in recess, the council should immediately be convened by the [president] who should be empowered also to initiate such emergency measures as may be necessary, subject to review by the council when it resumes session.³⁵

The director-general, on the other hand, was reduced to 'the chief administrative officer of the organization'.³⁶

In the spring of 1944, the public was also very much in favour of having an elder statesman, someone like Roosevelt or Winston Churchill, the British wartime prime minister, as the head of the new world organization.³⁷ Roosevelt himself had in fact toyed with the idea of leading the UN after the war.³⁸ However, State Department officials were unable to work out the relationship between the president and the director-general, and whether the president should be the chairman of the Council or the Assembly or both. Critics also argued that 'in a political organization of states, there was no place for an individual with authority in his own person, except to run the machine', and after April the idea of a president disappeared from American plans.³⁹ In the next comprehensive draft from July all the articles on the president had been deleted, while the articles designating the director-general as 'chief administrative officer' remained unchanged.⁴⁰ In dropping the idea of a president the State Department did not reconsider whether the director-general should return as the chairman of the Council. By this time 'other more pressing questions occupied the group'.⁴¹ But ideas about the secretary-general's political responsibility would return again in later discussions.

The next formal step in the drafting of the UN Charter was the Dumbarton Oaks conference in Washington DC from 21 August to 7 October 1944.⁴² The main issues of contention at this conference were the questions of veto in the Security Council and the Soviet Union's demand for 16 representatives in the General Assembly.⁴³ The main debate about the secretary-general concerned how he (and his deputies – and how many of these) should be elected.⁴⁴ The final text of the Dumbarton Oaks proposals suggested that the secretary-general should be elected by the General Assembly, on the recommendation of the Security Council, but said nothing about deputies.⁴⁵ This debate over the election of the secretary-general suggests that the great powers considered the office sufficiently important that they wanted to control who would hold it.

The Dumbarton Oaks proposals furthermore included a version of what we now know as article 99: 'The Secretary-General should have the right to bring to the attention of the Security Council any matter which in his opinion may threaten international peace and security.'[46] Before the conference, Britain had suggested that 'the head of the Secretariat should be given the right of bringing before the World Council any matter which in his opinion threatens the peace of the world'.[47] The Chinese draft had also included the following provision:

> Any use of force, or any threat of use of force, whether immediately affecting any member state or not, shall be deemed a matter involving the peace of the world. In such cases, the Secretary-General may, *on his own initiative* or at the request of any member state, immediately convene the Council to take effective measures to safeguard peace.[48]

Although the Chinese proposal was similar to article 11 of the League of Nations Covenant, an important difference lay in the inclusion of the phrase 'on his own initiative' which gave the secretary-general the right to convene Council meetings regardless of whether any member state had asked him to or not. At the conference, the US and the Soviet Union raised no objections, and this right was included in the Dumbarton Oaks proposals.[49] It was thus at the initiative of Britain and China, not of the US, that article 99 found its way into the UN Charter. Both states had experienced at first hand the shortcomings of the League of Nations during the interwar period when the organization was unable to prevent wars of aggression and conquest, and it is thus credible that article 99 was added so that the secretary-general could help defend the integrity of the new world organization. No longer should serious issues remain off the agenda just because no state wanted to raise them for political reasons. Giving the secretary-general this responsibility reveals that the four states intended him to be impartial and independent from the member states and their squabbles.

The San Francisco conference and the Preparatory Commission

After Dumbarton Oaks the four great powers decided to call a conference of all the allied states to agree on the Charter for the new world organization. At this conference, which met in San Francisco from 25 April to 26 June 1945, the main disagreement over the secretary-general continued to be the question of how he (and his deputies) should be elected.[50] This concern with the election, and the great powers' insistence on applying the veto to the Security Council's recommendation of a secretary-general, is evidence that the states saw the office, and the question of who would hold that office, as important issues. Rovine argues that this 'was perhaps the best evidence that the Office was to have more than simple administrative functions to perform'.[51] The question of the election of the secretary-general became tangled up in discussions of the relations between the Security Council and the General Assembly, as well as debates over voting rules in those bodies. More than one committee in San Francisco discussed this issue, but once agreement was reached on the Yalta voting formula for use of the veto in the Security Council, the question of the secretary-general's election was also finally settled. The veto would apply to the Council's recommendation, while the election formally was to be done by the Assembly.[52]

One of the subcommittees of the conference, however, also discussed article 99 in the context of examining all Charter provisions on the Secretariat. No-one argued that the article should be taken out. Rather, the discussion concerned two proposed amendments that would have expanded the article further. Venezuela proposed 'that the right of the Secretary-General in respect to matters which in his opinion might threaten international peace and security might be exercised before the Security Council, and/or before the General Assembly'.[53] The Venezuelan delegate argued that this would help strengthen the position of the Assembly in matters of peace and security.[54] This proposal was thus part of the attempt by smaller states at San Francisco to strengthen the General Assembly (and the secretary-general) at the expense of the Security Council (and the great powers). Uruguay further proposed expanding article 99 to allow the secretary-general to refer 'any matters which constitute an infringement or violation of the principles of the Charter' to the Security Council.[55]

States arguing against these two proposals thought they would 'extend to the Secretary-General wider authority than had been given to members of the Organization'. Furthermore, the proposals 'would place the Secretary-General in a very difficult position and would add to the very heavy burdens which have been placed upon him by the Charter', when he might have to 'decide between the Assembly and the Security Council ... and having to charge member states with violating the principles of the Organization'.[56] Interestingly, the US had also considered making an amendment allowing the secretary-general to bring matters to the General Assembly, but the idea was dropped without even raising it with the other three sponsoring powers because the technical experts thought it 'would confuse the respective jurisdictions of the two organs and would constitute a substantive change in the Secretary-General's authority'.[57] In the end the subcommittee also rejected both amendments, and adopted the text we now know as article 99. But a significant number of states (13 to 16 and 11 to 18) voted in favour of these amendments.[58]

Even though at San Francisco there was little discussion of the exact content of and limits to the secretary-general's political role, at various points in the debate states let slip comments about the secretary-general's political powers (or lack thereof). During a discussion on the election procedure some states took issue with the term 'election' itself, because it 'conveys the idea of representation. It was explained that the Secretary General is to be chief administrative officer, not a political representative; he will belong to the international community and his loyalty would be to the Organization.'[59] At another meeting the representative of the Netherlands felt the need to point out that 'the Secretariat would have only administrative functions and would not have any political functions', a view that 'was supported by several other delegates'.[60] And lastly, when the committee examining Security Council voting procedures had decided that the veto would apply to the recommendation of a secretary-general, the Netherlands wanted to reopen discussion on the secretary-general's terms of office and eligibility, prophetically stating:

> The new ruling ... would compel the permanent members to reach a compromise, and this might result in the appointment of a 'lowest common denominator'. Furthermore, the Secretary-General would work in the knowledge that his chances of re-election would be small if he were to incur the displeasure of one of the permanent members.[61]

The committee agreed, and took out any reference to the secretary-general's term of office from the UN Charter. At the same meeting the Soviet Union made another attempt to put reference to the secretary-general's deputies into the Charter, for, as the Ukrainian representative explained: 'The principal officers of the Secretariat would be, in his view, not experts or officials, but politicians, forming a kind of Cabinet. Acceptance of the proposal that there should be deputies would enable the small and medium powers to be represented in this Cabinet.' The suggestion was rejected by 24 votes against 12, with 1 abstention.[62] Clearly, the majority at this stage was of the opinion that the secretary-general had primarily administrative responsibilities. But other states argued in favour of giving the secretary-general more political responsibilities and rights, and even talked about the leadership of the Secretariat as 'politicians'. Thus, at the end of the San Francisco conference, although the majority favoured a mainly administrative secretary-general, in the absence of any in-depth discussion, the precise nature of his role had not been finally settled.

The Charter of the UN was signed in the San Francisco Opera House on 26 June 1945. Before adjourning, the conference agreed to set up a preparatory commission to meet in London and prepare for the first General Assembly of the organization. The UN Preparatory Commission[63] showed a greater awareness of the political functions inherent in the office of the secretary-general than had been evident in debates in San Francisco.[64] In its final report the commission wrote:

> The Secretary-General may have an important role to play as a mediator and as an informal adviser of many governments, and will undoubtedly be called upon from time to time, in the exercise of his administrative duties, to take *decisions which may justly be called political.* Under Article 99 of the Charter, moreover, he has been given *a quite special right which goes beyond any power previously accorded to the head of an international organization,* viz: to bring to the attention of the Security Council any matter (not merely any dispute or situation) which, in his opinion, may threaten the maintenance of international peace and security. It is impossible to foresee how this Article will be applied; but the responsibilities it confers upon the Secretary-General will require the exercise of *the highest qualities of political judgement, tact and integrity.*[65]

In earlier discussions the commission also pointed out that the need to invoke article 99 might not arise, because the secretary-general already had wide political powers under article 98 in his capacity to report on '*any* developments' in the annual report to the General Assembly.[66]

The preparatory commission had acknowledged that article 99 implied certain rights and responsibilities for the secretary-general, but its report did not spell them out beyond the quote discussed earlier. If the secretary-general is to be in a position where he can bring the Council's attention to a matter, he needs to be informed of what is going on in the world. This gives the secretary-general a right to ask questions of states or to form fact-finding committees and send them to various trouble spots to ascertain what is happening and whether he should invoke article 99.[67] Furthermore, article 99 uses the words 'may' and 'in his opinion'. These words reveal the extent of the secretary-general's independence and autonomy: he can form and articulate his own mind, and the opinion he holds can stand at odds with the opinions of the member states. He can also decide for himself whether or not to refer a situation to the Council or to do something else with the information he possesses. In this is revealed that the secretary-general has been given a discretionary right of political agency; the right to take initiatives and have opinions on political questions. Article 99 thus assigns clear autonomy and independence to the secretary-general's role.

The Preparatory Commission was served by a small secretariat headed by the British civil servant and diplomat Gladwyn Jebb. Jebb's official title was as executive secretary to the Commission. On 11 January 1946, at the opening of the first General Assembly, he was designated the acting secretary-general of the UN, a position he served in until the election of Trygve Lie on 2 February 1946. This meant that Jebb can be considered, 'effectively, the first UN Secretary-General'.[68] According to Urquhart, one of Jebb's first hires, 'Gladwyn was a skilled draftsman and was good at dealing both with the national representatives on the Executive Committee and with his own staff'.[69] Although he served as secretary-general for a short time only, Jebb did leave some impact on the new UN organization. As Chapter 6 will discuss, some of the staff of the preparatory commission would go on to serve in the UN Secretariat, thus forming the nucleus of the new organization's administrative apparatus. Jebb's most important contribution lay in drafting large parts of the preparatory commission's final report.[70] Although the report was the outcome of lengthy discussions among the member state representatives on the commission, as one of the principal drafters Jebb also influenced its content. On the subject of rules of procedure, for example, the rules suggested by the preparatory commission have remained largely unchanged to this day.[71] However, Jebb's primary focus during these months was on the administrative task of servicing the meetings of the preparatory commission and later the General Assembly. He resented the public attention that came with the position as acting secretary-general, and the constant request from the press to give 'statements' on various subjects, preferring to see himself as 'a temporary official only'.[72] Jebb did not serve in the role of secretary-general long enough to influence the role's political tasks.

The San Francisco conference left the question of terms of appointment for the secretary-general to the Preparatory Commission. The Commission suggested an initial five-year term, with the option of re-election. Giving the secretary-general a relatively short term, and providing for rotation in nationality, indicates the symbolic importance attached to the office.[73] The Commission's report also noted the importance of the secretary-general for the organization as a whole, as it talked about his 'moral authority' and stated that 'the Secretary-General, more than anyone else, will stand for the United Nations as a whole. In the eyes of the world, no less than in the eyes of his own staff, he must embody the principles and ideals of the Charter to which the Organization seeks to give effect.'[74] Thus the Preparatory Commission recognized the important aspect of the role of the secretary-general as a representative of the UN overall, or in other words, as a 'guardian' of the UN Charter. However, the Commission did not get much closer than earlier drafters and discussants to pinning down exactly what the secretary-general's role meant in practice. It has been suggested that the post was so important that 'the founders were unable, or unwilling, to describe it in any detail'.[75] Regardless, this left wide room for manoeuvre for the first holders of the office.

The election of Trygve Lie as the first UN secretary-general

On 2 February 1946 Trygve Lie was sworn in as the first secretary-general of the UN. Born in Oslo in 1896, Lie and an older sister grew up with their mother who ran a café and boarding house for workers from nearby factories. At an early age Lie became active in local Labour Party politics. He studied law at the University of Oslo, and worked for many years as a lawyer for the Norwegian Confederation of Trade Unions. In 1935 he was elected to parliament and joined the Norwegian government as minister of justice. When Germany attacked Norway in April 1940, Lie was the minister of supply and shipping, and he has been credited with saving the large Norwegian shipping fleet for the Allied war effort. From December 1940 Lie served as foreign minister in the Norwegian government-in-exile in London, where he built relations with politicians from Britain and other countries. Lie attended the San Francisco conference and the first General Assembly in London as head of the Norwegian delegation.[76] Lie himself felt that these experiences had not fully prepared him for the job of UN secretary-general, and later wrote in his memoirs:

> I had been nothing less than catapulted into the Secretary-Generalship of this new international organization, to preserve peace and promote progress in a world beset by unrest, poverty, and great-power rivalry. It was a challenge beyond my wildest dreams; but it was a nightmare as well. I hardly dared to think of the days ahead. Instead, I asked myself again and again, Why had this awesome task fallen to a labor lawyer from Norway?[77]

To find out why the job was given to Lie we need to look closer at the election process.[78]

The great powers had started discussing candidates for the post in the latter half of 1945. In practice the secretary-general would be elected by the five permanent members of the Council, because of their veto power, and because the Council and the Assembly wanted to avoid public debate about the nomination and election of the UN's top official.[79] The assembled delegates assumed that it could impede the legitimacy and effectiveness of the secretary-general – as a symbolic representative of the UN overall – if his election was preceded by public debate in which member states made their objections against him known.[80] In the great powers' discussion, the question of the secretary-general's nationality became tied up with questions of the location of the UN's permanent headquarters and the nationality of the first General Assembly president. In fact, the US had first approached Lie in August 1945 to ask if he would be willing to be Assembly president.[81]

Lie's name came up in debate among the big five for the first time on 8 October, on a list of candidates prepared by the US representative on the preparatory commission.[82]

In addition to considering the secretary-general's nationality, the five were looking for a great statesman to fill the post. As the Acting US Secretary of State, Dean Acheson, observed:

> We attach great importance to securing for the position a man of the highest ability who will be wholeheartedly devoted to his service as the chief administrative official of the United Nations and the head of its international secretariat. The position of SyG should be considered one of such importance and dignity and prestige as to attract an outstanding man.[83]

The General Assembly likewise agreed on the importance of finding a statesman for the position, and decided that 'the terms of the appointment of the Secretary-General shall be such as to enable a man of eminence and high attainment to accept and maintain the position'. He would therefore be offered an annual salary of $20,000 with a further representation allowance of $20,000, as well as a furnished house.[84] As noted before, the initial five-year term suggested by the preparatory commission was also part of the strategy to 'secure the best man' for the job.[85] Public opinion agreed that the office of secretary-general should be held by a man of eminence and repute, and names such as General Dwight Eisenhower, the Supreme Commander of the Allied Forces in Europe, or Antony Eden, foreign minister of Britain, were mentioned in public discussions.[86]

Despite agreement on the importance of the secretary-general, the great powers did not manage to agree on a candidate for the post during their meetings in 1945. In January 1946, the US' preferred candidate was Lester Pearson, the Canadian ambassador to the US, and his candidacy was also supported by Britain and China. The Soviet Union, on the other hand, argued that the secretary-general should come from Eastern Europe, and suggested Stanoje Simić, Yugoslavia's ambassador to the US, or the Polish foreign minister, Wincenty Rzymowski.[87] Another candidate favoured by the Western powers was Paul-Henri Spaak, the foreign minister of Belgium. Spaak was also one of the names being considered for Assembly president, and so was Lie. The US, the Soviet Union, and China had made an agreement to support Lie for the presidency, while Britain pressed for Spaak.[88] However, at this point in the proceedings someone talked to Spaak and learned that he did not want the job of secretary-general because he wanted to become prime minister of Belgium, and Britain, France, the US, and China therefore decided to offer Spaak the Assembly presidency instead, as that office could be combined with holding national office.[89]

The US (and China) had thus entered into two conflicting deals about the Assembly presidency.

This list of candidates tells us something about the characteristics the states were looking for in the new secretary-general. Eisenhower and Eden were famous in their own right because of the part they had played for the Allied cause during WW2, and were thus the candidates discussed by the media; however, the representatives on the Security Council also discussed these names in meetings, and included them on their lists of candidates under consideration.[90] Yet neither Eden nor Eisenhower held much chance of getting elected because the five permanent members decided early on that the secretary-general should not be one of their nationals.[91] When we look at the rest of the names on the list, one of the shortcomings of the election process of the secretary-general, as has also been pointed out by later researchers,[92] becomes obvious; since there was no formal search or nomination process, these were all people who were somehow known to the permanent five. Both Pearson and Simić were ambassadors in Washington DC, while Rzymowski and Lie were foreign ministers of their countries. The fact that these four were all in their countries' foreign service also points to the criteria for potential secretaries-general to have international experience. But as France pointed out, it would be preferable to choose 'a statesman rather than a diplomat, perhaps someone who had been foreign minister of his country', because 'this would bring to the post a broader experience than that of a diplomat'.[93] There was a tension here between wanting to attract a politician, ideally a cabinet minister, and the recognition, evident in Spaak's rejection of the offer, that being secretary-general of the UN was less prestigious than holding national political office.[94]

The manner of the election of the Assembly president would give the appearance that Lie was 'Moscow's man' while also opening the way for Lie to become secretary-general. At the first General Assembly meeting on 10 January 1946 Andrei Gromyko of the Soviet delegation spoke out in favour of Lie as 'a very capable and experienced statesman, enjoying respect not only in his own country, but abroad as well'.[95] Gromyko was followed by the Polish, Ukrainian, and Danish representatives. The American representative said nothing. As the Ukrainian representative suggested election by acclamation, and then proceeded to vote both for and against his own proposal, confusion about the procedure was complete. Spaak was never openly nominated by anyone, but still won the secret ballot by 28 votes to Lie's 23.[96] Lie was 'pleased by the demonstration of Soviet goodwill toward Norway', but 'embarrassed by the clumsiness of the Soviet attempt to push things through'.[97]

With Spaak elected Assembly president, the big five returned to the question of the secretary-general. The US still wanted Pearson,[98] while the Soviet Union insisted on Simić or Rzymowski. The US therefore offered

Lie's name as a compromise, and on 28 January the other four agreed.[99] In a private meeting on 29 January the Security Council nominated Lie for the office of secretary-general,[100] and he was duly elected by the General Assembly on 1 February with 46 votes in favour, 3 against, and 2 abstentions.[101] Lie's election was therefore a compromise between East and West in the early Cold War. He was probably elected because Norway was on a very short list of countries that could be acceptable to both sides.[102] Norway had not yet firmly joined the Western camp, and Lie had himself in speeches to the General Assembly talked about the need to build bridges between the two sides.[103] This theme of mediation between the great powers would reappear later on in Lie's thinking about his role as UN secretary-general, as we shall see in later chapters.

Conclusion

This chapter demonstrated that, contrary to the impression we might get from the UN Charter's description of him as merely 'the chief administrative officer of the Organization',[104] the UN secretary-general was expected to play a political role from the start. The office was designed with this goal in mind, and it can be discerned in statements by delegates at the San Francisco conference, and in the considerations that guided the search for the first holder of the office. The chapter furthermore argued that the office was inherently flexible because the exact implications of giving the secretary-general a more political role was never fully spelled out.

The foremost model for the office of the UN secretary-general was the secretary-general of the League of Nations. Although the claim that the UN secretary-general was to be 'more political' than the League secretary-general may lead us to believe that the League secretary-general was essentially non-political or administrative, Barros and others have shown that the League secretaries-general actually played an important political role behind the scenes.[105] The founders of the UN recognized that these political functions were there, and sought to formalize, institutionalize, and enhance them in the UN Charter.[106] However, it was also recognized that the League secretary-general had not been political enough, and so the UN secretary-general was given a specific task in helping to maintain international peace and security though article 99. At San Francisco, representatives of smaller states even argued that article 99 should be expanded to give the secretary-general (and the General Assembly) broader political scope.

Furthermore, beyond the political rights and responsibilities built into the office in the Charter, the search for the first secretary-general and discussions about the desired characteristics of the candidates, also reveal that the office was meant to be political. The founders of the UN were looking for a 'statesman' to fill the role. The press speculated freely about the possibility that Eisenhower or Eden would get the job. They were both famous and respected because of the role they had played during the war. The French representative in a meeting in January 1946 also said he would prefer a statesman to hold the office, preferably one who had been foreign minister, and not just an ambassador or civil servant.[107] Clearly, if the job went Eisenhower or Eden, one could not expect them to stay out of political matters that came before the institution. Such a person would necessarily take an active role in the organization's proceedings, beyond merely administering its Secretariat.

Yet, there were still those who saw the office as primarily administrative, as shown by committee discussions at San Francisco. And several government officials would have preferred to see article 99 remain a dead letter. As Lie later wrote in his memoirs; 'there were – and still are – many traditionalists in the foreign chancelleries of the world who would like to see Article 99 of the Charter, and all the implied power deriving from it, consigned to an unused constitutional corner to gather dust'.[108] The general expectation in 1946 was that article 99 would probably not be used much in its literal task (and indeed it has only formally been invoked twice[109]), because of the provision that the secretary-general should report annually to the General Assembly on 'any development'.[110] Leo Pasvolsky of the US State Department explained to a meeting of the US delegation to the General Assembly that 'this provision of the Charter was only for convenience in bringing situations involving non-members to the attention of the Council and that too much importance should not be attached to it'.[111] But as the following chapters will show, there is more to this article than its formal invocation, and quite often private consultations by the secretary-general with members of the Security Council on whether or not he should invoke the article is enough to make them aware of the issue and (hopefully) spur them to action.

The fact that the main debates about the secretary-general at the San Francisco conference, during the proceedings of the preparatory commission, and at the first session of the General Assembly concerned the election and terms of office of the secretary-general, also reveals that the office was considered important. The debate about election procedures reveals the states', in particular the great powers', concern to control who would hold the job. Later discussion about how many years his initial term of office should be, as well as comments about whether or not it would be possible to fire an unsatisfactory secretary-general,[112] point in the same direction. The office of UN secretary-general was important and not merely symbolic or administrative, and the question of who would occupy it mattered to states. The terms of office and the salary levels were eventually settled so as 'to enable a man of eminence and high attainment to accept and maintain the position'.[113]

Yet despite this concern to attract an outstanding candidate and a statesman, the office was still generally considered less prestigious than a national political office. Spaak turned the offer down because he wanted to become prime minister in Belgium, and US officials also frequently discussed this point in relation to the other candidates they considered. Furthermore, many of the actual candidates under discussion were diplomats (ambassadors or high-ranking officials in foreign ministries), not ministers or otherwise well-known political leaders. This offers an interesting parallel to the process of selecting the first League of Nations secretary-general in 1919, where the dream at first was to give the job to a politician from a small nation,[114] but the job was eventually given to a British civil servant.

This chapter has furthermore argued that the UN secretary-general was not only expected to play a political role from the start, but that this role was inherently flexible. Partly this flexibility came from the mere fact that there was disagreement and confusion about what exactly the role should be. Even the discussions about whether he was to be political or administrative contributed to the flexibility of the office. Because the role was not firmly settled, the holder of the office would have to interpret what the role dictated in each situation. The autonomy and independence this gave the role, meant that the office-holder would have room to expand the role if he wanted to. The flexible nature of the role also came from the existence of alternatives beyond the model provided by the League secretary-general. The ILO director played a much more active political part in proceedings of the organization, making his own policy proposals and defending them at meetings. He thus offered an example of what a more active political secretary-general could do. Likewise, the fact that earlier concepts, such as a 'mediator' or 'president' had been discussed in US plans, showed that there was room for taking the role in different directions. The proposals by some states at San Francisco to expand article 99 even further also reveals that the secretary-general would have allies in his quest to expand his role. On top of this, the wording of article 99 built this flexibility into the Charter by giving the secretary-general broad implied political rights – and the autonomy and independence that followed with these rights – and a basis on which to expand the scope and autonomy of the role even more.

All of this is to say that both the simple story that the UN secretary-general started out as administrative and that subsequent secretaries-general expanded the office to the political figure we know today, as well as the equally simple story that the UN secretary-general was to be 'more political' than the League secretary-general are wrong. They both touch on important parts of the story, but in simplifying the narrative they both miss the point. The UN secretary-general was expected to play a political role from the start, yet the exact implications of this were not recognized, and this made the role inherently flexible and open for subsequent secretaries-general to expand.

2

Establishing Precedents: The Iranian Crisis, UN Membership and the Greek Civil War, 1946

> My personal position in relation to the Security Council has also been highly floating and vague. I have a strong feeling that the eleven members of the Security Council do not wish any 'interference' from the secretary-general, despite article 99 ... the time had come to clarify my own position towards the Council. For me it was 'to be or not to be'. I felt the whole foundation of my future activities failing.[1]
>
> Trygve Lie (April 1946)

Introduction

Once a new IGO is established, it may develop in ways unintended or unanticipated by its state founders. Through the interplay of crisis decision-making, institutional constraints, and the individuals involved, new precedents emerge which build the foundations for the organization's later operations. As the previous chapter argued, when the UN started operations in 1946 the general expectation among member states was that the UN secretary-general would play some sort of 'political' role; however, the precise implications of this were never discussed or spelled out in detail. Article 99 gave the secretary-general the unprecedented right to 'bring to the attention of the Security Council any matter which in his opinion may threaten the maintenance of international peace and security'.[2] But what exactly did this article entail? What would be the relationship between the secretary-general and the Security Council, and what rights and responsibilities did the secretary-general have in the UN's efforts to maintain international peace and security? The UN founders had left these questions unanswered, but they quickly gained importance as the UN organization faced its first crises in Iran and elsewhere in 1946.

The lack of clarity and agreement on the practical implications of article 99 and the precise nature of the role of the UN secretary-general, meant that the first holder of the office, Trygve Lie, enjoyed considerable autonomy to explore his new position. From the start, Lie was determined to ensure that the UN, and the office of the secretary-general, should serve as 'a force for peace' in the world.[3] To this end he sought to clarify the rights and responsibilities of the secretary-general, and to seek the support of the member states for a range of new activities beyond those the League of Nations secretary-general had pursued. During 1946, as the Security Council grappled with crisis situations in Iran and Greece, and disagreements over membership admissions, Lie took advantage of the opportunities presented to establish firm precedents for the political activities of the UN secretary-general. Lie's interpretation of his powers under article 99 and his actions based on this interpretation, led to changes in the informal practices of the UN. Furthermore, for the first and only time, the expansion of the secretary-general's role was also formally recognized through changes in the rules of procedure of the Security Council, the General Assembly, and the Economic and Social Council (ECOSOC).

The most important changes to the secretary-general's role in 1946 happened as a result of Lie's actions in regard to the Iranian crisis. This crisis is therefore the main focus of this chapter. The chapter starts with a brief overview of the Security Council's treatment of the Iranian question from January to April 1946, when the secretary-general remained largely on the sidelines. The second section examines the events of April 1946 when Lie took the bold and unprecedented initiative to present to the Security Council a legal memorandum with his opinions on the Iranian case. The third part of the chapter then explores the memorandum's effects in precipitating a change in the Security Council's rules of procedure, leading it to formally recognize the right of the secretary-general to present oral or written statements to the Council. Finally, the fourth and fifth sections examine the establishment of two further precedents for the secretary-general's role vis-à-vis the Security Council. The fourth section examines the first time the secretary-general issued a clearly political statement on the question of UN membership in August 1946, while the fifth section discusses the recognition of the secretary-general's right to send investigative committees in the context of the Greek civil war in September 1946. Thus, less than a year after the organization started operations, the UN member states had recognized a number of important precedents for the political role of the secretary-general which laid the foundations for a further expansion of the office.

The Iranian crisis at the United Nations, January–April 1946

The Iranian complaint against the Soviet Union was one of the first questions on the agenda of the Security Council, and the discussion of the Iranian crisis would have lasting consequences for the relationship between the UN secretary-general and the Security Council.[4] The origins of the troubles in Iran lay in the joint Anglo-Soviet occupation of the country during WW2. The government in Teheran had been on friendly terms with Germany, prompting Britain and the Soviet Union to enter Iran in order to secure this vital supply route of aid from the Western states to the Soviet Union. The two occupying powers agreed they would both leave Iran within six months after the end of the war; that is, by 2 March 1946. But in late 1945 it became clear that the Soviet Union had no immediate plans to leave, and the presence of Soviet troops on Iranian territory became entangled with discussions over oil concessions and autonomy for Iranian Azerbaijan.[5] On 19 January 1946, during the first UN General Assembly in London, the Iranian government therefore asked the Security Council to examine the situation.[6] The first round of Security Council discussions ended even before Lie was appointed secretary-general, with a resolution requesting Iran and the Soviet Union to keep the Council informed of the progress of their negotiations,[7] but the question would return again in March 1946.

The deadline for all foreign troops to leave Iran came and went on 2 March, but Soviet troops remained in the country. During February the Iranian prime minister had travelled to Moscow to negotiate with the Soviet government, but no settlement was reached, and with promises of support from the US he instructed his representative to the UN and ambassador to Washington DC, Hussein Ala, to request renewed discussions in the Security Council.[8] On 18 March, just as Lie arrived in the US to establish the UN's new headquarters, Ala approached him to request that the Council resume discussion on Iran's complaint against the Soviet Union. A resumption of Council discussions did not suit the Soviet government, however, because it wanted to avoid public debate of the Iranian complaint. On 19 March the Soviet representative Gromyko therefore asked Lie to postpone discussions until 10 April,[9] but Lie felt the Security Council itself would have to decide whether or not to postpone discussion, and left the Iranian complaint on the provisional agenda.[10]

As the Council meeting approached, the Soviet government tried to force Teheran into an agreement by publicly announcing that such an agreement had already been reached, while handing the Iranian government three notes: one saying the Soviet troops would leave Iran within five to six weeks 'if no unforeseen circumstances occurred'; one to establish a joint Iranian-Soviet oil company; and one to offer Soviet help to negotiate autonomy for Azerbaijan.[11] The Soviet Union continued to call for the postponement of discussion, arguing that the Iranian complaint was baseless and that the Council had no justification to consider the question. Nonetheless, on 25 March a majority of Council members led by the US and Britain, decided to admit the item onto the agenda and turned down the Soviet request for a postponement. In protest, Gromyko marched out of the Council chamber, thus initiating the first Soviet boycott of the UN.[12] With Gromyko absent, the Council proceeded to invite the Iranian representative to give a statement, before deciding to adjourn until May, awaiting further information about the situation.[13]

On 4 April, the same day the Security Council deferred consideration of the question, Iran and the Soviet Union concluded an agreement: Soviet troops were to withdraw within five to six weeks from 24 March; a joint Iranian-Soviet oil company would be set up, subject to approval of the Iranian parliament within seven months; and the Soviet Union recognized Azerbaijan as an internal Iranian matter.[14] Two days later the Soviet Union again asked that the Iranian question be removed from the Security Council's agenda. The Iranian government at first instructed Ala to ask for the item to remain on the agenda, then argued that the Council itself should decide its course of action, before finally on 15 April instructing Ala to inform the Council that 'the Iranian Government has complete confidence in the word and pledge of the Soviet Government and for this reason withdraws its complaint from the Security Council'.[15]

The Soviet representative returned to the Security Council to argue that the question ought to be removed from the agenda, but received little support. The US, Britain, the Netherlands, Australia, Mexico, Brazil, and Egypt spoke out against the Soviet proposal, and argued that Iran no longer had the option of withdrawing its complaint, as the matter was now under the Council's jurisdiction. France and Poland supported the Soviet Union (and Iran). France noted that the matter could easily be brought back to the Council if a new situation should arise, and proposed that the secretary-general could be asked to continue collecting information and keep the Security Council informed. Poland argued that the purpose of the Council was to aid understanding between states, not to cause trouble for them after agreements had been reached, and furthermore it was important that the Council should protect small states from becoming pawns in the great powers' game.[16] Thus by the end of the Council meeting on 15 April, the Iranian question had turned into a procedural one, typical of a new organization trying to figure out what its rules and procedures meant in practice: could Iran withdraw its complaint once it was on the Council's agenda? The following discussions led to clarifications both on the procedures of the Security Council and on the nature of the relationship between the Security Council and the secretary-general.

Lie's legal memorandum, April 1946

When the Council discussion on 15 April entered the procedural realm, secretary-general Lie decided to present his opinions on the matter. Once the Soviet Union had given assurances that it would withdraw its troops, and Iran had stated its satisfaction with the Soviet promise and withdrawn its complaint, Lie 'saw no point in keeping the question on the agenda. The United Nations, I felt, should aim to settle disputes, not to inflame them. If both Iran and the U.S.S.R. agreed that their quarrel had been resolved, the Security Council should not indicate the contrary.'[17] Already on 8 April he had suggested privately to the president of the Security Council that Iran could 'volunteer to call it all off'.[18] Consequently, before the Council meeting on 16 April the secretary-general asked his legal advisers to prepare a memorandum setting out what he saw as the legal implications of the case. The memorandum argued for a restrictive view of the Security Council's agenda. Since the Council had not ordered an investigation under article 34, and had not under article 36 declared the existence of a dispute or a like situation under article 33, 'it may well be that there is no way in which it can remain seized of the matter', once Iran had withdrawn the complaint which was the basis for the Council's discussions.[19] In other words, the Council would have to take action on the Iranian complaint to gain ownership of it. Lie claimed he had prepared the memorandum merely for the discretionary use of the Council president. Although he did not expect that any state would change its stance on the matter, he felt it important to point out the Council's 'error' in deciding to keep the case on the agenda and to explain how this decision violated the letter and spirit of the Charter.[20]

Lie handed the memorandum to the Security Council president at the start of the meeting on 16 April, and the drama that followed would have lasting implications for the relationship of the secretary-general with the Security Council, even though Lie's argument about the Iranian question itself met little support. The president read out the memorandum before the Council agreed to send it on to the Committee of Experts – its procedural subcommittee[21] – for closer examination. After a brief debate on the Iranian issue, in which no one mentioned or engaged with the opinions contained in the secretary-general's memorandum, the president moved to call a vote on the original question – the Soviet Union's proposal to have the item removed from the agenda. But at this the French and Polish delegates protested that the Council could not move to vote before it had heard back from the Committee of Experts regarding the secretary-general's memorandum. 'The Secretary-General is an important official of the United Nations, invested by the Charter with special and important powers and … we cannot vote now as if his opinion did not count or exist', argued the Polish representative Oscar Lange.[22] The president of the Council, Quo

Tai-chi of China, admitted that he had made a mistake in calling for a vote, but argued against Lange's interpretation of the role of the secretary-general and pointed out that article 97 named him 'the chief administrative officer of the Organization'. Therefore, 'whatever observations we may receive from him – and I am sure the Council will wish to give due weight and due consideration to his observations – the decision remains with the Council'.[23] Soviet representative Gromyko then entered the debate with a sweeping argument in favour of a broad interpretation of the secretary-general's role:

> 'As regards the functions of the Secretary-General – a question which has arisen in passing – these are, of course, more serious and more weighty than was indicated just now. It is sufficient to recall [Article 99] of the Charter to realize the heavy responsibilities incumbent upon the Secretary-General ... Thus, the Secretary-General has all the more right, and an even greater obligation, to make statements on various aspects of the questions considered by the Security Council.'[24]

As Lie pointed out in his memoirs, no Council member challenged 'the remarkably broad interpretation of the Secretary-General's powers' presented by Gromyko.[25] Instead the Council adjourned for a few days to await the report of the Committee of Experts.

The 'memorandum fell like a bombshell', Lie later wrote in summary.[26] This was the first time the secretary-general publicly injected his opinion on a matter under consideration by the Security Council, and the action provoked strong reactions from many governments. The American representative, Edward Stettinius, was particularly angry, and wrote back to the Secretary of State that Lie's memorandum 'was drafted with other than purely legal considerations in mind', and furthermore, 'it was considered extremely dubious practice for the Secretary General to put in an unsolicited interpretation concerning a matter which should be decided by the Council alone'. In Stettinius' view, the secretary-general's opinion was particularly inappropriate in this case, because his view differed from that of the Council majority.[27] According to the *New York Times*, Secretary of State James Byrnes commented that Lie had 'overstepped the bounds of the Secretary General's authority' in submitting the memorandum.[28] Lie claimed that Byrnes later apologized for his remarks, and admitted he had not actually read the memorandum.[29] The British Foreign Office initially confined its discussion to the legal points raised by Lie and disagreed with his interpretation of articles 34 and 36 and the word 'investigation'.[30] Once the Committee of Experts had submitted its report, one Foreign Office official took pleasure in noting that 'it [was] encouraging that the Secretary-General [had] received a rebuke for his feeble and defeatist letter'.[31]

The Soviet government was the only one to enthusiastically welcome Lie's memorandum. At the Council's meeting on 23 April Gromyko praised its 'impartial and detailed analysis' and used it to support his arguments that the 'so-called Iranian question' should be removed from the Council's agenda.[32] It is significant that Gromyko gave such a positive characterization of the memorandum at this later meeting, rather than at the first meeting on 16 April, as it means he must have received explicit instructions from Moscow to endorse it.[33] In fact, Lie's actions on Iran probably caused the Soviet Union to see him as an ally within the UN, and thus to favour expanding his role to grant him broader scope for action and more autonomy.[34] In a 1950 assessment of Lie, two Soviet officials characterized the Iranian memorandum as a 'friendly' or 'neutral' stance by the secretary-general.[35]

Meanwhile, on 17 and 18 April the Committee of Experts discussed the secretary-general's memorandum. At the outset the Committee decided not the deal with the specifics of the Iranian question, but rather to discuss in the abstract the principle of retaining or removing agenda items.[36] The majority of the Committee of Experts, like the majority in the Council itself, criticized Lie's analysis of the Council's functions and competence, and argued against the idea that there could ever be any 'automaticity' in the removal of an item from the Security Council's agenda because the Council was master of its own agenda.[37] Given the identical national composition of the Committee of Experts and the Security Council proper, it was not surprising that the Committee reflected the balance in the Council, voting 8 to 3 in favour of the Council's competence to keep the item on its agenda.[38] As expected, on 23 April the Security Council rejected the Soviet proposal to remove the question from the Council's agenda.[39]

Even though the Iranian question remained on the Security Council's agenda, in reality the crisis was over. At the Council's request, Iran submitted reports on the progress of Soviet withdrawal. Not satisfied with the Iranian reports, the Council on 22 May decided to defer discussion indefinitely, but still retain the question on the agenda.[40] No further meeting was ever called on this question, and the matter was finally removed from the Council's agenda in 1976.[41] Once Soviet troops had left Iran, the Azerbaijan autonomy movement soon crumbled, and Teheran was able to reassert its control over the province within a few months. The following year, in October 1947, the new Iranian parliament also rejected the agreement for a joint Iranian-Soviet oil company, snubbing the Soviet Union of the oil concession it thought it had secured in April 1946. But by then the Soviet leaders had turned their attention elsewhere, and they merely objected verbally to the Iranian decision. Thus the Iranian crisis, the first crisis of the emerging Cold War, came to an end.[42]

Changes to the Security Council rules of procedure, May 1946

The most important consequence of Lie's Iran memorandum lay in its implications for the relationship between the secretary-general and the Security Council. As noted earlier, secretary-general Lie claimed to have been motivated solely by the need to point out the legal implications of the Security Council's 'error'. Writing to Halvard Lange, his successor as Norwegian foreign minister, Lie concluded that his memorandum had served the purpose he intended in this respect: 'the three members who were in the minority, were supported in the legal field by me as an objective judge, and the discrimination which was aimed at the Soviet Union, did not have the expected effects'.[43] Lie was surprised by the uproar his memorandum had stirred. He believed that article 99 already gave him 'not merely the right to submit legal opinions to the President, of which the latter would take notice, but that he should be able to address the Council on any question it might consider'.[44] In Lie's opinion, the discussion during the Council meeting on 16 April had recognized the secretary-general's 'right to have his own opinion and to submit it to the Council'.[45] James Reston, a journalist with the *New York Times* who followed the UN closely, likewise observed that the secretary-general's action had 'established the principle – which nobody questioned and which the Russians have now supported – that he has the privilege of addressing the Council on substantive matters'.[46] Nonetheless, although Lie argued that his 'right to intervene' had now been firmly established, he 'should be very happy' if that right could be written into the Council's rules of procedure.[47] To have the secretary-general's rights enumerated in formal rules would provide a firmer basis for the office's future activity than if they were solely based on informal practices.

The formal rules regulating the relationship between the secretary-general and the Security Council can be found in the UN Charter and the Security Council's rules of procedure. Article 99 states that 'the Secretary-General may bring to the attention of the Security Council any matter which in his opinion may threaten the maintenance of international peace and security', while article 98 says that 'the Secretary-General shall act in that capacity in all meetings of the ... Security Council ... and shall perform such other functions as are entrusted to him by these organs'. The preparatory commission working in the autumn of 1945 had drawn up a set of provisional rules of procedure for the Security Council, and one of the Council's first acts was to ask the Committee of Experts to examine these and present a suggestion to the Council.[48] On 9 April the Security Council had endorsed without discussion the four rules that described the roles of the secretary-general and the Secretariat. These four rules stated that the secretary-general 'shall act in that capacity in all meetings of the

Security Council' or appoint a deputy in his place, provide the staff required by the Council, give notice of meetings to all members of the Council, and be responsible for preparing the documents required by the Council.[49] In other words, the Council adopted four rules specifying the administrative tasks of the secretary-general in relation to the Security Council, but left undefined what rights and responsibilities the secretary-general enjoyed in the political field.

With the political role of the secretary-general still largely undefined, Lie found his position in relation to the Security Council 'highly floating and vague'. He had the strong impression that 'the eleven members of the Security Council do not wish any "interference" from the Secretary General'. In Lie's opinion, 'the time had come to clarify [his] own position towards the Council. For [him] it was 'to be or not to be'. [He] felt the whole foundation of [his] future activities failing.'[50] As a result, after presenting the memorandum in mid-April, the secretary-general and his staff started suggesting, informally, that there ought to be some rule recognizing the right of the secretary-general to present his opinions on matters of substance in the Security Council. According to Arkady Sobolev, the Soviet assistant secretary-general for Security Council affairs, Lie found it embarrassing that there was no written rule giving him the right to intervene in the proceedings of the Security Council when both the General Assembly and ECOSOC had them.[51] Secretary-general Lie and his executive assistant Andrew W. Cordier broached this question with the Americans, who were inclined to agree with the secretary-general that it would be desirable to have such a written rule in the Security Council rules of procedure.[52]

On 15 May, when the Committee of Expert started discussions on 'the powers and functions' of the secretary-general, Lie nevertheless took a back seat and allowed Sobolev, the assistant secretary-general for Security Council affairs, to take charge of the process. Sobolev suggested a new rule based on rule 24 of the rules of procedure of ECOSOC, which read as follows: 'The Secretary-General or his deputy may at any time, upon the invitation of the President of the Council or of the Chairmen of the Committees of the Council and subsidiary bodies, make either oral or written statements concerning any question under consideration.'[53] The US confessed its surprise at Sobolev's suggestion, as earlier discussions with Lie and his staff had led them to believe that rule 48 of the General Assembly rules of procedure would be acceptable.[54] The US representative proposed that rule as a model: 'The Secretary-General may at any time, upon invitation of the President, make to the General Assembly either oral or written statements concerning any question which is being considered by the General Assembly.'[55] The two suggestions differed over the question of subcommittees, but they both included the provision that the secretary-general would have to be invited by the president to give a statement. In his memoirs Lie claimed not to have wished for such a limitation on the right, and he felt this was not merely an academic point, as the president of the General Assembly had twice denied him the floor in debates in London. But at the same time both the Assembly and ECOSOC had this provision in their rules, and Lie therefore felt it would be 'impolitic to press openly for a more extensive right in the Security Council'.[56]

Fortunately for Lie, the Soviet and Australian representatives came to the secretary-general's rescue, and insisted on removing the words 'at the invitation of the president' from the draft rule. The ensuing debate on whether or not the secretary-general had an absolute right to intervene continued over the next two weeks and revealed interesting differences of opinion regarding the role of the UN secretary-general. Australia and the Soviet Union argued that the secretary-general was a 'co-equal with the Council',[57] and his right to intervene was therefore 'absolute and not limited', and should not be subject to an invitation.[58]

The Chinese representative took the lead on the opposing side, and insisted that the words 'upon the invitation of the president' should be included. Those who wanted to retain the phrase put forth four general arguments. First, they argued that this phrase was merely a formality, and that the Council should adopt only a minimum rule which would allow later interpretation and practice to develop in light of experience.[59] Second, these states argued that the Committee could not prejudice and prejudge the relationship of the secretary-general with the Military Staff Committee, the Atomic Energy Commission, and other subsidiary bodies of the Council. For this reason they also opposed Sobolev's suggestion to base the rule on the ECOSOC model.[60] Third, the US in particular questioned whether the secretary-general did indeed have an unlimited right to intervene, and in particular whether article 98 or 99 gave him the right to give statements on substantive and political matters.[61] Fourth, these states argued that the rule could not afford to the secretary-general greater powers than those possessed by the members of the Council, and that including the phrase would indicate that the president had discretion on the timing of the secretary-general's statements.[62]

The Australian delegation remained the strongest advocate for the view that the secretary-general had an unlimited right to give statements. Even when the Soviet Union and other states that had been supportive of these arguments gave in to the majority in the interest of consensus, the Australian delegate continued to insist on reserving his rights to reopen the question in later discussions in the Security Council proper. Other delegations put strong pressure on the Australian delegation to relent, pointing out that it would be embarrassing both to the secretary-general and the Security Council if this issue had to be discussed in a public meeting.[63] Nonetheless, Australia would not give in. According to Stettinius, even Sobolev joined in urging the Australian delegate to accept the inclusion of language on the president's invitation, and Sobolev would apparently also ask Lie himself to have a word with the head of the Australian delegation.[64]

After days of deadlock with the Australian delegation the last supporter of the secretary-general's unlimited right of intervention, new instructions to the British delegation caused a pendulum shift in the committee and adoption of a rule of procedure without the phrase 'at the invitation of the president'. Reports from New York had been doing the rounds at the Foreign Office in London. Philip Noel-Baker, Minister of State for Foreign Affairs, was the first there to point out that 'surely' the secretary-general should address the Council 'of *right*, and not by invitation of the Chairman'.[65] John Ward, head of the UN Department, agreed that although it seemed unnecessary to include this rule given the position the secretary-general already enjoyed under article 99, 'if he wants a rule there is obviously no objection ... he ought to be able to do it as of right'. The question of an invitation would presumably be a mere formality, and it was unfortunate that it had been raised as a matter of principle, 'but since it has I think the Australian delegation is in the right and that perhaps we should say so', Ward concluded.[66] The British Foreign Office consequently sent new instructions to its UN delegation to support the Australian committee member, because 'it seems to us quite wrong and inconsistent with the commanding position given by the Charter to the Secretary-General that he should be obliged to obtain an invitation before expressing his views'.[67]

When the British representative, who arrived late to the meeting, revealed his new instructions to the Committee on 23 May, several other states quickly changed sides too. By the end of the meeting, only the US, China, Egypt, and the Netherlands still insisted on the need for an invitation, and the Committee decided to adjourn to give these delegations time to consider a new draft rule.[68] By the next committee meeting four days later, all four had been authorized to approve the new draft, which the Committee adopted unanimously.[69] Finally, on 6 June the Security Council unanimously adopted the proposed new rule without any discussion. The new rule 21 of the Security Council's rules of procedure read as follows: 'The Secretary-General, or his deputy acting on his behalf, may make either oral or written statements to the Security Council on any question under consideration by it.'[70] The secretary-general's right to make statements to the Council was now formally recognized.

Although Lie had played an important role in this process, by submitting the legal memorandum on Iran that prompted the discussion, and urging for the rights he felt he already had to be recognized, the secretary-general cannot take credit for the unlimited right enshrined in the final rule adopted. Lie took a back seat in the process, and would have accepted the inclusion of the phrase 'upon the invitation of the president'.[71] Instead, as a result of the Australian delegation's tenacity, and the principled stand of the British

Foreign Office, the states on the Security Council in the end accepted that the secretary-general's right to offer statements was unlimited. The rules of procedure on the relationship between the secretary-general and the Security Council adopted in June 1946 remain unchanged to this day.

Once the Security Council had adopted this new rule of procedure, other UN organs soon followed. The General Assembly conducted a substantial revision of its rules of procedure during its second session, and adopted new rules on 17 November 1947. Going beyond rule 48 quoted earlier, the new rule 64 read as follows: 'The Secretary-General, or a member of the Secretariat designated by him as his representative, may at any time make either oral or written statements to the General Assembly concerning any question under consideration by it.'[72] ECOSOC undertook a major review of its rules of procedure before its eighth session in February and March 1949.[73] During these discussions the US proposed retaining the provision on invitation by the president, but the Secretariat's legal department insisted that the secretary-general considered this an important issue,[74] and the US dropped the idea. In the end ECOSOC adopted a new rule as follows: 'The Secretary-General, or his representative, may, subject to rule 47, make oral as well as written statements to the Council, its committees or subsidiary bodies concerning any question under consideration.'[75]

Despite the concern during discussions in the Committee of Experts on the role of the secretary-general in the Military Staff Committee, this committee was quite agreeable to allowing the secretary-general to participate, and adopted the necessary provisions in its rules of procedure in September 1946.[76] Alone among the principal organs of the UN, the Trusteeship Council declined to adjust its rules, leading Lie to speculate that some of the colonial powers might be hesitant to let the secretary-general and his deputies take full part in those discussions.[77] Nonetheless, with the changes in the Security Council, the General Assembly, and ECOSOC, the secretary-general's unlimited right to participate in political discussions had been established in all the major bodies of the UN.

Lie's statement on UN membership, August 1946

By the summer of 1946 the new rule of procedure which recognized the secretary-general's rights to submit statements to the Security Council was formally in place. Yet there would be other times when the secretary-general explored his implied powers. His memo on the Iranian question had dealt ostensibly with procedural matters, not with substance. In August 1946 the secretary-general took the opportunity to express his opinion to the Security Council, for the first time, on a contested political issue. He did so over the issue of UN membership.

Membership questions became a major headache for the UN throughout its first decade. Article 4 of the UN Charter simply stated that UN membership was open to 'all other peace-loving states which accept the obligations contained in the present Charter and, in the judgment of the Organization, are able and willing to carry out these obligations', and established the procedure for admission. New UN members could be admitted by the General Assembly, upon the recommendation of the Security Council.[78] As a substantive question, the five permanent members (P5) had the right to veto the Council's recommendation, and membership applications therefore quickly became tied up with Cold War politics. In May 1946 the Security Council decided to defer consideration of all membership applications until August, and in the meantime established a subcommittee to examine all incoming applications.[79] Finally, on 28 August the Council was due to start discussing the applications of Afghanistan, Albania, Iceland, Ireland, the Mongolian People's Republic, Portugal, Siam (Thailand), Sweden, and Transjordan (Jordan).

Leading up to the meeting, Council members discussed the issue informally, and the secretary-general took an active part in the proceedings. From the moment he was elected secretary-general, Lie had developed strong loyalty to the organization and its Charter and principles, and he felt strongly that membership had to be universal. On 23 August, Lie invited the P5 and the Council president to an informal meeting on the UN membership question. According to the US representative present, the secretary-general made 'an earnest plea for admission of all 9 candidates', and 'implored the members having the right of veto not to exercise this right in the case of applications for membership in the UN'. In Lie's opinion, 'use of the veto for this purpose would be damaging to the prestige of the UN and would further lower the esteem of the Security Council in the eyes of the world'.[80] The US, Mexico, and Brazil indicated that they would support the admission of all candidates, and the US let it be known that it would introduce a proposal to admit all nine when the Council met. The Soviet Union, on the other hand, continued to express doubts about some of the applicants, and gave its delegation strict instructions to oppose the admission of Ireland, Portugal, and Transjordan.

Given the secretary-general's strong opinions on the issue, it did not come as a surprise when he stated his unequivocal support for the American proposal to admit all nine applicants at the Council meeting on 28 August. If the UN was to fulfil its purpose, it would require 'the active support and co-operation of every respectable nation and of every decent man and woman in the entire world', Lie argued, and pointed out that the founding members of the UN, including the P5, had agreed that the organization 'must be as universal as possible ... For this reason, in my capacity as Secretary-General of the United Nations, I wish to support the admission to membership of all the

States which are applying today.'[81] At the time no state raised any objections to the secretary-general's statement, and the Council proceeded to discuss the subcommittee's report and the US proposal to admit all nine applicants.

It quickly became clear that the US proposal, supported by the secretary-general, would not carry. The Soviet representative Gromyko opposed admitting all states as one, arguing that 'countries cannot be regarded as things and dealt with in accordance with a standard measure', and the Council therefore had to consider the merits of each application separately.[82] The Australian representative likewise stated that although his country supported universality of UN membership, the proposed method of admitting them all as one was wrong. Although Brazil and China gave their unequivocal support for the US proposal, and the Netherlands indicated that it would vote in its favour, it was obvious that the proposal would not carry. The Soviet Union suggested that the US should withdraw its proposal in the interest of saving time, to which the US delegation agreed.[83]

Over two long meetings on 29 August, lasting more than ten hours in total, the Council discussed each individual case.[84] In the end the majority of the applications were turned down, while the Council agreed to recommend only Afghanistan, Iceland, and Sweden for membership.[85] This was the end of immediate Security Council discussion of UN membership for the time being, but further discussions and controversies would continue over the next few years. Soon the position of the US and the Soviet Union reversed, as the Soviet bloc started to support wholesale admission of all applicants, while the US and its allies insisted on treating each application individually. At one point or another, the deadlock kept 16 applicants outside the UN, until a package deal was agreed in 1955.[86] That year the Council finally agreed to admit Albania, Austria, Bulgaria, Cambodia, Ceylon (Sri Lanka), Finland, Hungary, Ireland, Italy, Jordan, Laos, Libya, Nepal, Portugal, Romania, and Spain,[87] soon leaving only the divided states of Germany, Korea, and Vietnam on the outside of the organization.[88]

As for the secretary-general's statement of UN membership, no state openly challenged his right to intervene in this matter of substance. Behind the scenes, however, some delegations muttered their annoyance at Lie's actions. Sir Alexander Cadogan, the British representative, wrote back to the Foreign Office that he had approached Lie after the meeting to suggest that the last phrase of Lie's statement was improper. Cadogan argued that the secretary-general should be allowed to make a statement on UN membership and the principle of universality, but felt that he had no right 'supporting' a proposal by a member state. Lie admitted that the use of the word 'support' might have been unfortunate, but went on to argue that his position as secretary-general of the UN was 'quite different from that of the Secretary-General of the League of Nations, and that he was entitled to participate in the discussion of any subject'. Cadogan 'remained unconvinced' and suggested to Lie in a friendly and personal way ... if he really had this right he should in his own interest, be very careful in his exercise of it. Secretary-General remained quite obstinate on the point of principle but conversation was quite friendly, and I do not think he took it amiss when I said that I was going to keep a look-out in the future to prevent him voting![89]

For some British diplomats, the bigger problem was that Lie's statement implied that he spoke on behalf of the UN overall. In their opinion, this assumption was incorrect; 'he has no right to intervene as if he, so to speak, spoke for the United Nations as a whole as opposed to a body which is one of the organs of the United Nations'. Cadogan had therefore been right to rebuke Lie for saying, 'in effect ... that the interests of the United Nations (of which he is not a judge) required a certain course of action and therefore he supported a particular proposal'.[90]

Nonetheless, the British kept their concerns private, and the episode passed without noticeable reaction from other delegations or the press. Other British diplomats pointed out the dangers of trying to limit the secretary-general's powers too much. Jebb, then Assistant Under-Secretary for United Nations Affairs, recalled that 'it was the intention of the drafters of the Charter to give substantially more powers to the Secretary General of U.N.O. than were vested in the Secretary General of the League of Nations', and that Britain should therefore be careful not to 'attempt to curtail the powers, real or imagined, of Mr. Lie more than is absolutely necessary'. Furthermore, should Lie abuse his powers, 'it will be his own funeral and I doubt whether our own interests are likely to suffer very much'. Ultimately, 'if on the other hand we clip his wings we may be prejudicing the position of his successor who may, for all we know, be an infinitely wiser and more powerful personality who will be able to get away with much more than the present Secretary General'.[91] Jebb thus recognized the importance of precedents being set in these early years, as well as Britain's long-term interests as a founder and member of the UN in allowing the office of secretary-general some autonomy and independence for the organization to function as intended.

The right to appoint investigative committees, September 1946

In September 1946, secretary-general Lie seized the opportunity to establish firm recognition of another implied power of article 99: the right of the secretary-general to appoint investigative committees. The opportunity arose during the Security Council's discussions of the Greek civil war. The civil war in Greece, like the Iranian question, was one of the earliest questions on the Security Council's agenda. On 21 January 1946, in retaliation against the Iranian complaint against Soviet troops in

Iran, the Soviet Union lodged a complaint against the presence of British troops in Greece, while the Ukrainian representative filed a complaint against British troops in Indonesia. Britain had sent troops to Greece in October 1944 as German forces were withdrawing, and almost immediately became embroiled in a civil war between the right-wing government in Athens (monarchist and supported by Britain) and left-wing armed groups who had fought against the Germans since 1941 (communist and supported by Albania, Bulgaria, and Yugoslavia).[92] The Security Council first took up the question of Greece on 1 February – the first meeting attended by the newly elected secretary-general[93] – but debate quickly ended on 6 February.[94]

When the Greek question reappeared on the Council agenda later in the year, however, the secretary-general would take the opportunity to assert his political powers. On 24 August the Ukrainian foreign minister sent a telegram to the UN secretary-general asking that the Security Council examine the situation on the Greek border where 'as a result of the irresponsible policy of the present Greek Government a situation had arisen ... which represented a grave danger to peace and security in this part of Europe'.[95] During Council discussions on the issue, the Soviet Union and its allies attacked the Greek government, while the Greek government responded with counter-accusations. Seeking a way out of the hostile debate, the US proposed sending a commission of three impartial individuals who could 'investigate the facts relating to the border incidents along the frontier' and submit an objective report to the Security Council.[96]

Before the US delegation formally introduced this proposal in the Council, it sought support for the idea in private consultations with other delegations and the secretary-general. On 17 September Lie informed Hershel Johnson, acting US ambassador to the UN, that if the American proposal for an investigative commission was vetoed by the Soviet Union (which seemed likely), the secretary-general would be prepared, 'on his own initiative and under his own authority as Secretary General', to send his own committee of three Secretariat officials to investigate the border incidents.[97] The US State Department agreed that Lie would be authorized to take such action, but cautioned against doing so in this instance, because they 'would not think it appropriate for the Secretary General to send a group of members of his own staff to investigate a subject which the Council had considered and rejected because of the lawful use of the veto'.[98] Furthermore, the State Department warned Lie that there was a danger that Albania, Bulgaria, and Yugoslavia would not allow his committee to enter their territories, and the 'prospect of the inability of the Secretariat group to accomplish anything' made it unwise to risk damaging the secretary-general's relationship with the Soviet Union for such uncertain returns.[99]

Nevertheless, before the vote on the American draft resolution at the Council meeting on 20 September, Lie asked for the floor and told the Council:

> 'Just a few words to make clear my own position as Secretary-General and the rights of this office under the Charter. Should the proposal of the United States representative not be carried, I hope that the Council will understand that the Secretary-General must reserve his right to make such enquiries or investigations as he may think necessary, in order to determine whether or not he should consider bringing any aspect of this matter to the attention of the Council under the provisions of the Charter.'[100]

Contrary to US fears, the Soviet representative immediately expressed his support for Lie's statement:

> 'I think that Mr. Lie was right in raising the question of his rights. It seems to me that in this case, as in all other cases, the Secretary-General must act. I have no doubt that he will do so in accordance with the rights and powers of the Secretary-General as defined in the Charter of the United Nations.'[101]

None of the other delegates present said anything to this, and Lie 'had thus established a solid base in the record' for his investigative powers.[102] These investigative powers are implied by article 99 of the UN Charter. If the secretary-general is to be in a position where he can bring matters affecting peace and security to the attention of the Security Council, he needs to be informed of what is going on in the world. This gives the secretary-general an independent right to ask questions and to form fact-finding committees.[103] It was this right that Lie and Gromyko referred to at the Council meeting on 20 September. Although some British diplomats would later object that 'in taking action of the sort contemplated ... the Secretary-General would be exceeding his functions as an official of the United Nations',[104] the secretary-general's right to investigate issues and seek information to decide whether or not he should use article 99 had now been firmly established. Lie never sent a committee to Greece, but the secretary-general's services as an investigator would become important to the UN in coming decades.

Conclusion

The role of the UN secretary-general was largely undefined when the UN started operations in 1946. This inherent flexibility allowed the role to expand during the tenure of the first secretary-general. During 1946, as the UN faced its first peace and security crises, important precedents were established for the relationship between the secretary-general and the Security Council. The member states recognized that the secretary-general shared in the responsibility to maintain peace and security as expressed in article 99, and that he must be allowed to enjoy certain rights to be able to perform his role. Most of these rights remain part of the informal rules of the organization, as precedents and procedures, but some are also enumerated in formal instruments. In 1946, for the first – and last – time, the Security Council changed its rules of procedure to recognize the rights of the secretary-general to present oral or written statements on any issue under consideration. Other rights, such as the right to appoint investigative committees, were recognized when no state protested against the secretary-general's statement on the record that he had this right.

During his first year in office, secretary-general Lie primarily sought recognition for the rights he considered that the Charter had already granted the secretary-general. In Lie's opinion, the secretary-general had a duty to inform the Security Council when it was committing a legal error in retaining the Iranian question on the agenda as a complaint of Iran against the Soviet Union. The storm of criticism and comment which his act unleashed took Lie by surprise. He believed the secretary-general's right to present his opinions to the Council was included in article 99. Nevertheless, he wrote in his memoirs that he was 'glad that these rights were secured at an early stage in the Organization's history when the fluid state of procedures lent itself to [his] initiative'.[105] As Lie saw the process, it was a question of recognizing the rights that the secretary-general already possessed and a matter of clarifying his position vis-à-vis the Security Council and the other organs of the UN, rather than trying to attain new and broader rights which he did not already possess.

This chapter further demonstrated that the secretary-general was not the only actor at the UN with an interest in recognizing the various rights of the secretary-general which allowed him a role in political discussion of peace and security. Indeed, in one instance other actors were responsible for expanding the secretary-general's role further than Lie himself had envisioned. When the Committee of Experts met in May 1946 to discuss inserting a rule to recognize the secretary-general's right to present oral or written statements to the Security Council, Lie took a back seat, and allowed one of his assistant secretaries-general to represent the Secretariat in the proceedings. Lie was also willing to accept that his right to intervene in the Council would be limited by requiring an invitation from the Council president. Such a provision was already included in the rules of procedure of the General Assembly and ECOSOC and Lie felt it would be unwise to push for broader powers in the Security Council. Instead, it was at the insistence of the Australian, Soviet, and later British delegations, that this provision was removed from the draft rule, and the Council recognized the unlimited right of the secretary-general to intervene in Council discussions. The General Assembly and ECOSOC followed up by aligning their rules with the Security Council's.

This chapter highlighted important changes to the secretary-general's role and his relationship with the Security Council and other UN organs during the first few months of the UN's operations. Faced with its first crises of peace and security, while trying to figure out how the UN Charter should be implemented in practice, the UN already in 1946 started to develop in unanticipated and unintended ways. Although article 99 was a clear indication that the UN secretary-general was expected to play a political role, at the start of 1946 it remained unclear what this would mean. During negotiations prompted by the Council's consideration of Iran, the Greek civil war, and UN membership, secretary-general Lie seized the opportunity to gain firm recognition for what he considered to be rights already implied in article 99. But as some of the quotes by state representatives showed, there was disagreement between the UN founder states on how far those rights should go. Over the coming years, as the following chapters demonstrate, secretary-general Lie would continue to act whenever he saw an opportunity, seeking to expand further the scope of action and the autonomy of the secretary-general's office.

3

Urging Forceful Action: 'The Palestine Problem' and Management of Regional Conflicts, 1947–49

> I regard the Palestine question as a crucial test for the United Nations. No greater challenge could be offered to the wisdom and statesmanship of this organisation. I believe that in this organisation are to be found the will, the wisdom and statesmanship necessary to break the horns of the Palestine dilemma and to bring long-delayed peace to the Holy Land.[1]
>
> Secretary-general's draft statement
> (February 1948)

Introduction

UN scholars often overlook Trygve Lie's contribution to the development of the political role of the UN secretary-general.[2] To the extent that he is remembered for his political actions, it is in the case of 'the Palestine problem'. Lie himself would later regard the State of Israel 'as his child', and he took pride in the part he played in helping to establish the Jewish state in Palestine.[3] Lie was an enthusiastic supporter of Israel's UN membership application in 1949 and sought to use every means at his disposal to ensure the necessary majority in the General Assembly. Ralph Bunche,[4] the acting UN mediator, described in his diary how, 'Lie phoned me in evening – very upset – said Israelis <u>had</u> to be admitted <u>now</u>; wanted me to make a statement in favor'.[5] Allegedly, Lie also passed 'secret' information to the Zionists/Israelis on several occasions,[6] and he attempted to leverage his contacts in Norway to ensure its delegation voted in favour of the Israeli membership application.⁷ These episodes have led contemporary observers and later researchers alike to accuse him of harbouring a pro-Zionist bias that came into conflict with what they perceive to be the proper way of fulfilling his role as UN secretary-general.⁸

Ironically, in the one instance that historians recognize Lie's efforts to expand the political scope and autonomy of his role – the case of Palestine – they hurl the adjective 'political' as an accusation against him. In regard to Palestine, Lie supposedly overstepped the boundaries of what was appropriate for the UN secretary-general by acting on a personal political bias. This chapter will argue, to the contrary, that although Lie may have supported the Zionist cause, there is not sufficient evidence to substantiate the corollary position that such support constituted the key driver of his actions. Instead, this chapter will show that in this particular case, Lie's personal pro-Zionism aligned with the secretary-general's interest in promoting and protecting the organization he had been entrusted to lead, and that it was this *institutional* interest that provided the main impetus for his actions.

What in the interwar years came to be known as 'the Palestine problem' – the question of the future organization and government of the territory that was the British mandate of Palestine – first appeared on the UN agenda in February 1947, when the British government referred the question to the new world organization. Since the late 1800s Zionists had arrived in Palestine with the aim of establishing a Jewish 'national home', a goal endorsed by Britain during WW1 and later confirmed by the League of Nations mandate for Palestine. The local Arab population resented this intrusion of newcomers, and nationalists demanded that Palestine be given independence as an Arab state. Tensions heightened in the 1930s, when more Jewish settlers arrived following persecution in Europe, and increased again after WW2, when Holocaust survivors tried to reach Palestine to start a new life. In an attempt to maintain peace and order within its mandate, Britain started sending 'illegal immigrants' to camps in Cyprus, but these policies caused much negative publicity in Europe and the US. Eventually the British government conceded its inability to govern Palestine and decided to refer the entire issue to the UN, in the hope that the world organization might succeed where Britain had failed.⁹ Presented with the Palestine problem, the secretary-general decided to view it as a 'test case', and an opportunity for the new organization to prove its worth. In his memoirs, published in 1954, Lie titled the chapter on Palestine 'The first major test'.¹⁰ Referring to Palestine as a 'crucial test … to the wisdom and statesmanship' of the UN organization was a common theme in the secretary-general's draft statements at the time.¹¹

Looking back at over seven decades of the Arab-Israeli conflict, we might today find Lie's designation of the Palestine problem as a 'test case' puzzling. Current scholarship generally agree that this conflict was intractable from the start, not least because of the Zionists' 'iron wall' policy.[12] Yet if secretary-general Lie chose to seize on the Palestine problem as an opportunity to prove the merits of the UN, he must not have shared this perception. Indeed, he would later go so far as to claim that the UN had solved the problem successfully.[13] In 1947 not only was there still significant uncertainty regarding the role of the UN secretary-general, but also the fate of the UN itself was far from determined. The young organization faced a number of challenges and setbacks in its first years of operation, not least due to the emerging Cold War, as the next chapter will discuss. Why, in the midst of such uncertainty, did Lie believe that Palestine — an intractable conflict — offered a good opportunity to prove the UN's abilities?

This chapter argues that Lie believed Palestine could demonstrate the UN's potential precisely because it was not yet a conflict between East and West. The secretary-general saw Palestine as a relatively minor regional conflict, and believed that if the UN could 'succeed in seeing through the plans here in understanding between the great powers ... it would have a tremendous psychological effect',[14] demonstrating the UN's abilities to governments and peoples alike. As he wrote in his memoirs, Palestine was a case where the great powers 'should still be able to act in unison' and 'do something positive through the United Nations'.[15] Hence, in relation to the Palestine problem Lie's main concern was neither the situation in Palestine itself, nor the Zionist establishment of a Jewish state, but rather the effects the UN's involvement with the Palestine problem might have on the UN organization and its place in the world.

When Lie wrote that Palestine was a 'test' for the UN organization, he actually identified two testing elements, though he never fully explicated them. The first related to the UN's ability to solve regional conflicts; it was a test of the organization's capacity to fulfil its explicit mandate to maintain international peace and security. The second test identified by Lie concerned the UN's potential to mediate and build bridges between the great powers. One of the main purposes of the new UN organization was to preserve the cooperation among the victorious powers of WW2, and it was intended to serve as a forum, or concert, for the great powers.[16] This chapter adds a third analytical test to those identified by Lie, and argues that in taking on the Palestine problem as a test case of the UN's capability to solve regional conflicts and create unity among the great powers, Lie also set himself a test. The Palestine problem was therefore also a significant test of the secretary-general as a 'guardian' of the UN, and his abilities to protect and promote the UN.

The chapter is divided into five sections largely arranged chronologically. The first sets the stage by looking at the UN's first involvement with Palestine and the process leading to the adoption of the partition resolution in November 1947. The second examines the secretary-general's efforts to push for implementation of the partition plan in the winter of 1947–48. The third considers the conflict that developed between the secretary-general and the US over the implementation of partition in the spring of 1948. The chapter then goes on to discuss Lie's efforts to encourage the Security Council to take forceful action in response to the outbreak of the first international Arab-Israeli war in May 1948. Finally, the chapter examines Lie's attempts to establish an armed guard to deploy to Palestine to enforce the partition plan during 1948.

Deciding what to do with Palestine, February–November 1947

The British government announced it would turn the Palestine problem over to the UN on 18 February 1947; just two days later, Lie raised the problem with his staff for the first time.[17] Shortly afterwards, Bunche, then a director in the trusteeship division,[18] wrote in a memorandum that the UN Secretariat had been given 'an unparalleled opportunity to take useful and constructive initiative' in preparing for the consideration of the Palestine problem.[19] Such an opportunity was a welcome change from the challenges and setbacks the organization had faced in its first years of operation. In March 1947, Lie was concerned by growing East–West tensions and the accompanying tendency of the great powers to sidestep the organization in dealing with these problems. These concerns regarding UN prestige were redoubled by the fact that member states ignored its recommendations on Spain[20] and South Africa.[21] The secretary-general complained that 'there was no doubt that the United Nations was at present going through a very serious political crisis',[22] and 'had suffered a series of serious setbacks in the last year'.[23] It was against this background that Lie and the Secretariat started to work on the Palestine problem, determined to achieve success at last.

Following Britain's referral, the General Assembly met in special session from 28 April to 15 May 1947 and appointed the United Nations Special Committee on Palestine (UNSCOP).[24] UNSCOP would examine the situation over the summer and make a recommendation to the regular session of the Assembly in the autumn. When UNSCOP held their first meeting in New York on 26 May, Lie reminded the committee that they represented 'the hope and faith of millions of people. Their confidence in the ability of the United Nations to fulfil its momentous mission will be greatly influenced by the results of your work.'[25] Already at this stage the UN secretary-general saw the coherence and survival of the UN as intricately linked to solving the Palestine problem.

By Lie's own account he did not interfere with the work of UNSCOP.[26] The secretary-general waited for the report to be finalized, but once it was public, he immediately started to lobby for the majority recommendation of partition,[27] which he felt duty-bound to promote:

> What had emerged was a *clear victory for the principle of partition*. The international community, through its chosen representatives, had decided that two states should be created. As Secretary-General, I took the cue and, when approached by delegations for advice, frankly recommended that they follow the majority plan. Behind-the-scenes discussions soon became hectic, and some Arab spokesmen attacked me openly; but I could not yield. The responsibility for solving the Palestine problem had been transferred to the United Nations, and the Organization had to act in conformity with its best judgment.[28]

The secretary-general's support for partition remained behind the scenes in this period. The US and the Soviet Union, on the other hand, both publicly stated their support for partition of Palestine.[29] This show of concord across Cold War boundaries and the sight of the two great powers working together, 'demonstrated with all clarity the potential unity of the great powers that had been dreamed of by the UN's founders'.[30] It gave Lie and other observers hope that the Palestine problem could be solved, and that the great powers might overcome their differences through the UN. As one observer noted, however, it was also a bittersweet experience, because such cooperation was not yet the norm.[31] Eventually, after months of debate, on 29 November 1947 the General Assembly passed a resolution recommending partition, with the support of two thirds of the UN membership, including the US and the Soviet Union.[32]

Implementing the partition of Palestine, December 1947–February 1948

The General Assembly resolution established a new Palestine Commission and tasked it with implementing the partition plan.[33] Before the commission's first meeting, Lie began manoeuvring, first to ensure that the Security Council would back up the commission, and second to sound out states' willingness to set up an international military force to accomplish the task. The secretary-general continued to work for the coherence of the organization, and sought to exploit any means at his disposal to reach his twin goals of implementing partition of Palestine and demonstrating the UN's abilities.

If the secretary-general had intended his manoeuvring to remain private, his plans were spoiled by a series of *New York Times* articles on his plans for a UN force in the new year.[34] Lie met informally with the permanent members of the Security Council on 5 January 1948 and expressed his concern that the members of the Palestine Commission could not travel to Palestine unless they were provided with adequate protection.[35] He had come to the meeting armed with a working paper prepared by the Secretariat, as early as October 1947, on precedents for the creation of international forces.[36] The secretary-general had also discussed the subject with the permanent five earlier in December,[37] and had already asked several smaller states whether they would provide troops for such a military force.[38] These consultations were part of the secretary-general's preparations for implementing partition of Palestine. He was determined to see the plan through, if necessary, by the use of an armed force.

At the first meeting of the Palestine Commission on 9 January 1948, Lie continued his quest to implement the partition plan, as he told the assembled members that they had a right to expect that the Security Council would 'not fail to exercise, to the fullest and without exception, every necessary power entrusted to it by the Charter in order to assist you in fulfilling your mission'.[39] The members of the Palestine Commission were similarly eager to secure the Security Council's help. According to Bunche, the Filipino representative on the committee was 'frightened to death' of going to Palestine, and prepared a suggestion to hand the case over to the Council within a few days of taking his seat.[40] Likewise, the Czech chairman, Karel Lisicky, in his first statement to the Security Council, begged for help and emphasized the need 'for assistance by non-Palestinian military forces available, not in symbolic form but in effective, adequate strength', for the Palestine Commission to complete its task.[41]

Behind the scenes, Lie mounted a campaign to get the Security Council to support the Palestine Commission. In his opinion, there was a real and urgent danger that, if the UN proved toothless in the face of opposition to its plans, states would come to believe that they could resist UN decisions by force and get away with it. The future of the organization itself seemed to be at risk if it could not deal with this relatively minor regional problem.[42] Lie prepared several draft statements containing his arguments, but he never officially delivered any of them to the Security Council. In his memoirs, Lie explained that he did not want to make a statement just for the record,[43] and Bunche also counselled him to withhold his statement until they could see 'which way the winds are blowing in the Security Council'.[44] In particular Lie wanted the US to take the initiative, as he realized that the opinions and initiatives of one of the permanent members carried more weight than those of the secretary-general.[45] Not content to wait passively, however, Lie prodded and lobbied the US delegation to urge them on. Bunche told the American UN ambassador, Senator Warren Austin, that Lie 'feels strongly that the Palestine issue is a basic one for UN'. The continued support of the US for partition was essential, and 'abandonment of the Palestine plan under these conditions would be a death blow to UN prestige'.[46]

Picking a fight with the US, February–April 1948

Despite the secretary-general's attempts to push the US to act forcefully in the implementation of partition, the US government decided to argue on legal grounds against the position preferred by the secretary-general and the Palestine Commission. The US argued that the Security Council had no legal right to implement a political solution recommended by the General Assembly. Lie, naturally, disagreed, as it would undermine the coherence of the organization if the Security Council disputed the decision of the General Assembly. On 24 February, Austin, the US ambassador, claimed that the Security Council was not empowered by the Charter to help implement a political solution; its only mandate was to deal with threats to international peace and security.[47] Lie was very disappointed: 'This attitude, I feared, would prejudice fundamentally the powers of the Organization, in addition to damaging its prestige. I was opposed in principle, as well as on practical grounds, to the position taken.'[48] In early March, therefore, he circulated a memorandum, prepared by the Secretariat at the request of the Palestine Commission, stating that the Security Council was within its rights, and even had a duty, to help implement partition. If necessary, it argued, the Security Council could establish an international force to do so.[49] The memorandum was leaked to the *New York Times*,[50] a move that may have been intentional on Lie's part,[51] as part of his strategy to use the media to rally support for his views and put pressure on states to act decisively to implement UN policies on Palestine.

The US reacted strongly to the secretary-general's circulating the memorandum because of the impression thus created that the Secretariat had prepared a counterargument to Austin's statement.[52] The Argentinean representative also raised the issue in a closed Security Council meeting on 9 March, claiming that the memorandum 'was the "bastard" product of "unbalanced minds", and, in principle, the Secretariat had no business producing such a document'. In response, Lie replied that 'as long as [he] was head of the Secretariat, it would have the right to give any opinion requested by organs of the United Nations'.[53] The other members of the Council supported Lie's right to circulate memorandums whenever he wanted.[54] This did not, however, necessarily mean that they agreed with the content of this particular memorandum regarding the Council's duty to implement partition.

The American arguments questioning the legality of Security Council enforcement of partition won out, or perhaps the other states did not want to take action any more than the US did. As a result, the Council decided to ask the P5 to consult with the Palestine Commission, the Jewish and Arab parties in Palestine, and the British mandate government as to what could be done to implement the partition plan peacefully.[55] Lie also took part in these consultations and even hosted some meetings in his office.[56] Simultaneously, the secretary-general continued his campaign to get the US to act. As Austin reported:

> As Lie left, he told us privately that he was convinced of our sincerity in our efforts to find a way, if there is any way, of implementing the partition plan by peaceful means. He was therefore doing everything in his power to support this effort by us. He was afraid we would find, however, that it would be impossible to implement the plan by peaceful means. Therefore, it would have to be enforced. Otherwise the UN would go downhill rapidly to nothing.[57]

In the end, the group concluded that it would not be possible to modify the plan to please both Jews and Arabs, and that the situation on the ground was likely to continue to deteriorate. It therefore recommended that the Security Council should firmly declare that it would not 'permit the existence of a threat to international peace in Palestine', and 'take further action by all means available to it to bring about the immediate cessation of violence and the restoration of peace and order in Palestine'.[58]

Coincidentally, the Security Council subcommittee presented its findings on how to implement partition on the very same day, 19 March, that the US decided to abandon the partition plan altogether and instead proposed the establishment of a new trusteeship over Palestine.[59] Again Lie's concern for the prestige of the UN came to the fore, as he threatened to resign over what he saw as an American betrayal. 'The American reversal was a blow to the United Nations, and it wounded me deeply. It showed a profoundly disheartening disregard for the organisation's effectiveness and standing.'[60] Although Lie had used the threat of resignation before,[61] and would do so again, this episode demonstrates the extent of the secretary-general's investment in implementing the partition of Palestine.

Furthermore, as if to confirm Lie's opinion as to the importance of the Americans, once the US abandoned partition the Security Council soon followed suit, and called a new special session of the General Assembly.[62] In a second resolution it called for a truce between Jews and Arabs.[63] 'For a long time now the situation has seemed promising', Lie wrote to a friend in Norway, 'but the Americans' right about-face has, in the meantime, darkened the prospects considerably'.[64] Even so Lie did not compromise his opposition to trusteeship, and continued his campaign to implement the partition plan by trying to persuade member states, such as the Nordic countries, to vote in favour of partition at the upcoming General Assembly special session.[65]

Overall, across this period Lie publicly articulated his opinions more strongly than before, and tried to use the media to his advantage, though the results were disappointing. Despite Lie's insistence the partition plan was not implemented, but rather abandoned altogether. In Lie's own words:

> For me, the General Assembly's decision in November last year has been law. I have done everything within my power to help the Palestine Commission, and have given that body the best members of the Secretariat. I also tried, in my speech before the opening of the Palestine Commission's first meeting, as well as in later press conferences, to establish the greatest possible bloc of authority behind this work ... Neither threats nor flattery were able to force my departure from what I considered the decision of the United Nations.[66]

Furthermore, Lie's efforts to establish an international force to send to Palestine also came to naught. Despite these setbacks the secretary-general refused to be dissuaded. The second special session of the Assembly, meeting from 16 April to 14 May 1948, repeated the call for a truce and asked the Security Council to appoint a mediator.[67] On 14 May, however, before the mediator could be appointed, the Jewish Agency took matters into its own hands and declared the State of Israel independent. The next day Egypt informed the UN that it had sent forces into Palestine to prevent the establishment of the Jewish state. This marked the inception of the first Arab-Israeli war, and represented a new phase in the UN's involvement with Palestine.

Persuading the Security Council to take forceful action, May 1948

Faced with the Arab invasion of Palestine, Lie increased his efforts to persuade the Security Council to take forceful action. In Lie's opinion, the Palestine problem had become a full-blown international war, which clearly constituted a threat to international peace and security. It was the first time since the signing of the UN Charter that any state had openly declared its deployment of armed forces into another territory. The Arab states' explicit purpose, moreover, was to prevent the UN partition plan from being fulfilled. The secretary-general viewed the attack on Palestine as an attack on the credibility of the organization itself, compelling the Security Council to either act, or risk enduring damage to the UN's reputation. 'A failure of the Security Council to act under these circumstances can only result in the most serious injury to the prestige of the UN and the hopes for its future effectiveness in keeping the peace elsewhere in the world', wrote Lie in a letter to the permanent five.[68]

Even before the invasion Lie had ordered an examination of the option of invoking article 99 to bring the issue to the attention of the Security

Council himself, and the Secretariat had dutifully prepared a formal letter which the secretary-general could send to the Council.[69] Just as with his earlier draft statements, however, the secretary-general held back to see whether the Security Council, and in particular the US, would act on its own, as 'it would be wiser to let [the US] have the public initiative'.[70] In its 15 May meeting, the Council had yet to reach conclusion, and Lie decided to redouble his efforts. He sent a private letter to the permanent five and also despatched his representatives, Robert Jackson, assistant secretary-general, and Andrew Cordier, the secretary-general's executive assistant, to the British and US delegations to implore them to take urgent action to halt the Arab aggression and restore the UN's authority.[71]

At the next Council meeting on 17 May the secretary-general's efforts came to fruition, as the US representative called the situation in Palestine 'a threat to the peace and a breach of the peace within the meaning of Article 39 of the Charter', and introduced an American draft resolution.[72] The secretary-general's actions were so influential that US officials felt the need to (humorously) point out 'that the Secretary-General should not take too much credit for what had happened that day'. To this Cordier 'facetiously retorted that in this kind of work it is rather dangerous for anyone to take credit less later events fly back into our faces', and pointed out that events had certainly moved faster than earlier suggested by the Americans.[73] It is thus fair to state that secretary-general Lie succeeded in persuading the Council to move towards taking forceful action on Palestine, and, correspondingly, addressing the twin tests to solve the conflict and create unity among the great powers. Lie's initiatives on the matter, however, did not end there.

During his consultations Lie noted sharp disagreements between the US and Britain, and he decided to take it upon himself to mediate these tensions so that the two Western powers could act together to bring peace to Palestine. For this reason, Lie went to see the British ambassador, Sir Alexander Cadogan, on 18 May, 'to pour out his heart to [him] about his discouragement at the prospects of the United Nations'. Palestine was just the latest episode in what Lie considered 'to be the progressive decline of the United Nations since its inception'.[74] The secretary-general also sent Jackson to London to elicit the Foreign Office's views and ask for guidance as to what the secretary-general could do to help. In a memorandum Jackson provided to the British while in London, he described the concerns of the secretary-general:

> If effective action cannot be taken quickly to deal with the situation in the Middle East, the Secretary-General fears (i) a spread of armed intervention in the Middle Eastern area; (ii) possible repercussions in Kashmir, Indonesia and the Balkans following clear proof of the

ineffectiveness of the Security Council; (iii) grave reactions on U.K./ U.S. relations; (iv) the beginning of the end of the United Nations.[75]

In London most officials dismissed Lie, although some admitted that he 'is probably more acutely aware of the effect of a complete failure in Palestine on the prestige of the United Nations than anybody else'.[76] Overall, the British diplomats felt Lie was 'misguided as to his proper powers and functions … but Lie has always dreamed of playing a dramatic individual part in international affairs'.[77] Back in New York, Lie also attempted to solidify his position with the Americans, dining with Secretary of State George Marshall and the American UN ambassador on 25 May.[78] At this stage, Lie's efforts to mediate between the US and Britain did not lead to further cooperation between the two Western powers on Palestine.[79]

Irrespective of Lie's attempts to bring about greater Anglo-American cooperation, the Security Council continued its Palestine discussions and on 29 May called for a truce, an arms embargo, and provided the mediator and the Truce Commission[80] with military observers to supervise compliance with the ceasefire. The Council also threatened further action 'under Chapter VII of the Charter' if either party failed to accept the resolution or later violated it.[81] In terms of practically negotiating the truce and coordinating its supervision, the Security Council largely allowed the mediator to run the field. Count Folke Bernadotte, the president of the Swedish Red Cross, accepted appointment as the UN mediator on 21 May.[82] Together with Bunche, as the secretary-general's representative, Bernadotte quickly negotiated an agreement on a four-week truce to start on 11 June.

Recruiting a UN armed guard, summer 1948

The second part of Lie's strategy for implementing partition of Palestine and thus meeting the UN's crucial tests was the establishment of an international armed force. In June, the secretary-general decided that the time had come to go public with his proposal for a designated UN force, and for its launch he chose the same venue where the Marshall Plan had been announced a year earlier.[83] On 10 June 1948, in a commencement speech at Harvard University, Lie began by speaking in general terms about the problems of the UN caused by the Cold War, and of the failure of the Military Staff Committee to reach an agreement on the forces to be made available under article 43 of the Charter. He then observed that even a small force could have been useful, suggesting 'a beginning could be made now through the establishment of a comparatively small guard force, as distinct from a striking force'.[84] Lie and his advisors felt that the absence of UN forces had 'hampered the work of the Security Council and diminished the prestige of the Organization'.[85] Following the Harvard speech, the secretary-general and Secretariat finalized a proposal for an armed UN guard and informally circulated it among the member states. They suggested a force of 1,000–5,000 men, largely drawn from smaller member states, to be recruited by the secretary-general and placed at the disposal of the Security Council, the General Assembly, and the Trusteeship Council. The proposal also emphasized that 'even more important than the practical usefulness of such a Guard would be the fact that it would symbolize the authority of the United Nations in troubled areas of the world', and could help counteract the growing doubts of the international public regarding the abilities of the UN, as 'the provision of even a very modest Guard force would give people the feeling that the United Nations was being given strength to fulfill its purposes'.[86] Creating a UN force would thus have directly supported Lie's overlapping goals. Lie believed it could have helped implement partition in Palestine specifically, as well as provide the UN with a general means of enforcement. Both were important if the UN was to meet its tests and prove that it could resolve regional conflicts and maintain international peace and security.

Over the summer of 1948, Lie's proposal for a UN guard, somewhat inevitably, became tangled up with developments on the ground in Palestine, leading the US to repeatedly feel the need to remind Lie not to confuse the question of armed guards for Palestine with his 'pet project' for a UN 'palace guard'.[87] The mediator had already recruited unarmed truce observers: soldiers on loan from the three members of the Truce Commission. This was unproblematic and covered by the Security Council resolution mandating the mediator to establish and supervise a truce.[88] These truce supervisors, soon to be organized as the United Nations Truce Supervision Organization (UNTSO) – a UN mission that remains in operation today – became the basis for the later development of UN peacekeeping.[89] UN plans for Palestine also included provisions for the internationalization of Jerusalem, and the mediator's first step was to negotiate the demilitarization of the city. To that end, on 19 June, Bernadotte asked the secretary-general to provide him with 1,000 armed guards to keep peace and order in Jerusalem following the conclusion of an agreement.[90] Jackson had already suggested to the secretary-general that Jerusalem would be an effective pretext to arrange for his UN guard:

> I do not under-estimate the difficulties of creating this force – but if you, as Secretary-General, could in fact become the saviour of Jerusalem I believe that the effect on the world as a whole would be electrifying, and the prestige of the United Nations would be vastly increased.[91]

But would the secretary-general have the authority to recruit such armed guards for Jerusalem? Surprisingly, Lie argued that he did not possess the requisite authority, and asked Bernadotte to take his request directly to the Security Council.[92] The US, in contrast, argued that Lie had all the authority he needed, stating it would be 'wise that this be a UN effort under the responsibility and powers of the SYG'.[93] Lie's hesitation may well have stemmed from the costs involved in recruiting a large armed force, for as Jackson wrote later in the summer (thereby inadvertently undermining Lie's entire idea of a UN armed force):

> It would obviously be much more economical for governments to lend detachments which could then be withdrawn when not needed rather than that the United Nations should organize such a force and its line of supply. The cost of mobilizing, training and the[n] demobilizing such a force would be much more expensive than the alternative of governments lending regular detachments.[94]

That said, Lie was comfortable with providing the mediator with a small force of 50 guards, which were sent as early as 20 June. These were volunteers from the guards normally employed at UN headquarters in New York,[95] and were thus already on Lie's payroll prior to their mission in Palestine. In the end, as the two sides failed to reach an agreement on the demilitarization of the city, no guards for Jerusalem were ever provided.

In the autumn of 1948 Lie put his UN guard proposal, as well as Bernadotte's last report, on the agenda of the General Assembly. Bernadotte himself was killed in Jerusalem on 17 September, and Bunche took over as acting mediator. The General Assembly reached no decision on Bernadotte's report, except to establish the Palestine Conciliation Commission to continue the work of negotiating a settlement between Israel and the Arab states.[96] On the issue of the UN guard, the General Assembly decided to refer the question to yet another committee due to report back to the 1949 session. In his memoirs, Lie called the UN guard proposal a 'positive by-product of the Palestine experience'. Although the end result, the United Nations Field Service, was 'not at all what [he] had originally intended', it did conduct useful work in transportation, communication, and guarding UN premises.[97] Following the latest Secretariat reform, today this branch of the Secretariat is called the Department of Operational Support.[98]

During 1949 secretary-general Lie gradually stepped back from the Palestine problem. The acting UN mediator, Bunche, negotiated armistice agreements between Israel and Egypt (signed 24 February), Lebanon (23 March), Transjordan (3 April), and Syria (20 July), thus containing the Arab-Israeli conflict.[99] Following the conclusion of these armistice agreements, Israel was admitted to the UN on 11 May 1949,[100] a decision strongly supported by the UN secretary-general. In Lie's opinion Israel had to be admitted to the UN to ensure consistency in the UN's policies.

The state had been established as the result of a UN resolution, and the UN could not now abandon it 'on the doorstep'.[101] With this granting of membership, the UN essentially legitimated the new status quo in the Middle East, despite the discrepancies between the new situation and the original partition plan. During the latter half of 1948, the 'Palestine problem' was essentially redefined into the Arab-Israeli conflict and the Palestine refugee problem, and three new UN organizations – the Palestine Conciliation Commission, UNTSO, and the United Nations Relief and Works Agency for Palestine Refugees in the Near East (UNRWA) – were established to manage the attendant day-to-day issues. This left the secretary-general and the Security Council free to move on to other, seemingly more pressing issues, including the Berlin Blockade and the conflicts in Indonesia and on the Indian subcontinent.

Conclusion

When preparing to publish his memoirs in 1953, Lie gave the following assessment of his own role in Palestine:

> My role in Palestine was impartial, but not detached. The issue was too passionate, the human tragedy too great, the challenge to the United Nations too grave, to admit detachment. I threw the weight of my office and my efforts behind the Organization's decision to partition Palestine. I did so with such ardor and constancy that my activity gave rise to charges of bias in the Israeli favor. I think I can reply that I acted consistently and honorably in favor of the ideals and integrity of the United Nations alone.[102]

Although leading scholars on the history of the Arab-Israeli conflict have disputed this assessment and claimed that Lie's actions evidenced a pro-Zionist bias, this chapter has provided evidence to the contrary. Lie may well have been pro-Zionist, but there is insufficient documentation to substantiate this as the main motivation for his actions. Instead, following an examination of Lie's actions and statements on Palestine in relation to his long-term goals for the UN organization and the office of the secretary-general, this chapter concludes that the secretary-general's actions were consistent with his own self-assessment that he had acted to defend the integrity of the UN.

From the moment the Palestine problem appeared on the UN agenda in 1947, secretary-general Lie viewed it as a crucial test of the UN's abilities. As argued in this chapter the Palestine problem presented three 'tests' for the UN. It was a test of its ability to solve regional conflicts, its ability to create unity among the great powers, and the secretary-general's ability to protect and promote the UN organization as its 'guardian'. Palestine was a regional conflict that developed into an international war, thus presenting an obvious test of the UN's ability to perform its mandate to maintain international peace and security. In this sense, Palestine offered a test of the UN's capacity to implement its proposals for a solution to the primary conflict between Jews and Arabs, as well as challenging its ability to effectively contain the fighting (and punish the aggressors) after the outbreak of international war in May 1948. In Lie's opinion, the UN organization passed this test. From 1949 onwards, the secretary-general would continue to view Palestine as an example of a UN success story,[103] a view shared by others at the time, as illustrated by the decision to award the 1950 Nobel Peace Prize to Bunche in recognition of his part in negotiating armistice agreements between Israel and its Arab neighbours.[104] In light of our knowledge of the more than seven decades of conflict that were to follow the events of 1948, and the continued struggle of the Palestinian people for its own independent state, today the accuracy of this view is called into question.

In relation to the second test posed by the Palestine problem, that of the UN's ability to unite the great powers for the common good, Lie similarly assessed Palestine a success. As it was not yet a Cold War issue, Lie believed the conflict in Palestine to be an excellent choice for his purposes. Lie believed that if the US and the Soviet Union could work together towards a solution to the Palestine problem within the UN framework, this might have a positive psychological effect on both sides. The emerging Cold War conflict between East and West was *the* major challenge of Lie's period as secretary-general, as the next chapter will go on to explore. Though the battles between the great powers, inside and outside the Security Council, made the secretary-general's job more difficult, Lie continued to hold out hope that a working relationship between the two sides could be maintained, and a Third World War prevented. The secretary-general argued that his main task was 'to keep the machinery going',[105] and to work toward stabilizing the situation so that the two sides might come 'to understand each other better and have more respect for each other than now'.[106] In the short-term, with regard to Palestine, the secretary-general's goal was to ensure that the great powers would work in unity in the Security Council, and once the Council adopted resolutions to condemn the fighting in Palestine, this goal was reached.

Yet as with Lie's assessment of the UN's success in relation to the first test, his assessment of a success in bringing the great power together must also be closely questioned. Although the US and the Soviet Union did work together to pass several Security Council resolutions on Palestine in 1948, this concord quickly ended. The 16 resolutions (of a total of 29) in 1948 would be followed by only 3 (of a total of 12) in 1949, with one of them the recommendation of Israeli UN membership. The number of Council resolutions would remain low throughout the balance of the Cold War.[107]

The apparent understanding between East and West in Palestine did not transfer into a general agreement to end the Cold War, as the secretary-general had hoped. Indeed, only a year after Israel's admission to the UN, the organization would be faced with an even more challenging test as the US and the Soviet Union faced off in the Korean War, as the next chapter will discuss.

Third, in taking on the Palestine problem with such enthusiasm, Lie also implicitly set himself a test of the secretary-general's abilities to maintain the coherence and prestige of the organization. These duties came with the secretary-general's role as a 'guardian' of the UN Charter. Although, in our assessment, when considered from a long-term perspective, the UN failed the two tests Lie identified, the secretary-general himself actually succeeded in his task. Through his active stance on the Palestine problem, secretary-general Lie took important strides towards carving out a space for an active secretary-general in both the UN organization and international politics in general. This was one case where Lie pushed to expand the UN secretary-general's role and to inject his office into all areas of UN activity on Palestine. The secretary-general in this chapter was confident about the role the UN should play in the world, and his own place within the organization. To reach his goals, Lie was not afraid to push and prod the great powers in the Security Council. He also openly advised member states on what policies to vote for and how to implement those policies. Even though some states disagreed with the course of action Lie advised, they accepted that he could have such opinions and advocate them, and that his concern for the organization's performance on this issue was legitimate. The secretary-general's actions here were close to those of an equal to the Council and the great powers; he was one of the actors on the stage, and the others accepted him as one of them. The secretary-general's primary emphasis throughout the UN's involvement with the Palestine problem was the coherence of the organization. He did his utmost to ensure the implementation of the UN's policies, and their continuity across the various UN organs involved in the process. Lie, as the first UN secretary-general, was an institution-builder, and his ultimate concern was to ensure the survival and, if possible, growth of the organization he led.

Another matter this chapter touched on was the role of media and public opinion, as well as the secretary-general's use of public versus private initiatives. Lie tried to balance his private and public roles and exploit them both to reach his ultimate goal. Recognizing that the voice of the permanent members carried more weight in the Security Council than that of the secretary-general (they have a right of veto), he sought in private to urge them to take the public initiative. But when things moved too slowly, as happened to Lie's proposal for a UN guard, he sought to rally public support by giving speeches and handing information to journalists. Just by talking to the media, much less trying to use the press and public opinion to his advantage, the UN secretary-general had moved a long way from the purely behind-the-scenes approach of the League of Nations secretary-general. The UN secretary-general's role as an advocate for global issues and his use of the 'bully pulpit' is an issue we will return to in Chapter 5.

Finally, this chapter dealt with Lie's proposal for an armed UN force. The secretary-general's urging for such a force tallies with his overriding concern for the coherence of the organization. In order to implement the UN's policies in the face of violent opposition, an armed force would be needed for enforcement and to protect the agents of the organization in their work. This issue also raised interesting questions about the authority of the secretary-general vis-à-vis the Security Council and the General Assembly. Would he have the authority to recruit such armed guards himself? As suggested earlier in the chapter, this may well have been a question of budgets and finances, because the secretary-general has no independent source of income. The General Assembly must approve the organization's budget, and it is up to states to foot their share of the bill (which they don't always do). This debate about a UN guard, as well as the provision of truce supervisors in UNTSO, point forward to the later establishment of UN peacekeeping after Suez in 1956.

At a press conference in February 1949, after Bunche had concluded the armistice negotiations between Israel and Egypt, Lie discussed his hopes for the UN in the light of the recent success. 'Conciliation, mediation and compromise are slow work', Lie argued, 'but they are – in the long run – the only firm foundation of a peaceful world'.[108] UN mediation between Israel and the Arab states had registered its first success with the conclusion of the armistice agreements and proven that the UN could play an important role in regional conflict resolution. Could the UN also achieve the same success with mediation on the global level to overcome the Cold War? As the next chapter will show, secretary-general Lie was not afraid to try. Just as he had hoped to bring East and West together over Palestine, he sought to mediate tensions between the US and the Soviet Union on a whole host of other issues.

Photo 1: On 2 February 1946 Trygve Lie of Norway was appointed by the General Assembly to be the first secretary-general of the United Nations. In this photo he addresses the Assembly after his election.

Credit: UN Photo/Marcel Bolomey

Photo 2: On 25 March 1946 the Security Council convened for its first meeting on US soil in the former gymnasium of Hunter College in New York. This gave Lie and the embryonic UN Secretariat less than two months to get all the facilities in order. In addition to administrative challenges, the spring of 1946 also saw the Security Council mired in heated discussions over the slow withdrawal of Soviet troops from Iran. In the context of this political conflict, secretary-general Lie submitted a legal memorandum which prompted a clarification of the secretary-general's political powers and his rights to participate in Security Council debates.

Credit: UN Photo

Photo 3: Trygve Lie played a central role in the process to get the UN headquarters located in New York. Through his close contacts with local government and business leaders, he was able to help secure a donation of $8.5 million from the Rockefeller family to purchase the plot of land on the East River in midtown Manhattan. Lie also helped assemble an outstanding team of international architects to design and build the headquarters. These buildings stand as a visible testament to Lie's contributions to the establishment of the United Nations. In this photo from 25 March 1947, Lie receives the check from John D. Rockefeller III (right) and signs the title for the East river site, while New York Mayor, William O'Dwyer (left) observes.

Credit: UN Photo

Photo 4: UN truce observers with children in Palestine, 1948. Although the normative principles of UN peacekeeping would be formulated in response to the Suez-crisis in 1956, the UN sent its first 'peacekeepers' to the Middle East in 1948. The United Nations Truce Supervision Organization is still active today. In the context of the conflict in Palestine, Trygve Lie also proposed the establishment of an international UN armed guard, but the member states did not support this suggestion.

Credit: UN Photo

Photo 5: In 1947–49, Ralph Bunche (left), played a key role in the UN's attempts to deal with the 'Palestine problem' and the first Arab-Israeli war. He meets here with Trygve Lie in New York on 18 April 1949 after successfully concluding armistice talks between Israel and Egypt, Lebanon, and Transjordan.

Credit: UN Photo/MB

Photo 6: As the 'guardian of the UN Charter' the secretary-general, more than anyone else, represents the UN overall. In March 1950, Trygve Lie proposed an ambitious 20-year peace plan, and set out on a tour to mobilize support from the world's governments and peoples. People from all over the world sent him letters and telegrams urging him to work for peace and to reduce international mistrust and conflict. In this photo taken on 23 June 1950 – less than two days before the outbreak of the Korean War – Lie re-reads some of the letters in preparation for a radio broadcast.

Credit: UN Photo/MB

Photo 7: On 1 November 1950, in the context of the Korean War, the General Assembly decided to extend Trygve Lie's term in office by three years. Lie was a staunch supporter of the US-led UN intervention in support of South Korea, and this earned him the hostility of the Soviet Union, who vetoed his re-election in the Security Council. But the US and its allies wished to express their support for Lie by extending his term, and they therefore used the General Assembly to bypass the Security Council. After this unorthodox re-appointment, the Soviet Union refused to have anything to do with Lie, and he was not able to function effectively as secretary-general. Lie resigned two years later in November 1952.

Credit: UN Photo

Photo 8: Secretary-general Trygve Lie often sought to enlist the support of the media and public opinion to put pressure on states. His frequent use of public speeches and close contacts with the press was novel compared to the role played by the secretaries-general in the League of Nations. He is seen here being filmed by a UN film crew on 30 June 1951.

Credit: UN Photo/MB

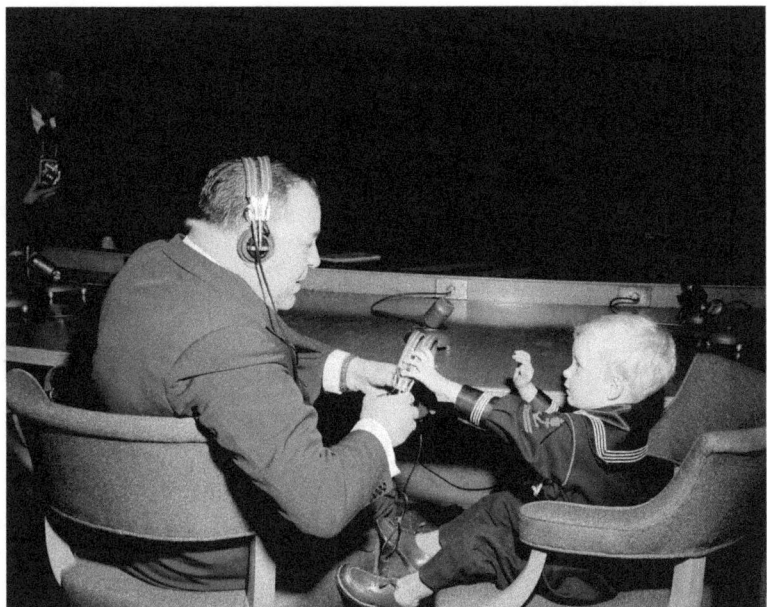

Photo 9: In this photo from 16 March 1950, secretary-general Lie demonstrates the earphones in one of the booths of the United Nations conference room to Rangvald Bratz, his three-year-old grandson.

Credit: UN Photo

Photo 10: On 9 April 1953, Trygve Lie welcomed his successor, Dag Hammarskjöld, at the airport with the warning that he was taking on 'the most impossible job in the world'.

Credit: UN Photo

4

Building Bridges: The Cold War from Berlin to Korea, 1947–50

> There is a dramatic and gigantic battle between East and West ongoing ... My motto is still: Patience. My main task is to keep the machinery going. I should be content as long as I have Mr. Vyshinsky and Mr. Marshall sitting around the green table at Lake Success.[1]
>
> Trygve Lie (November 1947)

Introduction

Trygve Lie had barely held the office of UN secretary-general for a month, when Winston Churchill, Britain's wartime prime minister, declared the descent of the 'iron curtain' from Fulton, Missouri, on 5 March 1946. The conflict between the US and the Soviet Union and their respective allies – commonly known as the 'Cold War' – was to become the defining feature of international politics for the next four decades. The Security Council held its first meeting on 17 January 1946 in London and come February it was already embroiled in heated debates over the slow withdrawal of Soviet troops from Iran and the presence of British troops in Greece. In Lie's own words: 'The hard realities of world politics intruded. Like gusts of wind warning of future storms to come, they blew in the door of the new-built house of peace before the workmen had finished.'[2] But what was the newly elected UN secretary-general to do in such a situation? How did the emerging superpower conflict impede or facilitate the development of the secretary-general's political role?

Within scholarship on the UN secretary-general a common observation is that the end of the Cold War opened new opportunities, allowing Boutros Boutros-Ghali and Kofi Annan to play more active roles than their Cold

War predecessors, particularly in the area of norm entrepreneurship.[3] Yet despite the constraints imposed by the Cold War, other scholars have also highlighted the way the Cold War paradoxically provided opportunities for the secretary-general, because it made Security Council agreement more elusive and allowed the secretary-general to balance the superpowers against each other.[4] Although this literature recognizes that the Cold War could be both constraining and empowering, few have undertaken in-depth studies of the mechanism behind this development.

This chapter explores how Lie as UN secretary-general sought to deal with conflicts between the member states, and how his role's autonomy and scope for action expanded as a result of it. It argues that Lie's actions were largely shaped by the institutional position of the UN secretary-general. The secretary-general, more than any other actor within the UN, 'represents' the UN overall. He can be described as a 'guardian' of the UN Charter and its principles and values. The secretary-general therefore has a duty to protect and defend the organization and its Charter. Lie clearly adopted this view from the moment he was elected, and based on this he would take action when he perceived a threat against the organization. The Cold War posed an existential threat to the UN. Not only was there a dire chance that the two sides might end up going to war against each other, but there was also an ever-present risk that one side (usually the Soviet Union) might decide to leave the organization altogether, thus condemning it to irrelevance. The secretary-general therefore sought as best he could to counter these dangers.

Three distinct strategies can be derived from the secretary-general's duty to protect the UN. The first can be called a 'bridge-building' policy: when the secretary-general mediates and negotiates between the two sides, seeking to ease tensions and differences between them, and overall to preserve the unity of the UN. A side-effect of the bridge-building strategy is that it tends to expand the autonomy and scope for action of the secretary-general, both as the secretary-general himself takes the initiative or because a 'vacuum effect' operates whereby the secretary-general is drafted into situations because 'someone' needs to do 'something'. During the Cold War, because the member states were unable to agree on common policies, this 'vacuum effect' operated to expand the secretary-general's autonomy and operational space. In this way, the context of the Cold War facilitated the expansion of the secretary-general's role. A second strategy, in extension of the secretary-general's concern to 'keep the machinery going',[5] is his emphasis on seeking cooperation on 'non-political' or 'smaller' issues, in the hope that any agreement on something might inspire agreement on bigger and more difficult questions. This strategy could also be discerned in Lie's activities in relation to Palestine, as discussed in the previous chapter. Lastly, because of the secretary-general's duty to protect the UN Charter, he will often have to take a stand on principle, even if this means siding with or against parties to a dispute. This balance is very difficult to thread, and the secretary-general must be careful how he does this, or the member states will no longer perceive him as impartial and legitimate.

This chapter is divided into four sections. The first examines secretary-general Lie's initial conception of the Cold War in 1946, and his views on the role of the secretary-general in relation to it. As explained in the introduction, the post-holder possesses considerable autonomy in the act of interpreting what his role dictates, and Lie's views on the Cold War are therefore relevant to understand the effects of this conflict on the development of the secretary-general's role. The second part looks at Lie's reactions to the Truman Doctrine and the Marshall Plan in 1947, and explores his attempts to reconcile these developments with the UN's purpose and framework. The third section examines the secretary-general's actions and initiatives on the Berlin Blockade of 1948–49, an instance where Lie took the initiative to mediate conflicts between the member states. Lastly, the fourth section examines the secretary-general's enthusiastic support for the US-led UN intervention in Korea in the summer of 1950, which he saw as taking a stand on principle in defence of the UN Charter.

Lie's 'Cold War' strategy

The UN was founded on the assumption that the great powers – the three victors of WW2 (later expanded to the P5) – would continue to cooperate to maintain international peace and security. Unfortunately for the UN and its new secretary-general, even during the UN's first months of operation, 'conflicts between the great powers [were] increasing rather than diminishing'.[6] Lie was conscious from the start of the dangers posed to the UN from the growing conflict between East and West, and already in his first annual report on the work of the organization took the opportunity to urge great power unity;

> I should be failing in my duty, in presenting this report, if I did not emphasize the absolute necessity that the Powers should seek agreement among themselves, in a spirit of mutual understanding and a will to compromise, and not abandon their effort until such agreement has been reached.[7]

As foreign minister of Norway during the war Lie had been a strong advocate for great power cooperation, and corresponding great powers responsibilities and special rights. In a November 1941 article in *The Times*, he set out his views on the need for post-war cooperation in the economic and political realm, and argued that 'the most important basis for extended international cooperation in the future is an amicable relationship between the British

Empire, the United States, Soviet Russia, and China'.[8] During the San Francisco conference and the first General Assembly session he continued to defend giving the right of veto to the permanent members of the Council because of their special responsibilities for the maintenance of peace and security.[9] Lie's views on these problems matter, because they influenced the way he interpreted his role as UN secretary-general.

The growing Cold War conflict made the position of the secretary-general even more exposed than it would have been otherwise. 'I'm in the middle of a hell of a job', he wrote during the winter of 1946–47. 'What is happening is a massive tug o' war between the two large victors … over markets and political and economic spheres of interest.'[10] He reported that 'I have had a damned difficult time … I have seen much evil and have, of course, made many enemies both here in the US and in Britain'.[11] Lie was convinced that his duty as secretary-general demanded that he should voice his opinions on matters before the organization. Often the great powers would disagree among themselves on those issues. In Lie's opinion, 'all three are making mistakes', and he would often tell them so. But because 'all three assume that those who are not with them, are against them … when I, as you'll easily understand, often disagree with one or more of the great powers in nearly every case, my work becomes of little significance'.[12] Lie would sometimes get the impression that 'they would prefer to do the job alone',[13] but his vision for the UN and opinions about the duties of the secretary-general would not allow him to play such a passive role: 'I have not allowed myself to be diverted, nor to be persuaded or pressured to do something I don't think is right. Many have attempted, but I'll rather fight than give in.'[14]

The specific task Lie saw for himself as secretary-general was to work as a negotiator and mediator who would seek to build bridges between the two sides. In his first annual report he admonished both sides for failing to cooperate, and argued it was his duty as secretary-general to draw attention to such problems:

> As the Preparatory Commission foresaw, the Secretary-General in certain circumstances must speak for the Organization as a whole. It is with a deep sense of responsibility that I appeal to the Members of the United Nations, and more especially to those Powers which have special rights and obligations under the Charter, to ponder the dangers to which I have called attention and to exert every effort to overcome them.[15]

Despite the growing dangers, Lie still believed that 'this balance of power can be stabilised', and that 'both sides will get so nervous about going to war, that we'll have peace for many, many years ahead … This is what I'm working for', he concluded.[16]

The task of being a 'bridge-builder' bears striking similarities to the role he argued for the small powers before he took office as secretary-general. As Norwegian foreign minister at the General Assembly in London he set out the duty of small states, because they 'are disinterested in many political disputes', to 'aim at making a sincere contribution to the mutual understanding and confidence of the Great Powers. The good neighbour policy should be the basis of their relations with great and small Powers alike.'[17] In the effort to build bridges and create unity between the great powers, the secretary-general would therefore find natural allies among the small- and medium-sized states, as well as among the world's peoples.

Although the situation was difficult, Lie did not give up hope that the conflict could be solved and better working conditions for the UN secured. In public and in private he continued to argue that an actual war between the two sides was unlikely: 'All concerned are, I think, too war-weary for that to happen, so we must go on living in the hope that reason will win through.'[18] Hope itself was an important tool for the secretary-general. He lectured to Norwegian students in Oslo in February 1946 on the need to be optimistic and realistic at the same time, because 'the work of the United Nations cannot be advanced without idealism, trust and faith', and brought in one of his favourite quotes from Fridtjof Nansen: 'A difficult thing is something that can be done immediately. An impossible thing takes a little longer.'[19] Lie also tried to argue that the 'airing of different views' in itself was good, and what was to be expected in a parliamentary system.[20] Overall, he decided he would have to try as best he could to keep the machinery of the UN going. 'The important thing is to keep going.'[21] 'I should be content as long as I have Mr Vyshinsky and Mr Marshall sitting around the green table out at Lake Success.'[22] For, after all, 'as long as we sit and talk together, at least there'll be no war'.[23]

The Truman Doctrine and the Marshall Plan, 1947

By early 1947 the Cold War was clearly under way, and the secretary-general had been caught in the middle of it. The US' Cold War policy would get its expression through two policy initiatives, known simply by the names of the men who introduced them; the Truman Doctrine and the Marshall Plan. Although neither of these policies were articulated or executed through the UN, they were the major topic of conversation in 1947, and Lie's reaction to them, and his efforts to bring them under UN control, aptly illustrates the secretary-general's views on the East–West conflict at the time and his goals for the world organization. Lie's actions on these issues conform to what we would expect of the UN secretary-general given the duties and responsibilities of his role.

The American president Harry S. Truman first articulated his doctrine in March 1947 in a speech to Congress where he asked for support for a programme of aid to Greece and Turkey. The US government had sought to adopt a more confrontational policy towards the Soviet Union for most of 1946, but the American public demanded demobilization and renewed focus on domestic American issues, and was unwilling to accept more sacrifices for foreign policy. The speech was therefore an effort by the US administration to use dramatic rhetoric 'to shock Congress and the public into providing the support necessary to implement a tough policy'.[24] Truman used the speech not only to argue for military aid to Turkey and Greece, but to present the East–West conflict as a choice between two 'alternative ways of life', and stating that 'it must be the policy of the United States to support free peoples who are resisting attempted subjugation by armed minorities or by outside pressures'.[25] This sentence has become known as the Truman Doctrine.

Secretary-general Lie was not persuaded by Truman's rhetoric. He felt the US' programme of aid to Greece and Turkey should have been presented in the Security Council, because Greece was at that time on the Council agenda. Whenever member states went outside the UN framework this was a setback to Lie, who sought to have the UN occupy a central position in international politics as envisioned by the UN's founders. He later wrote in his memoirs that the Truman Doctrine had 'burst like a bombshell upon the world with no advance notice whatever'. Even the US ambassador to the UN, let alone several 'friendly Member governments' and the secretary-general himself, had been unaware of the planned change of policy, Lie claimed.[26]

Lie visited Washington shortly after Truman's announcement, and reported back to a meeting of his staff that 'the general opinion was that for the moment the United Nations should not interfere in the new turn of events inaugurated by President Truman's statement'.[27] In his speech Truman had claimed the US policy 'will be giving effect to the principles of the Charter of the United Nations'. However, he also claimed that the UN itself was unequal to the task at hand, because 'the situation is an urgent one requiring immediate action and the United Nations and its related organizations are not in a position to extend help of the kind that is required'.[28] Lie disagreed with this negative assessment of the UN's capabilities, and expressed his 'surprise ... at the President's statement that the United Nations was not ready to organise relief when the [Food and Agriculture Organization] had in fact had a plan ready since the General Assembly designed to provide relief'.[29] The American programme of aid to Greece and Turkey announced in March 1947 was the first time the US deliberately chose to sidestep the UN, but it would not be the last.

Just three months later the US continued its policy change with an ambitious economic aid programme which has come to be seen as an extension of the Truman Doctrine from military to economic policy. In a commencement address at Harvard University on 5 June 1947, Secretary of State George C. Marshall promised American aid for European economic reconstruction. He argued that 'the United States should do whatever it is able to do to assist in the return of normal economic health in the world, without which there can be no political stability and no assured peace'. Marshall claimed that the proposed policy was not directed against any other states, only 'against hunger, poverty, desperation and chaos. Its purpose should be the revival of a working economy in the world so as to permit the emergence of political and social conditions in which free institutions can exist.'[30] This marked the start of the European Recovery Programme (ERP), or what has since become known simply as the Marshall Plan.

As with the Truman Doctrine, Lie's instinctive reaction was that the proposed aid programme should be executed inside the UN framework, in this case through the Economic Commission for Europe (ECE) which had been set up by ECOSOC in March 1947 precisely to coordinate and facilitate the economic reconstruction of Europe.[31] Whereas Lie after Truman's speech in March had refrained from giving any comments to the press, in the weeks following Marshall's speech Lie continuously told the press that he supported the plan and wished to see it executed as quickly as possible through the UN. At a press conference on 13 June he told the assembled journalists that he thought 'it was a very helpful step that was taken by President Truman and Secretary Marshall'.[32] On 19 June he went on to discuss the possible role the ECE could play in the process, and his belief that the European states would use the existing UN machinery for the purpose.[33]

Behind the scenes Lie also contacted the British Foreign Office to encourage them to guide the process in the direction of the ECE. In Barros' book, which largely reflects the Western view, Lie's belief that the ECE should play a role is described as 'wishful thinking at its worst', because of possible Soviet 'obstruction' in the ECE.[34] But in fact the US did consider using the UN for its proposed aid programme. In May George Kennan had pointed out that the programme 'will also have important connotations for the UN, and we should bear constantly in mind the need for maximum utilization of UN machinery'.[35] A week later Dean Rusk warned that 'unless we can demonstrate conclusively that [the ECE] cannot be used for this, the purpose of its creation, the ground swell of public opinion against again by-passing the U.N. might wreck and would certainly jeopardize any program'.[36] Ultimately, however, the US from the start was determined that the Soviet Union and its Eastern European satellites should not be allowed to influence the process – ideally they would choose not to take part at all – and that the best course of action would be to encourage key Western European states to decide on organizational questions.[37]

Britain and France therefore took the lead in crafting a European response to Marshall's speech. The French foreign minister, Georges Bidault, and his British counterpart, Ernest Bevin, invited all interested European states to a conference in Paris in late June 1947.[38] The Soviet Union and the Eastern European states were present at the start of the conference. Vyacheslav Molotov, the Soviet foreign minister, even brought along 100 technical experts, thus signalling his intent to stay and play an active part in the negotiations.[39] Within a few days, however, Stalin and Molotov changed their minds and on 2 July the Soviet Union withdrew from the conference.[40] The Eastern European states were at first allowed to stay, before the Kremlin changed its instructions to order its allies to leave the conference immediately.[41]

As secretary-general of the UN, Lie did not participate at the meeting in Paris, and neither did he send any representatives, but this did not stop him from continuing to urge the participation of the Soviet Union and the Eastern European states and the use of UN machinery for the execution of the recovery programme.[42] Once the Soviet Union had left the meeting and declared it would take no further part in discussions for the ERP, however, Lie had to recognize that the battle was lost. It would be impossible to use the ECE to execute the plan because of Soviet membership in the commission. Sir Alexander Cadogan, the British permanent representative to the UN, reported back to the Foreign Office that Lie 'quite understands the situation. He observed that the essential was to get relief quickly to Europe: all other considerations are subordinate.'[43] In a conversation with the British ambassador to Norway in mid-July, Lie argued that the Marshall Plan was necessary for Europe, and if the Soviet Union chose to remain outside, it would be to their own detriment.[44]

Although the ERP, despite the secretary-general's urging to the contrary, was executed outside the UN framework, the importance of European reconstruction was such that Lie could not long oppose the American aid. In the annual report for 1947–48 he praised the ERP for its 'great promise for the restoration of Western Europe to economic and political stability',[45] while in an article in the *New York Times* in May 1948 he included the Marshall Plan as part of the work for 'building a basis for peace that does not get into the usual headlines'.[46] However, there can be no doubt that Lie was disappointed that the plan had to be executed without formal UN participation or control. This went against his goal of having the UN play a central role in all aspects of international politics.

Furthermore, Lie's wish to have the Soviet Union participate speaks to his concern that nothing must be allowed to widen the tensions between East and West. As late as November 1947 he still expressed hope that the Soviet Union might join the programme, and wrote to his son-in-law: 'all in all I cannot understand that the Russian Communists could dare stand between Europe's millions in need of housing, food, clothes and work, and the aid which the powerful United States can give'.[47] In the annual report in July 1948 he warned that the Marshall plan 'can have lasting results only if present political divisions are not permitted to block co-ordinated action within Europe as a whole and an increase of trade between Eastern and Western Europe'.[48] The Truman Doctrine, on the other hand, could only serve to solidify the bloc formation, and Lie therefore claimed to have been opposed to it from the start. In his view, the Truman Doctrine was yet another example of how American policies were getting more extreme, and of how Washington had trouble distinguishing between socialism, communism, and the Soviet Union.[49] Lie's opposition to the Truman Doctrine would later continue in his hostility towards the formation of NATO.[50]

The Berlin Blockade, 1948–49

The Berlin Blockade was one instance where secretary-general Lie sought to mediate a high-stakes conflict between East and West. When the Soviet Union in June 1948 – ostensibly in response to the introduction of a new currency in the three western occupation zones of Germany – closed off all access to West Berlin, the most dangerous and tense Cold War crisis to date started. Gradually, the US, Britain, and France built up an airlift in response to the blockade, but the situation remained tense and unresolved. Secretary-general Lie followed the situation closely from the start and offered his services in negotiation to the four occupying powers, asking them if he should use article 99 to refer the matter to the Security Council.[51] The Soviet representative referred to article 107 of the UN Charter[52] and claimed that the question of Germany's future, and with it, Berlin, fell outside the UN's mandate. By the Western states, Lie was told bluntly that 'any action by the Secretary-General would not be appreciated at the present stage'. Lie nevertheless concluded that 'by merely drawing the attention of the representatives on the Council to the situation a certain amount had been achieved'.[53] The British Foreign Office 'appreciate[d] Mr. Lie's anxiety not to seem to be failing in his duty', but believed that this was 'not (repeat not) a matter for the application of Article 99 of the Charter'.[54] Over the summer, although he feigned ignorance to the press, and said that he thought the governments involved would find a solution on their own,[55] Lie kept in touch with the four states involved in the conflict, and in August even considered going to Berlin for a visit, if doing so might help find a solution.[56] Despite Lie's interest in the question, Berlin would not formally become a UN concern until October 1948. Once it was on the agenda, at various stages over the next few months, not only the secretary-general, but also the president of the General Assembly, the president of the Security Council, and some of the non-permanent members of the Council (the 'neutrals') would seek to negotiate an end to the Berlin Blockade.

The four-power negotiations having brought no results, on 29 September 1948 the US, Britain, and France, claiming that the Berlin Blockade constituted a threat to peace and security, asked that the matter be put on the Security Council's agenda.[57] From the start there were doubts both in the American delegation and among other delegations as to whether the US was really interested in a negotiated settlement or if it was merely looking for moral cover.[58] Nevertheless, regardless of the 'true' American motives, the US decided to forego its right to take the presidency of the Security Council for October, allowing the Argentine foreign minister, Juan Atilio Bramuglia, to take the presidency instead.[59] Over Soviet protests, the Council voted to take up the Berlin question on 5 October.[60] After a brief debate on 6 October, the process continued behind the scenes as Bramuglia and the group of neutrals started negotiations between the two sides.[61] The group addressed questionnaires to the US, Britain, France, and the Soviet Union, and drafted a resolution which was introduced in the Council on 22 October.[62] Throughout, the three Western states were kept well informed of the neutrals' progress by the Canadians, who also at one point stalled the resolution for a few days to allow the US and Britain to reach a common position with France.[63] Before the resolution was introduced in the Council, the three Western states were also given the chance to suggest changes.[64] It was therefore no great surprise that Britain, France, and the US, along with the six neutrals, voted in favour of the resolution on 25 October while the Soviet Union vetoed it, only supported by the Ukraine.[65]

When the Security Council rejected Bramuglia's suggested solution, Lie decided the time had come for him to take on a more active role in negotiating a solution to the Berlin Blockade. As secretary-general he felt a duty to do everything he could to build bridges between the two sides in the Cold War, and in Berlin there was an obvious need for someone to take an initiative. 'The result was as expected with the Berlin situation', Lie wrote to his daughter, but he remained hopeful for a solution; 'Sooner or later it will have to be solved, and as I have said many times before, I don't think it will lead to a war ... At the moment I'm in the middle of conversations ... to see if I can do something useful.'[66] In an early example of the secretary-general's use of special representatives,[67] Lie suggested using Abraham Feller, his American legal adviser, and Arkady Sobolev, the Soviet assistant secretary-general in charge of Security Council affairs, to work out a suggestion on the currency issue with American and Soviet economic experts. The goal was to find an agreement which would allow the blockade to be lifted simultaneously with the introduction of the Soviet-supported mark in all sectors of Berlin.[68]

The four states received Lie's engagement with caution, before ultimately rejecting the suggestion. Coincidentally, the US had already considered the option of asking a third party, like the UN, to work out a solution of the currency issue,[69] and Philip Jessup of the US delegation at first expressed cautious support for Lie's plan on 26 October.[70] On the other hand, Andrey Vyshinsky, Soviet deputy foreign minister, at first greeted Lie's suggestion negatively,[71] but a few days later he had obviously received different instructions from Moscow, and informed Lie that the Soviet Union now welcomed the secretary-general's efforts to mediate.[72] By this point, however, the US had decided against Lie's involvement, and the Western states started to create obstacles for the secretary-general. Jessup insisted that Britain and France be brought into the conversations,[73] and Lie duly informed Cadogan and Alexandre Parodi, the French ambassador. Parodi greeted Lie's suggestion positively, while Cadogan, 'as I had feared', wrote Lie, 'reflected the Foreign Office's traditional coolness toward any independent United Nations initiative'.[74] Britain and the US feared that Lie's involvement could not be kept secret,[75] and were furthermore 'anxious not to give the impression that they were running around looking for a settlement'.[76] Overall, the two Western allies were concerned not to be seen as consenting to 'negotiation under duress',[77] and wanted to leave all mediation to the Security Council and Bramuglia.[78] They therefore rejected Lie's offer of help.[79] Thus the secretary-general's proposal came to nothing, and when the *New York Times* learned of Lie's search for a currency plan on 9 November,[80] Lie was forced to issue a press release denying that he was participating in negotiations on Berlin. The secretary-general claimed that 'as part of his duty to keep himself informed of all matters before the United Nations', he had merely asked the Secretariat for a study of the currency issue.[81] Although Lie's offer to negotiate was rejected, the four great powers never challenged his right to make such an offer. This episode therefore provided one more step in the process of expanding the secretary-general's autonomy and scope for action to allow him an independent right to mediate and put forward proposals in international politics.

With the failure of his currency study proposal, which had been a behind-the-scenes initiative, secretary-general Lie adopted a new tactic – to issue a public appeal with the President of the General Assembly, Herbert Evatt of Australia. Evatt first learned of Lie's activity in Berlin when the British Foreign Office, against Lie's explicit request to keep the matter secret, informed all the Commonwealth countries of the secretary-general's proposals.[82] At first Evatt was quite upset with Lie because he had been kept in the dark, but the secretary-general responded that he had every right to do this without telling anyone, and furthermore Berlin was a Security Council matter, not a General Assembly concern.[83] However, neither Lie nor Evatt held a grudge for long, and within a few days they were talking of sending a joint appeal to the four states involved. Lie felt Evatt's reasoning in support of the appeal was 'quite good', and told his wife that 'as far as Evatt and I are concerned, that matter is now settled up most satisfactorily'.[84]

On 13 November 1948 the two UN officials sent a letter to the chairmen of the delegations of Britain, France, the Soviet Union, and the US, requesting that the letter be forwarded to their chiefs of government, thus sidestepping the foreign offices and foreign ministers.[85] The letter reminded the four states that they had all spoken out in favour of and voted for the General Assembly's 3 November resolution which had asked them to 'redouble their efforts ... to secure in the briefest possible time the final settlement of the war'.[86] Evatt and Lie went on to observe that in their opinion the first priority was to solve the Berlin problem. They therefore urged the four governments to start 'immediate conversations and [take] all other necessary steps toward the solution of the Berlin question, thus opening the way to a prompt resumption of negotiations for the conclusion of the remaining peace settlements'. They also encouraged the four states to 'lend their full and active support' to Bramuglia's mediation efforts and declared themselves ready to offer further assistance as and when needed, specifically mentioning the example of Lie's currency study.[87]

With their statement the two UN officials unleashed a storm of criticism which neither of them had expected, yet several smaller states agreed with the sentiment behind the appeal. Lie and Evatt had taken care to distinguish between 'immediate conversations' and 'resumption of negotiations' to forestall expected criticism from the three Western states; however, these carefully chosen words were not enough for Britain and the US. The American secretary of state and his aides saw the Lie–Evatt initiative as 'ill-advised and disturbing' because it seemed to apportion blame equally to the West and the Soviet Union,[88] and attributed the appeal to 'self-seeking'; Evatt had been eager for headlines and had 'duped' Lie into signing the letter with him.[89] The British reacted in similar ways. Lie wrote home to his wife and daughter that, 'needless to say, the English were little pleased with this initiative and the British press has been rather sour – naturally at the bidding of the British Government'.[90]

The Norwegian delegation to the General Assembly reported back to Oslo that many delegations, especially the Western states, were 'of the opinion that both the president and the secretary-general should have stuck to their tasks as respectively an elected representative and an official of the United Nations and avoid interfering in the delegations' politics'.[91] Indeed, the secretary-general had been in doubt about the wisdom and propriety in signing the appeal alongside the president of the Assembly. But Bramuglia, the Council president, had persuaded Lie to sign the letter, saying that in his opinion the secretary-general 'stood beside the President of the General

Assembly', and furthermore the letter would be 'a big help in his work in getting the Berlin crisis settled'.[92]

Bramuglia continued to support Lie and Evatt after the publication of the letter and defended them against criticism. The *New York Times* reported that the appeal 'reflected the general feeling of many nations not directly involved in the Berlin dispute', and that it had been 'heartily endorsed' by Bramuglia 'because it interprets the peaceful aspirations of the peoples of the world'.[93] The Soviet Union likewise welcomed the suggestion of Lie and Evatt for renewed conversations about a post-war settlement, and said it shared the belief that 'the solution of the Berlin question will have a positive effect on the settlement of other questions such as those of peace settlement for Germany, Austria and Japan'.[94] Summing up the whole affair, Lie wrote to his wife and daughter:

> On the surface the whole thing can look like a defeat for Evatt and me, but in reality our initiative means another step forward in that all parties have declared themselves willing to seek a solution to the Berlin crisis in the Security Council ... My purpose in signing together with Evatt was that we had to hoard as many glowing coals as possible on the heads of these statesmen in order to get them to understand that the world does not want war.[95]

Although nothing much came of the Evatt–Lie appeal, it represents one example of the emerging alliance between the secretary-general and the peoples of the world, as evidenced in the widespread public support for the secretary-general's letter. In this instance he served as 'a spokesman for the world interest',[96] seeking to put pressure on states to negotiate an end to their conflicts in the interest of world peace.

Lie's direct involvement with the Berlin negotiations ended in mid-November 1948, yet he was invited to send a representative to a currency committee formed by Bramuglia in late November. Bramuglia's idea essentially combined his group of neutrals with the secretary-general's currency study and established a committee of 'technical experts' to negotiate with the two sides and suggest a solution to the currency problems. The committee met in Geneva during the winter of 1948–49, but was unable to find a solution acceptable to both sides in the conflict. It ended its work on 11 February and sent a report to the Security Council.[97] Despite the fact that the failure of the committee was largely due to an American change of heart in January, when the report was finally published 'a carefully orchestrated Western public relations campaign' blamed the Soviet Union for the committee's failure.[98] Thus ended the UN's attempt to negotiate an end to the Berlin Blockade. By this stage, however, the US and the Soviet Union had started direct negotiations. Jessup and Yakov Malik held a number of secret informal meetings which eventually led to the lifting of the blockade in May 1949.[99]

Thus, the deal ending the Berlin Blockade was negotiated *at* the UN, but without the formal use of UN machinery or the involvement of UN representatives. Nevertheless, the Berlin Blockade demonstrated the usefulness of the UN. First of all, the UN provided a forum where representatives of the two sides could meet and work out their differences. This was an early example of the value of the Security Council as a 'concert' between the great powers.[100] The Berlin Blockade demonstrated 'the value of proximity' of diplomatic staff being present in New York and regularly interacting with each other.[101] Second, the earlier attempts by Lie, Bramuglia, Evatt, and the currency committee, all served to buy time and defuse tension, which allowed for a solution to be worked out. These UN efforts can be seen as 'a necessary failure' which prepared the way for direct negotiations on a more realistic basis.[102] In this case, therefore, the UN secretary-general, and others within the UN system, had helped in solving a dangerous Cold War problem.

The outbreak of the Korean War, 1950

So far during the Cold War secretary-general Lie had sought to play the role of impartial mediator between East and West; however, his stance would change when the Korean War broke out. At that time the secretary-general interpreted his duty to protect and defend the UN Charter and organization as dictating that he strongly oppose the North Korean aggression and urge UN support for South Korea.[103] The Korean issue had been a concern of the UN since 1947, and in early 1948 a UN commission supervised elections in the southern part of the country (the Soviet Union would not let them operate in the north) which led to the establishment of the government of the Republic of Korea. South Korea had thus been established as a result of UN involvement, and this was important when the Korean War broke out in June 1950.

Shortly before midnight (New York time) on 24 June 1950, John D. Hickerson of the US delegation called Lie at his home to discuss the invasion and the UN response. According to Hickerson, Lie's immediate reply was: 'My God, Jack, that's against the Charter of the United Nations!'[104] The secretary-general forthwith requested a report from the UN commission in Korea, and asked the Secretariat to prepare for an emergency Security Council meeting. Later at night he had further telephone conversations with the American delegation, which formally requested that he convene the Security Council.[105] When the Council met in the afternoon on 25 June, the secretary-general spoke first, recounting the history of the UN's activities in Korea, and stating that the reported military actions were 'a direct violation of the resolution of the General Assembly ... as well as a violation of the principles of the Charter. The present situation is a serious one and is a threat to international peace ... I consider it the clear duty of the Security Council to take steps necessary to re-establish peace in that area.'[106]

It was highly unusual for the secretary-general to speak first, and it was neither 'necessary [n]or expected' in this situation.[107] Although Lie later claimed to have decided during the night to invoke article 99, legal historians argue that article 99 was not invoked because the US had asked for a Council meeting to be called.[108] This should not detract from the important role secretary-general Lie would play over the coming weeks to legitimate and coordinate the UN response in Korea.

One of the duties Lie saw for himself in the situation was to coordinate the UN response and serve as an 'executive' of the Security Council's decisions.[109] To this end, already before the first Council meeting on 25 June, Lie met with Ernest Gross of the US delegation to formulate a plan for the meeting and discuss the statements they were each going to make.[110] In the interest of unity, Lie also claimed to have helped persuade the Egyptian and Indian delegations, which both lacked instructions from their home governments, to vote in favour of the US draft resolution.[111] Over the next few days Lie continued to urge member states to come to the aid of South Korea, and he took it upon himself to send out telegrams asking member states to inform him of what help they could give. Referring to the Council's second resolution of 27 June[112] Lie's telegram asked all governments, 'in the event that your government is in a position to provide assistance ... if you were to be so good as to provide me with an early reply as to type of assistance'. The secretary-general would then submit the states' replies to the Council and to the Korean government.[113]

Lie sent the telegram in the interest of coordinating the UN's response and to facilitate the process of providing aid to South Korea. He may also have thought it more likely that states would respond in the positive when the request came from the secretary-general rather than one of the member states. Indeed, some states later complained that Lie had overstepped his authority and that they were embarrassed when they had to say no to the secretary-general's requests.[114] The US government was happy to have the secretary-general send out the telegram because it thought 'it was a good idea to use the United Nations umbrella as much as possible', but the State Department also 'felt however that Lie should function as no more than a post office'.[115] Not content to serve merely as a 'post office', Lie continued to urge greater coordination of the Korean operation, and increased use of UN machinery. He set about drafting a new Council resolution to give the US formal responsibility for directing the UN response; give the American command the right to use the UN flag; and to establish of a coordination committee (consisting of Australia, France, India, New Zealand, Norway, the UK, and the US) which could receive all offers of aid, review them, and transmit the offers to the US government.[116] No state challenged the secretary-general's right to draft Security Council resolutions, and the episode therefore served to further expand the secretary-general's toolbox and to assign him a role of near-equal status with the members of the Council. In the end, however, on 7 July the Council chose to adopt a similar resolution proposed by the US, which designated the US as UN command, but without establishing a coordination committee.[117]

In addition to the interest in coordinating the UN response because of his executive responsibilities for the Secretariat and coordination between UN organs, Lie's actions were motivated by his concern to protect and defend the UN Charter and for greater unity of the UN member states. As the quote from Lie's statement on 25 June revealed, the secretary-general saw the North Korean invasion as a clear breach of the UN Charter. He therefore chose to speak first at the Council meeting 'because the response of the Security Council would be more certain and more in the spirit of the Organization as a whole were the Secretary-General to take the lead'.[118] Lie's understanding of his role in the proceedings would therefore fit well with the reason the US sought the support of the UN – 'to rally the world community's support' and give 'international sanction to what the United States would have done anyway'.[119] In this particular instance, therefore, the interests of the US and the UN secretary-general overlapped, and in this period Lie worked closely with the US delegation to coordinate the UN response. There was by itself nothing unusual in this, because the US and the secretary-general had a close working relationship and would share information and exchange views on most issues on the UN agenda.[120]

The secretary-general's active support for the American policies in Korea helped give legitimacy to the US-led intervention and ensure that it truly was a 'UN' response. In doing so, Lie would become the focal point of UN policies in Korea, and a symbol of the organization's unity in the face of North Korean aggression. This strengthened his position as an overall representative of the UN and a 'guardian' of the UN Charter, and provided the main motivation behind the General Assembly's decision to extend Lie's term in office in November 1950, as will be discussed in the next chapter. Simultaneously, however, Lie's actions completely destroyed his relationship with the Soviet Union, and even though he would serve as secretary-general until April 1953, he could not really function effectively in his job because of the Soviet boycott. The Soviet government also saw the secretary-general as representing the policy of the majority of the UN, yet because it disagreed with that policy, the logical conclusion was to also oppose the secretary-general. This illustrates how narrow a space the secretary-general had in which to operate as the Cold War hardened. Whatever he did, one or more of the superpowers were bound to disagree and resent him for trying to meddle in their affairs. Nevertheless, because of the importance of stopping North Korean aggression in contravention of the UN Charter, Lie would later 'consider [his] stand on Korea the best justified act of seven years in the service of peace'.[121]

Conclusion

Because the secretary-general more than anyone else 'represents' the UN and is a 'guardian of the UN Charter', he has a duty to protect and defend the organization. As the Cold War hardened, secretary-general Lie would therefore seek to mediate and negotiate between the two sides in the interest of UN unity. If the organization, and in particular it's most high-profile organ, the Security Council, were unable to operate, this would be damaging to UN prestige, and therefore to the very survival of the UN, because the organization relied on public support. This provided Lie's motivation for his actions in trying to mediate between the US and the Soviet Union in the Berlin Blockade, between the US and Britain over Palestine (as discussed in the previous chapter), and for his efforts to solve the question of Chinese representation and to propose an ambitious peace plan (as will be discussed in the next chapter). Another way in which the UN might stop functioning would be if one party decided to leave the organization altogether. The UN was built on the principle of universality of membership, and could only succeed if all states were members.

A side-effect of the secretary-general's attempts to mediate and negotiate in the interest of UN unity, was that his actions expanded both the secretary-general's autonomy and his range of possible tools and actions. Although the majority of Lie's proposals failed to bring about his desired objective – the Marshall plan aid remained outside the UN framework, Lie's currency proposal in Berlin was rejected, his joint appeal with Evatt ignored, no coordination committee for Korea established – because the member states did not significantly protest against Lie's attempts to influence them in these matters, the secretary-general's right to do so was recognized. In several instances Lie sought to 'push' his own suggestions for a mediated solution, but in other instances the institution would 'pull' him into this expanded role. Examples of the latter from the present chapter include the inclusion of a representative of the secretary-general in the technical currency committee on Berlin in the winter of 1948–49, and the obvious need for someone to coordinate the UN response in Korea in the first few weeks. Although the UN Security Council on 7 July handed responsibility for the operation in Korea to the US, in the weeks before, Lie had performed an important function in coordinating and serving as a channel of communications between the member states.

A second way in which Lie sought to fulfil his duty to protect and defend the UN, was to 'keep the [UN] machinery going'.[122] Even if for the moment the P5 were unable to agree on most political issues, at least the UN could remain the centre of negotiations between them. Furthermore, if it could be possible to reach agreement on other 'non-political' issues, such as the Marshall plan aid for the reconstruction of Europe, or indeed on 'smaller' political problems like Palestine as discussed in the previous chapter, this might have an important psychological effect and inspire agreement on other issues as well. In continuation of this line of thinking, Lie proposed a peace plan in 1950, as will be discussed in the next chapter.

Lastly, in protecting and defending the UN and its Charter, the secretary-general would sometimes come to take a stand with one group of member states against another. When, in his opinion, North Korea, supported by the Soviet Union, attacked South Korea in a clear breach of the UN Charter, Lie would happily work with the US to mobilize the rest of the UN membership in aid of South Korea. In standing on principle, the secretary-general became a symbol of the UN's policies and unity in Korea – he strengthened his role as 'representing' the UN overall – while also earning himself the hostility of one of its most powerful member states. Lie's strong principled defence of the UN, as well as the adverse consequences this had for his ability to function effectively in his role, will be explored further in the next two chapters.

5

Advocating Global Interests: Trygve Lie's Peace Plan, 1950

> I have unshaken faith in the good sense and understanding of the people in all countries. I believe they know that the United Nations stands between them and destruction. I believe they will insist that all governments, by word and action, uphold the United Nations and use it for the great purposes for which it was established – the prevention of war and the creation of peace.[1]
>
> Trygve Lie (February 1950)

Introduction

Today the UN secretary-general is widely considered to be a 'norm entrepreneur' or an 'advocate' for global issues.[2] The UN website describes the secretary-general as 'a spokesperson for the interests of the world's peoples, in particular the poor and vulnerable among them',[3] while the civil society campaign '1 for 7 billion' argues that 'as the UN's top official, the Secretary-General embodies the high values of the Charter and represents the hopes and concerns of the world's seven billion people'.[4] This highly visible, politically and symbolically important role has developed over time, but the foundations for this public role were set up while Trygve Lie was in office.[5] Lie himself described this part of his role as 'a spokesman for the world interest'.[6] As previous chapters have shown, Lie frequently sought to enlist the public and the media in his efforts to put pressure on states to act the way he wanted them to. This chapter examines Lie's most high-profile and ambitious attempt at acting the norm entrepreneur or advocate: his 1950 proposal for a 20-year peace programme.

In 1950 the hardening fronts of the Cold War caused trouble for the UN. Protesting the Western states' refusal to allow the communist Chinese government to assume the Chinese seat in the UN, the Soviet Union boycotted the Security Council and other UN organs from January 1950. In 1949 the Soviet Union tested its first atomic bomb, while in January 1950 President Truman announced that the US would develop the more powerful 'H-bomb', thus signalling a new phase of the arms race between East and West.[7] And within the UN, negotiations in the Military Staff Committee and the Atomic Energy Commission had completely stalled. In an effort to reinvigorate the UN, and with a genuine hope of easing tensions between the two Cold War blocs, Lie put forward a peace plan with ten suggestions in March 1950. He then set out on a month-long 'peace tour' to Europe to argue his case directly to world leaders and the public.

In the end, Lie's peace plan failed, like so many of his other initiatives. With the outbreak of the Korean War in June 1950, hope for an immediate reconciliation between East and West dwindled further. The General Assembly discussed Lie's proposal and requested other UN organs to consider the plan and report back on their progress on relevant issues,[8] and for a few years the item remained on the annual agenda of the Assembly. But although the specific peace plan may have failed in its immediate objectives, the episode served to demonstrate the secretary-general's authority and autonomy and to expand this further. Although the specific plan failed, the underlying procedural norms took further hold. Building on the foundations established by Lie in relation to this and other episodes, later secretaries-general could propose their own ambitious plans and use the 'bully pulpit' to urge states to action.[9]

As previous chapters discussed, the intention of the UN's founders was for the great powers to work together to keep world peace, primarily using the tools and forums available in the Security Council and its subcommittees. Unfortunately, the emerging Cold War quickly poured cold water on those dreams. From the Iranian crisis to Berlin to the Korean War, conflicts between the two superpowers and their allies hampered the work of the organization. Yet, unexpectedly, freezes and deadlocks in the Security Council and conflicts among the member states simultaneously opened up space for the UN secretary-general to take on a more active role. Partly this role expansion was the result of Lie's activist stance as a secretary-general, and partly the development occurred through a 'vacuum effect' which demanded action from the secretary-general and Secretariat to cover up for inaction in other parts of the UN. These effects can be detected also in the dynamics surrounding Lie's peace plan proposal of 1950.

This chapter examines the peace plan episode from beginning to end. It starts with a discussion of the background to Lie's proposal in the Cold War situation in 1950 particularly related to the Chinese representation issue, the nuclear arms race, and the troubles this caused for the UN. The second section details the content of Lie's suggested peace plan, while the third describes Lie's efforts to promote the plan and his 'peace tour' to Europe. Finally, the chapter considers the aftermath of the proposal and its implications for the development of the secretary-general's role as an advocate or norm entrepreneur.

Background: the Cold War in 1950

This chapter explores the highpoint of Lie's activist stance as secretary-general in his 1950 proposal for a 20-year peace plan. The Cold War context and its consequences for the UN organization and its work explains why secretary-general Lie felt the need to put forward such a proposal at this time. Two important developments, in particular, provide the immediate background and motivation for the secretary-general's actions in 1950: the accelerating nuclear arms race and the question of Chinese representation.

During the early Cold War, people all over the world lived in fear of the consequences of another nuclear attack or, worse still, of an all-out nuclear war between the two superpowers. As one researcher later noted: 'During the first few years, people did not fear anything specific or immediate. The public simply felt that the ground had fallen away from under them.'[10] The US deployed the first atomic bombs on the Japanese cities of Hiroshima and Nagasaki in August 1945, ostensibly to end the war with Japan, yet growing rivalry with the Soviet Union already played a part in the decision to deploy the new weapon in this way.[11] American scientists and decision-makers knew that the US would likely be unable to keep a nuclear monopoly. The knowledge of how to build the bomb would spread, and it was probable that the Soviet Union, at least, could get hold of the necessary raw materials of uranium and thorium.[12] Experts estimated it would take approximately four or five years for the Soviet Union to produce its own atomic bomb,[13] an estimate that proved accurate as the Soviet Union conducted its first test on 29 August 1949.

In the 1945–49 period, while the US held a nuclear monopoly, American and international actors sought to establish an international framework under the UN to control nuclear technology. Scientists involved in the creation of the bomb became some of the earliest and most ardent supporters of the antinuclear movement and proponents of international control mechanisms. As historian Petra Goedde notes, 'acutely aware of the enormous power of the bomb they had created, they felt a sense of moral responsibility to curb its destructive power'.[14] To this end, scientists wrote reports and articles warning against the use of the atomic bomb and arguing for the need for a world government or some form of international system to contain the destructive potential of this new technology.[15] The most well known of these proposals was the Baruch Plan.

The so-called 'Baruch Plan' was a proposal by the US made at the first meeting of the UN Atomic Energy Commission on 14 June 1946.[16] The Atomic Energy Commission was a subcommittee of the Security Council established by the General Assembly with the task of making recommendations on the exchange of scientific information, necessary controls of nuclear energy for peaceful means, the elimination of atomic weapons, and effective safeguards to protect states against violations and evasions of the agreements.[17] The American proposal built on an earlier proposal known as the Acheson–Lilienthal plan that was largely drafted by the scientist Robert Oppenheimer.[18] The American plan proposed the establishment of an International Atomic Development Authority which would be given complete control of all phases of development and use of atomic energy to prevent its misuse and facilitate its use for peaceful purposes. In his speech to the commission, Bernard Baruch, the American representative, stressed that 'no system of safeguards that can be devised will of itself provide an effective guarantee against production of atomic weapons by a nation bent on aggression'.[19] However, an international authority and cooperation between all states offered the best hope of preventing the destructive use of atomic energy for military purposes.

Unfortunately, the proposal failed as negotiations in the Atomic Energy Commission soon stalled. The Soviet Union put forward its own proposal for an immediate ban on nuclear weapons three days after the American Baruch Plan,[20] but the two superpowers disagreed on the mandates for international control. The General Assembly passed resolutions urging the Security Council and the Atomic Energy Commission to speed up negotiations, but no agreement was forthcoming. Then, on 29 August 1949 the Soviet Union conducted its first nuclear test, and on 21 January 1950 President Truman announced that the US would proceed to develop a more powerful bomb – a 'superbomb' – based on hydrogen technology. The nuclear arms race sped up and prompted widespread concern.

When asked a few days later to comment on Truman's statement, secretary-general Lie responded:

> We all know that new developments can be expected from time to time to result from the work of scientists of a number of countries. Clearly this fact makes it more and more necessary to continue the search for agreement among the Great Powers, not only on a United Nations system of control of atomic energy, but also on other issues that divide the world and hamper the United Nations in its efforts to make the world more secure against war.[21]

The worsening atomic arms race thus provided one motivation for the secretary-general to reinvigorate the UN as a forum for negotiations between

East and West. A second important motivation came from the deadlock caused by the Soviet walkout in response to the Chinese representation issue.

The question of Chinese representation in the UN was yet another instance when Lie pushed his own opinion on a political matter. This was also an occasion when Lie went too far. In openly going against the wishes of one of the P5 – even if only Nationalist China, the weakest of them – Lie caused irreparable damage to his relationship with the Security Council. From January 1950 until the outbreak of the Korean War the question of Chinese representation dominated proceedings at the UN. After Mao Zedong declared the establishment of the People's Republic of China (PRC) on 1 October 1949, it was only a matter of time before the question of which Chinese government should hold the permanent seat in the Security Council would come to a head. The Nationalist Chinese government led by Chiang Kai-shek, now in exile on the island of Taiwan, had the support of the US, while the communist government in Beijing was supported by the Soviet Union.

The question was first raised in the Security Council[22] on 29 December 1949 by Yacov Malik of the Soviet delegation. Malik argued that the government of the PRC was the only legal representative of the Chinese people, and that the Soviet Union therefore would not recognize Tsiang Ting-fu, the current Chinese representative in the Council, as a legitimate representative of China. When the Council president, after short statements by China and the Ukraine, declared the matter closed, Malik accepted the decision without further protest.[23] But this was only a dress rehearsal for what was to follow. When the Council reconvened on 10 January 1950 – with Tsiang in the president's chair – Malik raised the issue of Chinese representation once more, and introduced a proposal to remove Tsiang from the Council. The proposal received support from India and Yugoslavia, but was defeated by 6 votes to 3, with 2 abstentions.[24] During the debate Malik had frequently threatened that he would leave the Council unless his proposal was adopted, and this was exactly what he did after his defeat on 13 January.

The Soviet walkout created a new crisis for the UN secretary-general to deal with. At the time no one knew if this was the first step to the Soviet Union leaving the organization altogether, as over the next few weeks the Soviets walked out of more than 20 other UN committees and commissions. In discussions with American diplomats, Lie expressed his fears that the Soviet walkout might lead to a new situation with three competing organizations: one consisting of the Soviet Union and its allies, one for the emerging bloc of nonaligned states led by India, and the 'rest' in the UN.[25] Secretary-general Lie felt he had to do something to prevent the break-up of the UN. He talked to his staff and had them prepare a legal memorandum. This was not the first time Lie sought to depoliticize an issue by presenting his opinion in legal terms rather than openly admitting to the political nature of the question.

The memorandum argued that the question of Chinese representation was essentially one of credentials, and therefore a procedural matter. This meant that the veto would not apply in the Security Council, and all that was needed to solve it would be an affirmative vote of seven members. Five Council members had already recognized the new Chinese government, and would presumably vote in favour of seating them in the Council.[26] The memorandum argued that it was incorrect to put any criteria on membership or representation in the UN beyond those listed in the Charter. Specifically, it was incorrect to use recognition of a government (an individual act) as a criterion for membership (a collective act). States could vote in favour of admitting a state to membership without this automatically translating to recognition of that state, as the admission of Burma in 1948 had demonstrated. The only valid legal basis was to determine which state was *able* to fulfil the obligations of UN membership, and this was purely a question of observing which government had effective control over the territory of the state in question.[27] As Lie later wrote in his memoirs: 'Without being happy that the Communists had won the Civil War in China, I did not feel that approval or disapproval of a regime was in question: it was a matter of recognizing the facts of international life.'[28]

Armed with his legal memorandum Lie set out to talk to the states on the Council to see if he could convince an additional two to vote in favour of seating the representative of the communist Chinese government.[29] These discussions did not bring about any solution. Although France and other states confessed to agree with Lie's analysis, they could not vote in favour of the Chinese communists for political reasons. France was particularly upset that the Chinese communist government supported Ho Chi Minh in his struggle against the French colonial government in Vietnam. The Soviet tactics moreover alienated many states, and the British delegation believed the Soviet end-goal might actually be to isolate the Beijing government further to make them easier to dominate.[30]

The Chinese representation debacle provided a further motivation for Lie's decision to develop and promote his ten-point 20-year programme for peace to try and rally the organization around positive goals.[31] Ultimately though, the Chinese representation issue itself receded into the background after the Soviet Union returned to the Council in August 1950, thus accepting the status quo. Once China intervened in the Korean War, Lie also shelved his efforts. 'In short, troops of the People's Republic of China had gone to war against the United Nations', Lie wrote, and 'for the duration of the fighting, that ended my interest in seating the Peking government in the United Nations'.[32] The Beijing government would not take its seat in the UN until 1971 after the US–China rapprochement. The issue nonetheless had lasting consequences for Lie's position as UN secretary-general. In this case, Lie essentially disputed the right of one of the P5 – Nationalist China – to sit in the Security Council. No other secretary-general has ever done the same so brazenly. For the remainder of Lie's tenure, he did not enjoy Chinese support. Furthermore, Lie's campaign against the US' close ally, also caused damage to the secretary-general's relationship with Washington DC, and provided new material to conservative newspapers and Congressmen who already believed Lie to be 'Moscow's man'.

In the midst of worries over the worsening nuclear arms race and the freeze of UN activities due to the Chinese representation conflict and the Soviet walkout, Lie decided he had to step up with a bold proposal. A memo prepared by Lie's close advisors in early March 1950, summed up the problem: 'The effect of the deadlock on the prestige and health of the United Nations is obvious. Some resumption of discussions is essential to stop the rapid draining away of public confidence, not only in the United Nations as an organization, but in the whole idea of peaceful settlement and international co-operation.'[33] New atomic developments would occur as technology progressed, each time prompting 'the same worries [to] come to the surface again and again'.[34] The legal approach had failed to solve the Chinese representation issue, and Lie therefore concluded that 'new ways had to be found to resolve the crisis. Was it possible to bring the parties together again on other issues than that of Chinese representation?'[35] In an effort to bridge the divide and end the deadlock, Lie decided to put forward a bold proposal for a 20-year peace plan.

'A twenty-year program to win peace through the United Nations', March–June 1950

The question of Chinese representation and the Soviet walkout from the UN inspired Lie to think deeply about the UN's purposes and the organization's future, and prompted him to propose an ambitious peace plan in the spring of 1950. On 21 March in a speech to the B'nai B'rith, a Jewish community organization, in Washington DC, the secretary-general called for the development of a 'twenty-year program to win peace through the United Nations'.[36] Lie and his advisers then proceeded to prepare a memorandum with the following ten suggestions for developing such a 20-year peace programme:[37]

1. Inauguration of periodic meetings of the Security Council, attended by foreign ministers, or heads or other members of Governments, as provided by the United Nations Charter and the rules of procedure; together with further development and use of other United Nations machinery for negotiation, mediation, and conciliation of international disputes ...

2. A new attempt to make progress toward establishing an international control system for atomic energy that will be effective in preventing its use for war and promoting its use for peaceful purposes ...
3. A new approach to the problem of bringing the armaments race under control, not only in the field of atomic weapons, but in other weapons of mass destruction and in conventional armaments ...
4. A renewal of serious efforts to reach agreement on the armed forces to be made available under the Charter [article 43] to the Security Council for the enforcement of its decisions ...
5. Acceptance and application of the principle that it is wise and right to proceed as rapidly as possible towards universality of membership ...
6. A sound and active program of technical assistance for economic development and encouragement of broad-scale capital investment, using all appropriate private, governmental, and intergovernmental resources ...
7. More vigorous use by all Member Governments of the Specialized Agencies of the United Nations to promote, in the words of the Charter, 'higher standards of living, full employment, and conditions of economic and social progress' ...
8. Vigorous and continued development of the work of the United Nations for wider observance and respect for human rights and fundamental freedoms throughout the world ...
9. Use of the United Nations to promote, by peaceful means instead of by force, the advancement of dependent, colonial, or semicolonial peoples, towards a place of equality in the world ...
10. Active and systematic use of all the powers of the Charter and all the machinery of the United Nations to speed up the development of international law towards an eventual enforceable world law for a universal world society.

Several of the ten proposals called for renewed attention to a problem, or increased use of programmes already in place. The last six points of the plan thus called for continuous efforts to promote universality in UN membership, international law, economic and social development, human rights, and 'the advancement of dependent, colonial, or semicolonial peoples'. These were all areas identified in the UN Charter as important to improve overall conditions in the world and thereby to facilitate a more peaceful and just world. Despite their importance, throughout his tenure as secretary-general, Lie focused most of his energy and attention on the more openly political issue of peace and security, and his 1950 peace plan was no exception. Four of the plan's ten points directly related to the UN's work for peace and security. Lie called for renewed negotiations for international control of nuclear energy and for broader arms control, and he attempted once again to prompt the states to provide the armed forces promised under article 43 of the UN Charter.

The most specific suggestion was the call for the Security Council to inaugurate 'periodic meetings'. Article 28(2) of the Charter provided for such meetings, but none had ever been held. Lie suggested calling a meeting in 1950 attended by foreign minister or heads of government, to be held away from UN headquarters, and devoted to a general review of 'outstanding issues in the United Nations, particularly those that divide the Great Powers'.[38] In a separate memorandum drafted in March 1950, the secretary-general proposed including on the agenda for such a meeting discussion of Chinese representation, atomic energy, armed forces under article 43, conventional armaments, and admission of new members. He admitted that it would be difficult to reach agreement on any one of these issues, and that it would probably be impossible to hold any such meeting until the question of Chinese representation was settled. Nevertheless, Lie's hope was that progress could be made through intense negotiations in private in the months leading up to the meeting. The meeting itself would thus become an opportunity to implement new agreements and to announce progress to the world.[39] Holding a periodic meeting was therefore primarily a means to spur on private negotiations between the P5, in the hope that some progress could be made in the long run.

According to Andrew Cordier and Wilder Foote, who were both part of the small group of Lie's advisors who drafted the peace plan proposal and associated memos,[40] the immediate goal of the proposal was to 'restore the United Nations as a center for negotiations between the West and the Communist countries'. Its long-range goal was to remind the member states that their long-term interests lay in 'devoting a higher proportion of their available resources of brains, leadership, and power toward increasing the effectiveness of the United Nations as a universal institution for ameliorating conflicts and extending areas of cooperation'.[41] The short-term goal thus related directly to easing the Cold War tensions, while the long-term goal was an attempt to remind member states of their long-term interest in the continued functioning of the organization.

Lie's peace tour

Lie, by this time highly experienced in the role of secretary-general, decided to employ all the tools at his disposal to promote his idea of a peace plan. He had two audiences in mind, both the governments of the member states, and public opinion. Armed with his memorandum of ten suggestions, Lie decided he would have to seek out the presidents, prime ministers, and foreign ministers of the permanent Council members (minus China) directly, rather than merely relaying his information through their UN delegations. To this end he set off on a widely publicized 'peace tour' at the end of April, spending nearly a month on the road. A trip to Europe to visit UN offices and attend UN meetings in Paris, Geneva, and The Hague was on the books already, but now widely publicized stops in Washington DC, London, Prague, and Moscow were added to the itinerary.

During April and May 1950 Lie discussed his plan with President Truman and Secretary of State Acheson of the US, Prime Minister Clement Attlee and Foreign Minister Ernest Bevin of the UK, President Vincent Auriol, Prime Minister Georges Bidault, and Foreign Minister Robert Schuman of France, and Prime Minister Josef Stalin, Vice-Premier Vyacheslav Molotov, and Foreign Minister Andrei Vyshinsky of the Soviet Union, as well as other government representatives from those four countries plus Switzerland, the Netherlands, and Czechoslovakia.[42]

Seeking to increase the legitimacy of his proposal, Lie further decided to enlist the support of the executive heads of the specialized agencies of the UN, scheduled to meet in Paris in early May as the UN Administrative Committee on Coordination (ACC).[43] Bringing on board the leaders of the specialized agencies would 'create the widest possible front on a purely international basis', argued Tor Gjesdal, one of Lie's closest advisors, and 'the moral value of such a joint action will be indisputable, and ... will awaken sympathy all over the world'.[44] Although the ACC had never before issued any political statements, normally limiting itself to administrative matters, because it brought together the executive heads of the various organizations in the UN system, many of them well known and respected in their own right, Gjesdal argued the ACC could be likened to 'an "international cabinet meeting" on a very high level'.[45] Chaired by Lie, the meeting on 2–3 May was attended by Jaime Torres-Bodet, director-general of UNESCO; David A. Morse, director-general of ILO; Norris E. Dodd, director-general of the FAO; Brock Chisholm, director-general of WHO; Edward Warner, president of the Council of the International Civil Aviation Organization; Eugene R. Black, president of the World Bank; A.N. Overby, representing the managing director of the IMF; F. Blanchard, representing the director-general of the International Refugee Organization; G.C. Gross, representing the secretary-general of the ITU; Fulke Radice, representing the director of the UPU; and E. Wyndham White, executive secretary of the interim committee of the International Trade Organization.[46] The 12 executive heads endorsed the following statement, drafted by Lie's staff:

> The present division of the world and the increasingly serious conflicts of policy among the Great Powers have gravely impaired the prospects for world peace and for raising the standards of living of the peoples of the world. It is of particular concern to the administrative heads of the organizations that these conditions threaten the very basis of their work ... We also believe that it is necessary for all Governments to renew their efforts to conciliate and negotiate the political differences

that divide them and obstruct economic and social advancement. Specifically, we believe that it is essential to the future of both the United Nations and the specialized agencies that the present political deadlock in the United Nations be resolved at the earliest possible moment. The peace and wellbeing of all peoples demand from their Governments a great and sustained new effort by the nations of the world to achieve a constructive and durable peace.[47]

Lie recorded his elation with the ACC meeting's support in a letter to his family, noting that 'it has never happened before that the administrative chiefs of the specialised agencies of the UN have dared to take a political step', and concluding that it was 'the most eventful ACC meeting [he had] ever attended'.[48]

Returning from Europe, Lie finally submitted his memorandum to all the UN member states on 6 June and later placed it on the agenda for the upcoming General Assembly. The secretary-general's suggestions met with mixed responses. The smaller states warmly endorsed Lie's plan, as evidenced in the widespread support for the Assembly resolution asking the various organs of the UN to make note of Lie's proposals and report back on what they were doing to meet those goals.[49] Nine countries jointly proposed this resolution, which was adopted by 51 votes in favour, 5 against, and 1 abstention.[50]

The permanent Council members – Lie's primary target – nevertheless expressed some reservations. By this point Lie had no relationship with Nationalist China, and he never attempted to win this government over to his ideas. The British government questioned the usefulness and wisdom of Lie's suggested agenda for a periodic meeting of the Security Council, but realized that 'from purely tactical and propaganda considerations we would not wish to be accused of pouring cold water on Mr. Lie's suggestion, thus appearing to share with the Russians the blame for the present deadlock'.[51] During Lie's meetings in London, therefore, British representatives were careful to appear positive, so much so that Lie's impression was that Britain actually supported his proposals, and he recorded satisfaction with the meetings in his letters.[52]

Lie's impressions from his first meetings with the French government, on the contrary, were much more negative, as he reported afterwards that France seemed to be 'for sale'.[53] In Lie's opinion, what French leaders wanted above all else were American weapons, and they would sacrifice UN interests to get them.[54] Lie's impression contrasts sharply with the report from the American embassy in Paris that the French president had given the secretary-general 'a very warm welcome and strongly encouraged him to do everything in his power to avert the danger of another war'.[55] Likewise, at the end of his second visit to Paris in the latter half of May, foreign minister Schuman expressed general support for the majority of Lie's proposals and told him that 'France saw in the UN the only organization that could lead the world to a lasting and stable peace', and would therefore 'do whatever it could to end the present unmaintainable conditions'.[56]

Like its British ally, the American government was careful not to give Lie either 'yes' or 'no' during their two meetings in Washington DC in April and May.[57] After Lie's publication of the memorandum in early June, however, Secretary of State Acheson stated the US' reservations against Lie's suggestions, and argued that the real problem was not the question of Chinese representation, as Lie claimed, but the general Soviet attitude towards the UN and cooperation with the West. Slipping into Cold War rhetoric, Acheson cautioned 'the free nations of the world' to be patient and 'carry forward in our own determination to create situations of strength in the free world', as this would be the only way to achieve a lasting settlement with the Soviet Union.[58] Still, Acheson took care to note his support for the secretary-general, saying that it was 'proper for Mr. Lie in his capacity as Secretary General of the United Nations to take whatever steps he thinks desirable in his effort to reduce the existing tensions in the world. The Secretary General of the United Nations occupies a unique position and deserves our encouragement and support.'[59]

Lastly, the Soviet Union, although it criticized Lie's memorandum as 'one-sided' and biased in 'Anglo-American' favour, agreed to Lie's proposal to hold periodic meetings of the Security Council, and indicated that Lie's ten suggestions could serve as a working paper for deciding on the agenda for such a meeting.[60] Likewise, during the General Assembly's discussions in November 1950, despite introducing an alternative plan with a number of changes, Vyshinsky still expressed his support for 'the views expressed in the memorandum to the effect that it is possible to take steps, through the UN, to end the so-called "Cold War", and promote the strengthening of peace'.[61] This was significant because this partial support for Lie's plan came *after* the extension of his term as secretary-general, which the Soviet Union strongly opposed – a topic we will return to in the next section.

Aftermath and Lie's re-appointment

Lie officially submitted his proposal to the member states on 6 June, less than three weeks before the outbreak of the Korean War, discussed in the previous chapter. Although this latest instalment in the Cold War condemned the prospects for finding an immediate solution to the question of Chinese representation, and made the holding of a periodic meeting of the Security Council increasingly unlikely, Lie did not abandon the idea of a peace programme. If anything, the Korean War made solving the Cold War even more urgent, as he told reporters at a press conference on 26 June: 'The

Korean crisis, in my opinion, does not detract from my programme. It only points it up more sharply. It is a symptom, an effect of the deadlock that divides the world ... it only serves to support my conviction that a start must be made towards settling the differences between the major Powers.'[62]

Furthermore, although the outbreak of the Korean War meant that some of Lie's suggestions would have to be postponed, one immediate effect could be observed even in 1950: 'My mission received a degree of publicity surpassing anything I had expected or desired', wrote Lie. 'Millions of men and women who had previously heard little or nothing of the United Nations now became aware of its vital significance in the struggle for peace, and immediately responded with demonstrations of support.'[63] At every stop during the tour, Lie was inundated with flowers, notes, and letters, so that he 'had flowers all the time, so many that [he] had to give them away as the journey progressed'.[64] Among the many well-wishers were the famous scientist Albert Einstein, who sent Lie a handwritten letter in April 1950 to wish him 'luck and success in [his] great task', and to commend Lie as 'one of the very few who are able to see clearly in the confusion of our days, and who is not to be daunted by any hinderances [sic] or bounds in your desire to help'.[65] In London, the secretary-general received a delegation of women and children, bearing flowers, letters, and small notes and drawings.[66] Such public support was an important goal of Lie's peace plan in and of itself. As the secretary-general wrote in an open letter in reply to the numerous letters he had received in the past few months: 'Public understanding, public knowledge, is one of the strongest foundations upon which the United Nations rests ... The United Nations is the only real road to peace. It is a road which you and I – all of us – can build together.'[67]

Support for Lie's peace proposal also contributed to his re-appointment as secretary-general in November 1950. This had been an eventful year for secretary-general Lie. This chapter has discussed his attempts to solve the question of Chinese representation and to promote an ambitious 20-year peace plan to end the Cold War. The previous chapter discussed Lie's strongly principled defence of the UN Charter in relation to the Korean War in June 1950. Lie's seeming crowning moment came in November 1950 when the General Assembly re-appointed him to the office of UN secretary-general for a new three-year period. Yet if we look closer at the re-election process we discover that most states were merely lukewarm supporters of Lie, and that the re-election widened the rift between the secretary-general and the Soviet Union which had appeared in June 1950. From this point onwards, the Soviet Union and its allies refused to recognize Lie as a legitimate secretary-general, and he was therefore unable to function effectively in his post.

It was not immediately obvious that Lie would get a second term as secretary-general. Although over time this has become something of a norm, for the first secretary-general there were no precedents or expectations surrounding reappointment for a second term. Both the UN Preparatory Commission and the first General Assembly session in 1946 had left the question open, the General Assembly merely deciding that the *first* secretary-general should be appointed for a five-year term, 'the appointment being open at the end of that period for a further five-year term'.[68]

The most obvious obstacle to Lie's re-election was the opposition of the Soviet Union. Because of his strong principled stand on the Korean War, in diametrical opposition to the Soviet Union's views of that particular conflict, the Soviet Union was strongly opposed to renewing Lie's term as secretary-general. The Soviet Politburo on 10 September instructed its UN delegation to 'raise objections and vote against the reelection of Trygve Lie to the [position] of the UN Secretary-General'.[69] Likewise, the Chinese Nationalist government were deeply unhappy with Lie's attempts to unseat them from the Security Council, as discussed earlier in this chapter, and would likely oppose his re-election. Since both the Soviet Union and China possessed a veto over the Security Council's recommendation of a secretary-general, their opposition made Lie's reappointment highly unlikely. Nevertheless, at the start of the Assembly Lie thought the Soviet Union might still be open to voting in his favour, or at least to abstain, because the delegation gave him no indications of hostility upon their arrival in New York.[70] As late as May 1950, Lie had still been the Soviet Union's preferred candidate, because its officials believed it would be impossible to come to agreement with the Western states on anyone better than Lie, and Lie, despite his flaws, had been 'friendly' towards the Soviet Union on a number of occasions.[71] This indicates that Lie's actions on the Korean War were the decisive factor in swaying Moscow against reappointing him for a new term as secretary-general.

In addition to Soviet and Chinese opposition during the Assembly session in 1950, Lie also had a somewhat uneasy relationship with the British and American governments which would seem to make his re-election appear unlikely. As discussed throughout earlier chapters, the British government had been unhappy with Lie's performance as secretary-general since 1946, and Foreign Office files are riddled with snide and derogatory remarks about Lie's personality and abilities. During the fourth Assembly in the latter half of 1949, rumours about possible replacements for Lie circulated freely among the assembled delegates, and prompted an outflow of negative remarks about Lie in the British Foreign Office. Britain's permanent representative to the UN, Sir Alexander Cadogan, hoped Lie would not be re-elected 'for I really think Lie is rather a disaster'.[72] Hector McNeill, a junior minister in the Foreign Office, agreed: 'like everyone else I have no use for [Lie]. He is cowardly, inept and vain, and has brought no ability or morality to his job. One would not want to see him again Secretary General.'[73]

The Americans too, had discussed the possibility of replacing Lie, and thought it might be desirable to establish the precedent that the secretary-general should serve only one term, at least in the initial years.[74] At one point some circles in the State Department even discussed the possibility that Ralph Bunche – then a director in the UN Trusteeship Division, formerly of the US State Department, celebrated mediator of armistice agreements between Israel and the Arab states, and a prominent African-American – might become UN secretary-general. They speculated that Bunche might be acceptable to the Soviet Union because he was African-American.[75] Thus by early 1950, the support of the US and the UK for Lie's re-election was far from guaranteed.

Even more importantly, Lie himself had emphatically declared that he would not be a candidate for re-election, and that he desired nothing more than to retire and return to Norway upon completing his five-year term in February 1951. At a press conference in December 1949 he stated as much: 'When I have completed my term of service as Secretary-General, I shall be very happy to have been able to serve the United Nations for five years, and I am not a candidate for re-appointment.'[76] Lie even bought a new house for himself and his family by the Oslo Fjord, and told people how much he was looking forward to returning 'to his beloved Oslo'.[77] Note that Lie by this point had lived outside Norway for ten years, apart from the short eight-month period between the end of WW2 and his election as secretary-general, and his desire to return home may well have been genuine. Nevertheless, many state representatives continued to believe that Lie ultimately desired a second term, and indeed saw his peace tour in May 1950 as proof of an election campaign.[78]

All these things considered – Lie's declaration that he wanted to retire, Britain being eager to replace him with someone else, China's opposition because of Lie's initiative to seat the communist government in the UN, and the Soviet Union's opposition because of the Korean War – we would expect Lie's term to have ended in February 1951, and the Security Council and the General Assembly to have elected some other compromise candidate. Perhaps we might have seen an earlier entry for Dag Hammarskjöld or some other Swede? However, this was not to happen, and instead the General Assembly on 1 November 1950 re-appointed Lie for another three years.[79] What had happened?

The answer in short is Korea. Just as the Korean War had changed the Soviet Union's opinion of Lie as secretary-general, so the Korean War too strengthened the US' desire to see Lie re-elected. Despite earlier hesitation about re-electing Lie, in April 1950 the US State Department reached the same conclusion independently being reached by the Soviet Foreign Office at the same time – Lie was the only candidate likely to be acceptable to both sides, and it would probably not be possible to replace him with someone better.⁸⁰ The US also informed Lie in June 1950 that he was their candidate for re-election.⁸¹ Lie's strong and principled defence of the UN Charter and his active support for the US-led UN intervention to aid South Korea demonstrated Lie's usefulness to the US, and confirmed them in their decision to see him re-appointed.

Moreover, the US decided on principle to support Lie because the Soviet Union wanted to get rid of him. As Secretary of State Acheson explained on 24 October: 'We were taking a position on principle; we could not permit the Soviet Union to use its veto to punish Mr. Lie for his position on Korea.'⁸² Lie also decided to accept re-appointment because no one state (the Soviet Union) should be allowed to determine UN policies, and because he didn't want to leave the UN in the middle of its challenges in Korea. As he later wrote in his memoirs: 'With the Assembly's vote returning me to office, the immediate political objectives had been won: United Nations action in Korea had been reaffirmed, the continuity of United Nations administration had been assured, and the independent position of the Secretary-General had been preserved against the threats and pressures of a great power.'⁸³ After some discussion back and forth, Britain and France acquiesced to the American desire to extend Lie's period, while China agreed to abstain in the interest of isolating the Soviet Union in its opposition against Lie and the Korean intervention.

This left a deadlock in the Security Council, however, as the Soviet Union declared it would veto Lie⁸⁴ while the US would veto anyone *but* Lie. President Truman informed the UN delegation that the US Government 'were prepared to make a real fight on this matter and that we would insist on the election of Mr. Lie. We were prepared to *threaten* to use the veto and to go further and *use* the veto itself if that became necessary.'⁸⁵ The Council held a number of private meetings during October, but in the end was unable to agree on any one candidate. The question was therefore transferred to the General Assembly *without* the recommendation called for by article 97 of the UN Charter. Nonetheless, the majority of the General Assembly decided 'that the present Secretary-General shall be continued in office for a period of three years'.⁸⁶ The resolution passed on 1 November 1950 by 46 votes in favour, 5 against (the Soviet bloc), and 8 abstentions (China because of Lie's position on the question of Chinese representation, the Arab states over Lie's support for Israel, and Australia for legal reasons).⁸⁷

Lie's re-election therefore came about mainly at the behest of the US, who at this time still commanded a majority in the General Assembly. The high number of abstentions, however, indicates the internal struggle in the anti-Soviet bloc over whether or not to go along with the American wish to re-elect Lie. For some states Lie was unacceptable politically, while others objected to the procedure of the US in pushing its will through over the objection of the Security Council. As British and French hesitation about following the American plan reveals, several members of the majority still held objections against Lie, yet in the interest of unity they agreed to vote in his favour.

The re-appointment of Lie to a second term as secretary-general by the General Assembly without a recommendation from the Security Council thus aligns with the general trend at the time of the General Assembly assuming powers previously reserved for the Security Council, and the Western states' attempt to bypass the deadlock in the Council. This was another example of how a vacuum effect operates; when one actor is unable to perform its tasks, someone else will take over either voluntarily or by force. The fifth Assembly session also passed the 'Uniting for Peace' resolution on 3 November,[88] and the American UN ambassador explicitly recognized the continuity of the various resolutions on Korea, the extension of Lie's term, and the 'Uniting for Peace' resolution in a letter he sent to Lie on 7 November. Austin called Lie's re-election 'an integral part of the gains made by the United Nations beginning with June 25, 1950 ... which gives promise for the future ... to consolidate the unity of the non-communist members of the United Nations'.[89] Indeed, the US would increasingly in this period view the UN as a means to isolate the Soviet Union. However, even its closest allies protested against this trend,[90] arguing that 'primary emphasis should be placed upon the UN as a world forum for discussion and for east–west rapprochement'.[91] This was precisely what Lie had sought to do throughout his first four years in office, culminating in the 20-year peace plan in early 1950. Ironically, his re-election served as a step in the opposite direction towards turning the UN into an arena for the Cold War struggle.

Despite the symbolic importance of Lie's re-election as standing on the principles of the UN Charter, in the long term this was no victory for the secretary-general. The Soviet Union declared the re-election illegal, and henceforth refused to recognize Lie as secretary-general or to work with his office. Already during the General Assembly discussions, the Soviet representative warned that if Lie were reappointed, 'the Government of the Soviet Union ... will have no dealings with him and will refuse to regard him as the Secretary-General'.[92] Once Lie's original term expired on 1 February 1951, the Soviet government followed up on its threat, and thereafter addressed all communications to 'the Secretariat' rather than Lie, and also refused to invite him to their social events, or to reply to Lie's invitations to them.[93] Therefore, as Lie later admitted, the benefits of the principled victory in his re-election would have to be

> weighed against the serious impairment in the usefulness of my office that followed. The Soviet boycott limited my activities to a small part of the political role intended for the Secretary-General by the Charter. It was not a happy state of affairs, and I sincerely hope

that future Secretaries-General of the United Nations will be spared such tribulations.[94]

The Soviet boycott thus directly contributed to Lie's decision to resign from office a mere two years later in November 1952.

Conclusion

Lie's 1950 peace plan saw the secretary-general making a bold proposal to seek to overcome the divisions of the Cold War. In the context of worsening East–West tensions, an intensified nuclear arms race, and deadlock at the UN over the Chinese representation issue, Lie attempted to mobilize the peoples of the world and their governments to rally around the UN. The UN was established to provide a forum for solving potential conflicts that could threaten international peace and security. The UN's founders intended the great powers to work together for this goal through the Security Council. Yet by 1950 this machinery was breaking down. Lie feared the Soviet walkout was the beginning of the end of the UN as a global organization. He therefore sought to enlist public support in defence of the UN and its ideals.

Lie's 1950 peace plan thus represents an early example of the secretary-general's important role as an advocate for the UN,[95] or a 'norm entrepreneur'[96] on global issues. As a 'guardian' of the UN Charter the secretary-general has the right and responsibility to promote the principles and purposes of the UN, and to educate and mobilize the peoples of the world in the organization's defence.[97] This episode furthermore served to strengthen the role of the secretary-general as the overall representative of the UN. Lie himself described this aspect of his role as being a 'spokesman for the world interest'.[98] Later scholars have recognized the secretary-general as 'a living symbol and embodiment of the United Nations'.[99]

With his actions in this period Lie set important precedents for the public, political and symbolically important role of the secretary-general. In contrast to the League of Nations secretary-general, the UN secretary-general has come to play a much more public role, a development which started under Lie. Furthermore, serving as a 'guardian of the UN Charter' also provides an important foundation for the secretary-general's authority to act in other contexts. The 1950 peace plan proposal saw Lie seeking to mobilize the support of the world's peoples. Public opinion provides the secretary-general with an independent power base and source of legitimacy separate from the member states. Later secretaries-general have also sought to utilize public support by making public appeals, a practice that started during Lie's tenure in office.

6

Administering the International: The International Civil Service and the UN Secretariat, 1946–53

> The degree in which the objects of the Charter can be realized will be largely determined by the manner in which the Secretariat performs its task. The Secretariat cannot successfully perform its task unless it enjoys the confidence of all the Members of the United Nations ... appropriate methods of recruitment should be established in order that a staff may be assembled which is characterized by the highest standards of efficiency, competence and integrity.[1]
>
> Report of the Preparatory Commission of the United Nations (December 1945)

Introduction

Issues of peace and security, so-called 'high-politics', frequently take centre stage in debates on the UN. This book has been no exception, as the previous chapters all focused on the repeating cycles of high-level political crises, and Lie's attempts to deal with these as secretary-general. Lie chose to focus most of his attention and energy on the political role of the UN secretary-general and the questions of peace and security discussed by the Security Council. Yet, to understand the process by which the UN Charter was transformed from paper to practice, the establishment of the UN Secretariat itself is also of crucial importance. As the previous chapters showed, in these early years after an organization has been established, while the rules are still fluid, individuals working in the organization have wide room for manoeuvre and can influence the establishment of precedents for the future. It therefore matters also what kind of organizational structures are set up and which formal and informal rules develop for the secretariat itself.

This chapter examines the initial establishment of the UN Secretariat, focused particularly on the norms associated with the International Civil Service (ICS). The ICS is both an empirical and a normative concept.[2] As an empirical concept it refers simply to the staff working for international organizations. The term as such was first adopted by the League of Nations and later continued in the UN system. But with the designation of staff as ICS in purely descriptive terms, there also follows certain normative expectations. The ICS offers an ideal vision for how staff should act and who they should be. This vision combines ideas of liberal internationalism with a Weberian ideal of a professional and efficient bureaucracy.[3] From liberal internationalism comes the idea that the ICS should be neutral, impartial, and loyal only to the international organization, while the Weberian tradition entails that staff be hired and promoted based on merit and an organizational structure with division of work and clear channels of authority.

In the administration of the UN Secretariat, the UN Preparatory Commission suggested 'a robust vision of an international civil service, not unlike those to be espoused by would-be UN reformers in the years to come'.[4] The UN Charter, in articles 100 and 101, formalized the vision of an international staff loyal only to the organization that had developed through the practice of the League of Nations. Article 100 established that the secretary-general and his staff should 'not seek or receive instruction from any government or from any other authority external to the Organization', and that member states should 'respect the[ir] exclusively international character'. Article 101 further stated categorically that 'staff shall be appointed by the Secretary-General', and that 'the paramount consideration in the employment of staff ... shall be the necessity of securing the highest standards of efficiency, competence, and integrity. Due regard shall be paid to the importance of recruiting the staff on as wide a geographical basis as possible.' In the League, the ICS ideals were expressed and developed through internal Secretariat reports and discussions, here the UN's founders 'elevated [them] to the constitutional level of the UN and enshrined [them] in the Charter'.[5] Yet, despite this apparent strengthened position for the ICS in the UN, in the area of administration, unlike in the political areas described in earlier chapters, the freedom of the UN secretary-general would actually become more limited than initially envisioned. Whereas the secretary-general's political autonomy and authority expanded, his administrative freedom was restricted, somewhat counter-intuitively considering the UN Charter primarily describes the secretary-general as the UN's 'chief administrative officer'.

Furthermore, the role and position Lie adopted in these questions remains something of a puzzle. In the high-profile case of McCartyhism, Lie has been accused of 'selling out' the (American) staff of the UN Secretariat to the US government. In the midst of the frantic communist witch-hunt, Lie allowed the FBI onto UN premises to interview and fingerprint American nationals working in the Secretariat, and when some staff members 'pleaded the Fifth' and refused to testify to a Senate Committee, Lie fired them. The secretary-general thus failed to protect and defend these Secretariat staff, and failed to stand up for the integrity and independence of the ICS. Why did he make this choice?

These choices are puzzling when considered against Lie's personal background. Lie started his political and professional life working for trade unions and the Norwegian Labour Party. After completing a law degree at the University of Oslo in 1919, in 1922 Lie was hired as general counsellor for the Norwegian Confederation of Trade Unions, a position he held until he was elected to parliament in 1935.[6] Over the next few years Lie defended workers in conflicts with employers and fought for the right to unionize and to strike. He defended workers who faced criminal charges under the so-called 'hostile' labour laws; for example, for attempting to prevent strike-breakers or for giving financial support to workers engaged in 'illegal' strike action.[7] Lie became one of the leading Norwegian experts on labour dispute law ('*arbeidstvistlov*') in this period, and also published a short book on the subject.[8] The period 1920 to 1935 saw the most intense and drawn-out conflicts between employers and workers in Norwegian history, leading up to the adoption of the first Basic Agreement ('*Hovedavtale*') – the 'labour market constitution' – in 1935.[9] As a general counsellor for the trade union and active Labour Party politician, Lie held a central position in this transition period in Norwegian society, and he stood squarely on the side of workers' rights. Yet when the US Senate and FBI came looking for 'un-American' citizens in the UN Secretariat, Lie gave in to their demands and fired staff members. What explains this apparent about-face? How and why did Lie seemingly surrender and fail to defend his staff, when in the past he had been a staunch defender of workers against employers and government interference?

This chapter examines the establishment of the UN Secretariat while Lie was secretary-general, with a particular emphasis on the ICS ideals. The first section describes the initial hiring of staff for the new Secretariat. The second section looks closer at the organizational structure of the Secretariat and Lie's relations with the senior staff. Third, the chapter considers the search for and building of a permanent headquarters for the new organization. The fourth section turns to the process of McCarthyism and its impact on the UN and implications for the ICS. Finally, the chapter also discusses Lie's resignation from office in November 1952.

Staffing the Secretariat

The establishment of the UN and its secretariat in 1946 naturally brought numerous administrative challenges. Upon taking office on 2 February 1946, secretary-general Lie had to hire staff for the Secretariat, move the organization's headquarters to a new city, find office and meeting space, and prepare for and provide support to meetings of UN organs. Where the League of Nations had been given nearly two years to prepare for the first meetings, Lie wrote, 'the central problem was that the United Nations was already a going concern which had to be serviced continuously, and with no delay whatever'.[10] The General Assembly and Security Council were already in session, while ECOSOC was scheduled to start its first session in May with various committees and commissions also due to meet during the spring.[11] Thus the UN had to 'hit the ground running'.[12] Already on 25 March the Security Council held its first meeting in New York,[13] thus giving Lie and his staff less than two months to get the Secretariat operational nearly from scratch. The process took its toll both on Lie and his assistants. He wrote to a colleague in Norway that his work had been 'very exacting ... I have had to reconstruct the administration from the bottom'.[14] But even worse, the consequences of this initial scramble would linger in the Secretariat for decades. 'It was an ill-organized and frantic start, the impact of which would never fully be erased', concluded one later study.[15]

Certain administrative resources were already in place. The executive committee of the UN Preparatory Commission had been operating in London since August 1945 and in February 1946 possessed a staff of approximately 300 people. Lie arranged for this staff to continue to service the General Assembly and the Security Council in London, while he concentrated on establishing the new permanent Secretariat.[16] Some staff from the London secretariat soon went on to work for the UN Secretariat, including such well-known figures from UN history as David Owen and Brian Urquhart.[17] Furthermore, the UN could build on the experiences of the League of Nations in setting up the new Secretariat. The Preparatory Commission and the General Assembly, building on the League example, had drawn up detailed plans for the Secretariat, which was now presented to the new secretary-general. But as Lie later wrote, 'despite this help, my initial task was far more complicated than Sir Eric Drummond's had been, not to mention the fact that the instructions were so detailed that they limited my freedom of action'.[18]

The UN Preparatory Commission had suggested procedures for recruitment and management of the Secretariat. This entailed setting up a complex system of examinations, in-house training, and testing which would allow for the recruitment of staff of 'the highest standards of efficiency, competence and integrity' while taking into account the need for a geographical balance among staff.[19] The Secretariat was designated one of the principal organs of the UN, and, as the Commission and other observers at the time noted, this position entailed an important responsibility. Thus, the Commission wrote, 'the degree in which the objects of the Charter can be realized will be largely determined by the manner in which the Secretariat performs its task'.[20] Lie agreed:

> I needed the best possible staff, to share the burdens of my office and prove its worthiness of being a principal organ of the United Nations ... The staff ... would be entrusted with responsibilities in carrying out their tasks that would require a high level of judgment, ability, and devotion to the objective international standards of Article 100 of the Charter.[21]

Yet, when Lie set up office in the spring of 1946, none of the envisioned hiring and training procedures were in place. The problem facing Lie was not a shortage of candidates. Both in London and New York the embryonic Secretariat received letters from thousands of men and women seeking employment with the UN.[22] The problem was thus primarily one of screening the applicants to find the most qualified among them.

To assist in this process, Lie sought the help from member states in screening and running background checks on applicants. Certain states, foremost at this time the Soviet Union, took this to the extreme and only offered one name for each position,[23] while others, most notably the US, refused to give such assistance.[24] Providing background information on applicants had been an established part of the procedure in the League of Nations, yet the US now refused to do so. Those opposed to asking member governments for information argued that the secretary-general should be free to make his own decisions on staffing without any government interference, in line with the provisions of articles 100 and 101 of the UN Charter.[25] At several occasions from early 1946 onwards, Lie sought through various channels to obtain information about American staff and applicants from the US government, but time and again the US government refused to comply with his request.[26] The US Secretary of State reportedly responded that the US 'would neither tender any recommendations, support officially, nor give clearance on the appointment of American nationals to subordinate positions in the secretariat'. Taking into account the experience of the League, Barros argues, 'it was a naive stance'.[27] This initial American refusal to screen applications also aggravated problems during the later McCarthy era, as discussed later in this chapter.

With inadequate time and resources, Lie had limited options available. As Jebb, then in charge of the London secretariat, wrote, Lie 'had no choice but to recruit quickly, extensively and indiscriminately'.[28] It was impossible to do thorough background checks and run staged recruitment processes, so the only solution available was to offer everyone temporary contracts in the beginning. Yet Lie notes in his memoirs, 'a high proportion of these temporary appointees fully proved their worth and later joined the career service'.[29] Nonetheless, the rapid and hectic pace of hiring during the first year resulted in certain long-term problems for the UN, not least of which was the skewed geographical balance of the Secretariat staff, since a majority was hired on the spot among available candidates in London and New York.

Many key decisions of lasting consequence were taken during the early months. One important aspect concerned the salary scale for the new staff. Early on, a practice emerged of linking the salary of UN Secretariat staff to the scales used by the US federal government. Yet not all UN officials agreed with this decision. In April 1946, newly appointed Assistant Secretary-General for Social Affairs, Henri Laugier of France, wrote a memo to Lie and the group of assistant secretaries-general warning that this practice could 'entail disastrous consequences for the future of the Secretariat and its effectiveness, and consequently for the future of the entire United Nations Organisation'.[30] Laugier was afraid that linking to the US federal scales would be setting a too low level of remuneration and thereby signify lower status for the Secretariat. He felt strongly that Secretariat staff should be considered 'on a level which should be in all respects equal at least, and I think on certain points superior to that of the temporary diplomatic missions or permanent Embassies', and therefore Secretariat salaries ought to be comparable to the diplomatic staff at the major embassies in the US.[31] If UN salaries were set at too low a level, Laugier warned, there would be a danger that the Secretariat would attract only 'candidates of mediocre abilities' who would be 'unequal to the world task and responsibility entrusted to [them]'.[32] Nonetheless, despite Laugier's dissent, UN Secretariat salaries would be linked to the US federal government, a decision which has not been entirely without problems.[33]

Another challenge of the early phase was finding office and meeting space. Initially, the Secretariat worked out of various hotel rooms and a few offices it inherited from the UN Information Organization at the Rockefeller Center. Many meetings took place at the Waldorf-Astoria, where Lie also stayed with his family.[34] It soon proved impossible to locate any suitable office space in midtown Manhattan, however, and a lease was signed on Hunter College, a former women's college in the Bronx, on 8 March.[35] On 25 March the Security Council was able to open its first meeting on American soil in the former gymnasium.[36] From there on, the UN would move on to an old factory at Lake Success, where Council chambers and Secretariat offices were established, while the General Assembly met in a hall at the grounds of the former World's Fair at Flushing Meadows.[37] The process of finding permanent headquarters will be discussed later in this chapter.

Locating housing for the staff of the new organization also proved to be challenging. The housing market in New York was already tight and returning soldiers and other young families were competing with newly hired UN staff for the few available homes.[38] The problems of inadequate working and living conditions took its toll on the staff, and 'the secretariat's morale began to sag'.[39] Lie and his family could finally move into their new house in Forest Hills in Queens, New York, on 1 September after months in hotel rooms.[40] In June 1946, Lie reported that

> things remain very difficult with regard to solving both practical and political questions. The accommodation situation is just as difficult here as in any other country which was involved in the war and I am waging a daily fight to try to obtain offices, conference accommodation, and houses for my personnel, but these purely practical and physical problems will be solved gradually, although they are taking rather a long time.[41]

Faced with these challenges, UN staff and government diplomats alike began comparing New York and its facilities unfavourably to Geneva, London, and San Francisco. But in Lie's opinion private considerations had to take second place behind the important political work of the organization. 'Regardless of deficiencies in climate, personal comfort, and the like, [n]one of us was here on vacation', he wrote in his memoirs.[42]

Lie continued to hold out hope that the administrative structures of the Secretariat could be improved with time. Taking stock in the summer of 1946, he noted that 'things have gone slowly, and I'm not entirely satisfied with the results. But in a year's time I expect the organisational apparatus to be in order.'[43] Unfortunately, the administrative problems of the Secretariat would never be solved during Lie's term in office, and his problems with recruiting suitable candidates for the top leadership positions, discussed in the next section, would only compound the difficulties.

Organization and leadership in the Secretariat

On the face of it, the UN Charter clearly assigned the secretary-general independence in the administration of the Secretariat. Article 100 established the 'exclusively international character' of the secretariat staff, while article 101 categorically stated that 'staff shall be appointed by the Secretary-General'. The UN Charter thus assigned the secretary-general authority to hire his own staff to all levels of the Secretariat. Furthermore, during negotiations in San Francisco a proposal to specify the number and process of election of the secretary-general's deputies was defeated, as the majority of governments supported the secretary-general's freedom to decide on this subject for himself.⁴⁴ However, once Lie took office in February 1946, he soon discovered that the member states had nonetheless found a way to limit his options. The General Assembly, adopting a recommendation from the Preparatory Commission, had decided that the Secretariat should be organized into eight departments each headed by an assistant secretary-general.⁴⁵ Behind the scenes, the P5 had further agreed that five of these top-level positions should be reserved for their nationals.⁴⁶ Lie had no choice but to comply.

The Soviet Union laid a claim to the assistant secretary-general for Security Council affairs, which Lie took as a positive sign of Moscow's devotion to the new organization. He was further pleased by Washington's agreement to let the Soviet Union control this important post.⁴⁷ After consulting with the Soviet delegation, Lie appointed Arkady Sobolev as assistant secretary-general for Security Council affairs. As examples from the previous chapters have shown, Lie and Sobolev enjoyed a good working relationship, and Lie would often use Sobolev as a go-between to communicate with the government of the Soviet Union. According to Barros, Sobolev was the only one of Lie's eight assistant secretaries-general who 'satisfied' Lie.⁴⁸ Sobolev also met with the approval of long-time Secretariat member, Urquhart, who later wrote that Sobolev 'managed with considerable style to walk the tightrope between being the senior Soviet official and being an international civil servant in a particularly sensitive post, and we all became very fond of him'.⁴⁹ Sobolev returned to the Soviet Union in 1949 and was succeeded by Constantin Zinchenko as the new Soviet assistant secretary-general for Security Council affairs.⁵⁰

The appointments of Laugier of France as assistant secretary-general for social affairs, and Victor Chi-Tsai Hoo of China to head the Department for Trusteeship and Non-Self-Governing Territories went fairly quickly while Lie was still in London. Also in London, Lie appointed Benjamin Cohen from Chile as assistant secretary-general for public information, Ivan Kerno from Czechoslovakia as assistant secretary-general for legal affairs, and Adrian Pelt from the Netherlands as assistant secretary-general for conference and general services.⁵¹ Finding the two assistant secretaries-general from Britain and the US, however, proved more complicated and took a somewhat longer time. As Lie complained in his memoirs:

> The British took an approach which was so solicitous of my right to appoint whatever British subject I chose as Assistant Secretary-General, as to be not quite helpful. The United Kingdom was diffident in its suggestions, and my requests for Englishmen either in government service or in prominent private positions failed to meet with any positive response.⁵²

Finally, months later on the day before the opening of the first ECOSOC meeting in New York in May 1946, when an assistant secretary-general for economic affairs needed to be present, Lie decided to promote David Owen, who was then serving as his executive assistant. Owen was an economist by training, but by age and experience more junior than the other men appointed to the rank of assistant secretary-general.[53] Nonetheless, Owen would prove his skills in the post and later went on to serve in other senior roles within the UN system for development aid.

The US had reserved for themselves the post of assistant secretary-general for administrative and financial services, the post concerned with the internal administration of the Secretariat. This assistant secretary-general would have many important tasks to fulfil in the initial establishment of the Secretariat, when thousands of new staff had to be hired rapidly, as discussed in the previous section. It was therefore unfortunate that the process of hiring this particular assistant secretary-general also dragged out in time. Lie approached Stettinius, the American UN ambassador, to ask for suggestions, but was informed that Secretary of State Byrnes, wanted to deal with this appointment himself.[54] Weeks passed without any recommendation from Byrnes. In private conversations and letters Lie received suggestions of several prominent Americans, including Milton Eisenhower, the general's brother, but none proved willing and able to accept the position. Eventually, Byrnes suggested the job be given to John B. Hutson, then Under Secretary of Agriculture, and he was quickly appointed.[55] Unfortunately for Lie, Hutson proved inadequate to the task. Jebb described him as a 'complete dud'.[56] Urquhart reported that the Department of Agriculture 'had evidently been delighted to get rid of ... "Potato Jack" Hutson'.[57] This was the man Lie had to rely on for assistance in establishing the Secretariat during the first year.

Everyone was relieved when Hutson resigned in early 1947, but this meant the appointment process had to be repeated again. Once more, Lie approached several men who were unable or unwilling to accept, before finally appointing Byron Price. During the search Lie complained that 'it has its difficulties getting the people we in the United Nations consider the best qualified for the positions'.[58] Fortunately, Price proved to be a better fit for the job than his predecessor. Price had previously worked for the Associated Press, the Office of Censorship, and the Association of Motion Picture Producers, and as Lie wrote in his memoirs, he 'left a much higher salary ... to come to the United Nations. He proved to be an administrator of solid integrity and efficiency. His complete reliability soon won him confidence and trust equaled by few of my close associates.'[59] Despite Price's competent service from 1947 onwards, the initial lack of leadership and early change of personnel during the initial frenzied hiring of Secretariat staff was unfortunate and contributed to the administrative chaos of the Secretariat.

The eight assistant secretaries-general constituted the top leadership of the UN Secretariat. During the San Francisco conference they had been likened to 'not experts or officials, but politicians, forming a kind of Cabinet'.[60] In his memoirs, Lie used similar language: 'The group of Assistant Secretaries-General was to be my official "cabinet", available for advice on all matters ... I delegated to them broad administrative authority from the very beginning.'[61] That the member states considered these positions of importance can best be judged from the five great powers' insistence that they each be given one assistant secretary-generalship. Yet despite the importance of staffing these positions with highly competent people, particularly during this crucial early phase of the UN's establishment, the member states did not always supply Lie with their best and brightest. Urquhart's characterization of the group was scathing: 'Having put Lie in a new and extremely challenging job, the UN's member governments did little or nothing to provide the qualified, top-level assistance that would have lightened his burden.' With the exception of Sobolev, Urquhart continued, the assistant secretaries-general 'were at best mediocre and at worst grotesque ... Lie, who met with this dismal crew once a week, was increasingly frustrated and disgusted, and he had every right to be.'[62] Already in April 1946, Lie complained of the difficulties of getting qualified assistance and worried about the lasting consequences of this initial lack of leadership:

> I have had considerable difficulties in appointing personnel. Some governments have refused to let me have the first-rate people I wanted in the top positions. I therefore have had to choose the next best. The top positions have consequently been filled partly with quite excellent people, but, unfortunately, also partly with people who should have been placed further down the ladder. I am, therefore, afraid that the result of the UN's work in the first period will prove unsatisfactory and uneven.[63]

Fortunately, Lie had somewhat more freedom in appointing staff at the lower levels of leadership, and these people were to some extent able to take up the slack. Important among these was Andrew W. Cordier, an American history professor who served as Lie's (and later Hammarskjöld's) executive assistant after Owen was promoted to assistant secretary-general. In this post, Lie wrote in his memoirs, he 'was my strong right hand throughout my term as Secretary-General and filled a significant role in many of the developments' of this period.[64] As earlier chapters have shown, Lie would often rely on Cordier for advice and assistance, and also despatched him to talk to governments on his behalf. Urquhart described Cordier as 'a tough, bumbling figure who was always prepared to dive in, no matter how shallow or muddy the water might be', and acknowledges that 'Cordier did a great deal to mitigate or short-circuit the confusions caused by the Assistant Secretaries-General'.⁶⁵ Also highly able was the American Ralph Bunche, who, like Cordier, was a scholar of international relations, and had previously worked in the US Department of State. During Lie's tenure, Bunche formally served as Hoo's number two in the trusteeship department, but as discussed in Chapter 3, Bunche played a key role as mediator in the Israel–Palestine conflict. Under Hammarskjöld and U Thant, Bunche would go on to play a key role in the efforts to mediate several other high-profile conflicts from Suez and the Congo to Kashmir and Vietnam, before leaving the UN Secretariat in 1971 at the rank of under secretary-general for special political affairs.⁶⁶

When Lie first established the UN Secretariat in 1946, he followed the suggestion of the General Assembly and the Preparatory Commission to organize the work under eight departments, each headed by an assistant secretary-general. Lie did not have a designated 'deputy', although the question had been discussed earlier. During the spring of 1947 in the search for a new assistant secretary-general to replace Hutson, the question of a separate 'deputy secretary-general' arose once more. Neither the UN Preparatory Commission nor the General Assembly had suggested the need for a deputy secretary-general separate from and above the assistant secretaries-general. Instead, the General Assembly proposed that 'there shall always be one Assistant Secretary-General designated by the Secretary-General to deputize for him when he is absent or unable to perform his functions'.⁶⁷ But during the first year of the UN's operations, the desire arose for a separate official who could help Lie with coordination of the various UN organs, committees, and commissions. Some of the men offered the post of assistant secretary-general for administrative and financial services, such as Milton Eisenhower, were primarily interested in the potential of a more senior 'deputy secretary-general' role in the UN system.⁶⁸ During early 1947 nothing came of the suggestion, and Adlai Stevenson, then a member of the US delegation to the UN, counselled Lie and his advisers to focus on the immediate task of replacing Hutson and then to revisit the question of a deputy: 'I know something of the obstacles to [creating a deputy position], but they may have to be hurdled somehow to get the kind of man he wants and needs.'⁶⁹

In parallel to the debates in New York and Washington, the British Foreign Office in London had also become convinced that Lie needed to appoint a deputy – 'a strong and able man' – to help with some of the administrative tasks and coordination of the Secretariat.⁷⁰ Lie was initially hesitant towards the British suggestion because of expected opposition from the Soviet Union and the US. The US feared that appointing a deputy secretary-general might undermine the responsibilities and position of Cordier, Lie's executive assistant, and Price, the assistant secretary general for administrative affairs, as well as damage their relationships with Lie. Both these men were American nationals.[71] Eventually, Lie gave in to British pressure and appointed Robert Jackson, an Australian national who had served as deputy director of the United Nations Relief and Rehabilitation Administration (UNRRA), to the deputy post in December 1947. As expected, the appointment caused some friction within the Secretariat and among Lie's team of advisors and close colleagues. Jackson 'had proven managerial skills', but his relationship with Lie 'proved awkward'.[72] Jackson's time as deputy at the UN included, for example, the Palestine conflict when Lie sent him as his representative to discuss with various governments, as discussed in Chapter 3 of this book. But already in August 1948, after less than one year, Jackson was dismissed when Lie abolished his position.[73]

Problems of administrative chaos and confusing lines of leadership and responsibility would continue to plague the Secretariat throughout Lie's tenure as secretary-general. In 1952 Lie prepared a proposal for reorganization of the Secretariat, but his ideas were never put into practice before Lie resigned and a new secretary-general took over.[74] Hammarskjöld implemented the first reorganizations of the Secretariat in 1953 and 1955.[75] Since then numerous reform have been proposed, and some implemented, but the UN Secretariat is still criticized for its ineffective practices and cumbersome organizational structure.

Finding headquarters

In December 1945, the UN Preparatory Commission decided that UN headquarters should be established in the eastern part of the US. The question of the eventual location of UN headquarters was deeply political, and many European states wished to see headquarters established in Europe. As discussed in Chapter 1, the question was also linked to decisions on the nationalities of the first secretary-general and other UN officials. Hearing the rumour that the UN might come to the US, public officials, business leaders, and private individuals from more than 200 American cities and towns campaigned for the establishment of UN headquarters in their hometowns or regions during the 1944–46 period. Large cities like New York, Chicago, San Francisco, and Philadelphia figured on the list of hopefuls, as did the Black Hills of South Dakota and the small town of Tuskahoma, Oklahoma.[76] Numerous Americans travelled to London to seek to influence the delegations to the UN Preparatory Commission and the first General Assembly to favour their bids to host UN headquarters. 'Be it said that they were liberal hosts in the Church House lounges',[77] Lie noted dryly in his memoirs.

Secretary-general Lie supported the decision to establish headquarters for the new world organization in the US because he hoped this would ensure that the US remained a member of the organization, and that the new world organization thus avoided the fate of the League of Nations.[78] Lie was therefore happy when the Preparatory Commission recommended the US, and even happier with the choice of New York for temporary headquarters. Wishing to remain in New York, Lie reasoned that 'men and women being what they are ... once Headquarters were set up – even though temporarily – considerable effort would be required to move them again'.[79] Nonetheless, the search for a permanent site and the eventual decision to locate the UN on the East River in midtown Manhattan would not be a straightforward process. The final decision came about as the result of an insistent campaign by prominent New Yorkers, their close coordination with secretary-general Lie, resistance and hostility from the residents of the suburban counties north of New York, and a last-minute gift from the Rockefeller family.

Based on an initial survey and site visit conducted in late 1945, the General Assembly had decided that Westchester County in New York and/or Fairfield County in Connecticut offered the best options for permanent UN headquarters.[80] 'What the builders of the UN have in view is one of the finest things that the world has ever seen', said Stoyan Gavrilovic of Yugoslavia, head of the UN inspection team, in a January 1946 radio interview. 'The idea is to build a place that will be reserved entirely for the United Nations, a place which will become the Capital of the World.'[81] Local American officials and UN government delegates alike favoured a vision of a new international city or enclave with enough space to host UN conference facilities and offices, state delegations, and housing for UN staff and government diplomats, all set in a tranquil pastoral setting to facilitate their work for a more peaceful world.[82] Early estimates indicated the need for a site of up to 40 square miles.[83] Despite some objections that the search for a 'world capital' would result in 'a pompous, pretentious palace',[84] and that the UN 'must impress itself upon the world through its deeds and through its articulate conscience – not with its physical magnificence and its monumental bricks and mortar',[85] the majority at this time favoured the vision of headquarters as an international enclave in a suburban setting.

New York officials, like secretary-general Lie, hoped that the UN would remain in the city. Unfortunately, lack of housing and office space and long commuting times caused dissatisfaction among the first UN staff and diplomats in the spring of 1946, and the city had to boost its campaign. New York Mayor William O'Dwyer invited hundreds of prominent businessmen, philanthropists, and socialites to join the 'United Nations Committee of the City of New York'. Among those who accepted were Arthur Hays Sulzberger, publisher of the *New York Times*, Winthrop Aldrich, president of the Chase National Bank, Thomas J. Watson, president of IBM, and Broadway producer Billy Rose. The mayor headed the committee himself, with Nelson A. Rockefeller, former assistant secretary of state and then president of the Rockefeller Center, as vice chairman. The women of

New York also got involved with the campaign to welcome the UN to the city, including the former First Lady, Eleanor Roosevelt, and the newspaper columnist and celebrated hostess Elsa Maxwell.[86] Robert Moses, city planner and parks commissioner, and the architect Wallace K. Harrison were also part of the group. Shortly before the scheduled opening of the first Security Council meeting at Hunter College in March 1946, O'Dwyer gave greater authority to Rockefeller and Moses by officially naming them chairpersons of two subcommittees, 'but they might as well have been named as Trygve Lie's official new best friends', argued historian Charlene Mires.[87] When the secretary-general arrived in the city on 21 March, Rockefeller and Moses welcomed him with a lunch, where he was also introduced to other prominent New Yorkers.[88] 'On that day began seven years of fruitful and heart-warming co-operation between New York City and the UN', Lie later wrote in his memoirs.[89] Together the secretary-general, the New York mayor, and the rest of the group would cooperate closely to ensure the UN stayed in New York.

O'Dwyer and Moses wished to see the UN stay permanently at Flushing Meadows in Queens. The former site of the World's Fair in 1939 had been refitted to host the General Assembly which opened its first session in New York in October 1946. Yet, as the Assembly session progressed, Flushing Meadows proved increasingly unpopular with UN delegations. In the counties north of New York, the UN's plans also faced increasing resistance from local residents who feared the congestion and changes to their community that would follow the establishment of a large and dominating world capital in their neighbourhood.[90] As a decision on the permanent location was moving closer, the British delegation and others prompted for a reopening of the site question. Yet another site inspection committee set out on a new tour to view potential sites in Boston, New York, Philadelphia, and San Francisco. Now more perceptive to the benefits of a city centre location, on 2 December 1946 the committee ended up recommending two locations as equally suitable: the Presidio in San Francisco and a location in the Belmont Plateau and Roxborough area of Philadelphia in shared first place, with Westchester County north of New York second.[91] New York City appeared to be out of the competition because the city's only offering, Flushing Meadows, had been rejected as unsuitable.

Over the next couple of days, Lie and other supporters of New York scrambled to search for an alternative so that the UN could stay in the city. 'Who literally first had the idea to put the Headquarters on the East River site is not too important. As happens often, events moved several of those involved to recognize concurrently a combination of factors which could bring a solution', wrote George A. Dudley, Harrison's associate, in his review of the process.[92] On 6–10 December, a flutter of meetings and telephone calls between Lie, O'Dwyer, Moses, Harrison, Nelson Rockefeller and his brother Laurence and father John D. Rockefeller Jr, Eduardo Zuleta Angel who was chairman of the Headquarters Committee, Austin of the American UN delegation, and the real estate developer William Zeckendorf, resulted in a generous offer from John D. Rockefeller Jr to grant the UN US$8.5 million to purchase a site on the East River from Zeckendorf.[93] Zeckendorf had planned to develop the site in a grand project called 'X-City', but had been unable to secure the necessary funding and some of his options were about to expire. The area currently housed slaughterhouses and dilapidated tenements and was widely considered an eyesore to the city.[94] As the UN Headquarters Committee convened for another meeting on 11 December, Austin could read out the Rockefeller letter to the astonished delegates, and that same afternoon another site inspection team toured the proposed site on the East River.[95] Already on 14 December, the General Assembly passed the necessary resolution accepting the gift by 46 votes to 7.[96] Noting its 'feeling of sincere gratitude' for the gift, earlier opposition towards New York vanished. The Indian representative noted that although they had originally preferred a different location and wanted to reject the offer, they had been persuaded by the majority view. 'We hope that we shall learn to love New York and that New York will learn to like us', he concluded.[97]

Once the Assembly reached final agreement to establish headquarters at the East River site in New York, it handed over responsibility to the secretary-general, who was asked to prepare a plan for buildings, construction costs, and financial arrangements before 1 July 1947.[98] In January 1947, Lie appointed Harrison, the New York architect who had been intimately involved with the search for a site and the Rockefeller gift, as UN Director of Planning and chairman of the international Board of Design. A few remarked that Harrison '"went with the deal" – a reference to his close association with the family that had donated the land to the UN',[99] but Lie wrote in his memoirs that he 'never regretted' the choice of Harrison for this job. 'His forthrightness, common-sense approach, and diplomacy with fellow architects, delegates, and building contractors alike were fully as valuable as his architectural skills; and he and his wife became close and admired friends besides.'[100] Dudley, one of the architects who assisted Harrison during this time, also argued that Harrison was a perfect fit for the job: 'Few could match his knowledge of New York City, particularly the East River site, and his many friendships with governmental leaders and architects from other nations. Less known were his skills as a leader and developer of consensus, which would shape the result.'[101]

Harrison quickly proposed that the UN should appoint an international Board of Design for the initial design of the new headquarters, and in the interest of speeding up the process, Lie and the Headquarters Commission agreed.[102] Member states were asked for suggestions, and together Lie and Harrison made the final selection of ten architects from around the world: Gyle Soilleux (Australia); Gaston Brunfaut (Belgium); Oscar Niemeyer (Brazil); Ernest Cormier (Canada); Liang Sicheng (China); Le Corbusier (France); Sven Markelius (Sweden); Howard Robertson (the UK); Julio Vilamajo (Uruguay); and Nikolai Bassov (the Soviet Union).[103] Between 17 February and 9 June 1947 the board held 45 meetings where it considered and discussed more than 40 plans.[104] Working with Le Corbusier, the world-famous architect proved somewhat difficult. 'In so many ways, Corbu was all but impossible to deal with', Harrison's deputy, Max Abramovitz, noted. 'No sooner had he arrived than he sought to take charge of the entire operation.'[105]

The final design for UN headquarters was a team effort. The plan originated in an early sketch by Le Corbusier showing a tall, thin secretariat building at the southern end of the plot, rising from a low, large building housing the General Assembly and the various councils and committees.[106] The idea of placing a tall secretariat at the southern end of the site in a north-south orientation won approval from the rest of the board, but many remained sceptical of housing all remaining functions within one building. At a board meeting in March, when Le Corbusier was absent to attend business in Paris, Robertson, the British architect asked '[i]s the conference bloc getting too big in proportion, using up too much space of the site?', while Bassov, the Soviet engineer, urged that the scheme 'should have more dynamic masses than the present composition. Now it's one up and the rest is a pancake!'[107] Harrison was determined that the board should not reach a decision too soon and encouraged everyone to develop and present their own ideas over the following months. Several board members were also delayed and did not arrive in New York until later in the process; therefore, conversations and presentations of new schemes continued among a varying cast of architects, designers, and engineers.[108]

Niemeyer, the Brazilian architect, was one of the late arrivals. On 25 April he was finally ready to present his ideas for a modified version of Le Corbusier's scheme. Instead of one large conference and assembly building connected to the Secretariat slab, Niemeyer moved some of the functions below ground and separated the General Assembly from the other meeting rooms. The board was immediately drawn to Niemeyer's scheme. 'It literally took our breath away to see the simple plane of the site kept wide open from First Avenue to the [East] River', wrote Dudley, and compared the idea favourably with Le Corbusier's: 'As different as night and day, the heaviness of [Le Corbusier's] block seemed to close the whole site, while in Niemeyer's refreshing scheme the site was open, a grand space with a clean base for the modest masses standing in it.'[109] Niemeyer himself emphasized the value of open space: 'In this way a huge square of the United Nations was created: a large civic square, which would give the plot the necessary importance.'[110]

With the deadline to report back to the General Assembly approaching, on 30 April Harrison gained the board's consensus to concentrate on Niemeyer's scheme.[111] The final design was a joint effort combining input from several ideas into the plan presented to Lie in June 1947.[112] Le Corbusier later claimed that he had created the design for UN headquarters and tried to take credit for it. 'The project is 100 percent the architecture and urbanism of Le Corbusier', he wrote in a November 1947 letter to Lie, Harrison, and Nelson Rockefeller.[113] Harrison was diplomatic in his reply: 'I am delighted that you feel that you are the one who designed the United Nations Headquarters. It pleases me equally that other members of the Board have that same satisfaction. After all, the combined work was to be symbolic of the unity and selflessness of the United Nations.'[114]

Construction and building work on the new site started as soon as possible. In October 1947 the US government offered a US$65 million interest-free loan to the UN for construction of headquarters,[115] which the General Assembly accepted on 20 November.[116] Once the US Congress approved the headquarters loan bill on 11 August 1948, construction work on the site could start in earnest.[117] On 24 October 1949 Lie and other dignitaries, in front of an audience of some 16,000, attended the cornerstone laying ceremony, with the steel skeleton for the Secretariat building already rising tall behind them.[118] The first Secretariat staff moved into the new building on 20 August 1950, and on 1 January 1951, less than two years after building work commenced, UN headquarters was formally transferred to the new site.[119] In October 1952 the General Assembly convened in its new hall. 'I was deeply moved', Lie recalled. 'Here, at last, was a United Nations program that had been completed.'[120]

Lie took an active interest in the headquarters issue from the start. His close collaboration with local government officials and prominent New Yorkers helped to ensure the permanent headquarters was located in New York on the East River site. His interest in the project continued through the building process. Although he delegated day-to-day coordination to assistant secretary-general Price, he continued to, in his own words, 'lend assistance and advice, taking part in the numerous conferences and discussions, and seeing that the political wheels remained well greased'.[121] Lie wrote in his memoirs:

> Just as the location of the United Nations had concerned me from the first in London, so now I felt a personal responsibility for getting the building completed and occupied, a visible United Nations achievement. It was but one of the Secretary-General's countless problems during those six years, but it was the most cherished one. In contrast to the disappointments and the deterioration of the world political scene, the sight of Headquarters rising day by day was a source

of strength and confidence. With expectancy I could send for the Headquarters file or attend a meeting of the Headquarters construction group. Its worries were good worries; its problems, healthy problems.[122]

The final headquarters rising by the river in central Manhattan stands now as a testament to the efforts of Lie and those working in the UN Secretariat in the beginning of the UN's activity. Urquhart, former Secretariat member and UN scholar, praised Lie's role in getting the UN settled in New York City, 'one of the world's most vibrant and cosmopolitan cities, thereby avoiding a number of totally unsuitable rural sites'. He further highlighted Lie's role in arranging the Rockefeller donation, for coordinating with city authorities, and for assembling 'the outstanding team of architects that designed the now famous UN Headquarters building'.[123] 'This was a major achievement, and Lie deserves all credit for it', concluded Urquhart.[124]

The International Civil Service under attack from McCarthyism

As discussed earlier in this chapter, the initial establishment of the UN Secretariat was a challenging task. Thousands of new staff had to be hired very rapidly, without established recruitment and selection procedures, and Lie's difficulties with securing competent candidates for the top leadership positions in the Secretariat compounded the problems. Already during the summer of 1946, the morale of the Secretariat began to drop.[125] But the worst attack on the Secretariat during Lie's tenure came from McCarthyism. The American McCarthyism process caused tension in the secretary-general's relations with the UN's host state, and also lost Lie the support of the Secretariat staff as they resented him for not defending their interests. Forever connected with the name of US Senator Joseph McCarthy, the American hunt for communist spies hit the UN Secretariat with full force in 1952. The American instance that no American communists be allowed to work in the Secretariat would seem to be contrary to articles 100 and 101 of the Charter which established the independence of the international civil service, and yet Lie nonetheless decided to cooperate with the American government in their search for communists inside the UN Secretariat. Why did Lie seemingly compromise the independence and integrity of the Secretariat in the face of American pressure?

The secretary-general had already in 1946 asked the American government for help in screening American applicants for the Secretariat, as discussed earlier in this chapter, but Washington said no despite repeated UN pleas over the next few years. Assistant secretary-general Byron Price outlined Lie's thinking to the US government in June 1949: (1) there should not be spies of any nationality in the Secretariat as that would be contrary to article 100; (2) no American communists should be allowed to work in the Secretariat, only communists from communist countries was appropriate; and (3) the UN did not have the ability to investigate the background of applicants; could the FBI therefore kindly help screen all American applicants, 'or at least to indicate informally whether the [FBI] knows anything of a derogatory nature regarding such applicants?'[126] As this document revealed, Lie's and Price's primary concern was to avoid having spies of any kind in the Secretariat – being a spy would be contrary to article 100 which stated that Secretariat staff should not 'seek or receive instructions from any government or from any other authority external to the Organization [and t]hey shall refrain from any action which might reflect on their position as international officials responsible only to the Organization'. But in June 1949 the US government once again turned down Lie's request for help in screening American applicants, before finally agreeing to an informal procedure for sharing information in September 1949.[127]

Over the next few years, 'fanciful witnesses and professional informers testified to Senate subcommittees about a Communist-dominated U.N. Secretariat hiding hundreds of agents engaged in subversive activities', and created the impression that the UN had been overrun by communist spies.[128] Morale in the Secretariat, already low due to general administrative chaos, plummeted, as Lie reluctantly initiated harsh policies, including terminating staff contracts, because he wanted to retain the US' support for the UN. During 1950 and 1951 the secretary-general ended some contracts because he claimed the employees had engaged in undermining activities. Among some of the first employees fired, were central members of the trade union, prompting talk that Lie, the former trade union lawyer, was now engaging in 'union busting'.[129] The fired employees complained to the Administrative Tribunal, but the tribunal supported the secretary-general, and the Assembly agreed that the secretary-general should be allowed to end contracts without any other reason than this 'being in the UN's interest'.[130]

During the autumn of 1952 two competing US hearings made matters worse for the UN. Accusations of communist spies in the UN resurfaced, and some American Secretariat staff called to testify pleaded their Fifth Amendment rights. The subpoenaed witnesses only represented 1 per cent of the staff in the Secretariat, but in the public imaginary the impression that the UN was full of communist spies continued to spread, and the morale of the Secretariat suffered.[131] Lie decided once more to rely on legal help, and asked an independent jurist committee to advise him on whether he was allowed to end the contracts of those who had refused to testify. In November 1952 the jurists supported Lie in this; refusing to testify was a breach of the staff regulations, and Lie would be within his rights to dismiss them. The secretary-general immediately sent a letter to the nine employees in question, giving them four hours to accept to testify again. One of them resigned, and the other eight refused to give up their constitutional rights, and were subsequently fired by Lie.[132] Eventually, in January 1953, after a US presidential executive decree, secretary-general Lie opened up the UN headquarters to the FBI to interview and fingerprint all US nationals employed at the UN.

Critics argued that Lie thereby surrendered to the US government, and that he should not have allowed the FBI to enter UN premises. As one of the dismissed Secretariat staff later said: 'by his conduct in this affair, Trygve Lie compromised the integrity and independence of the international civil service'.[133] Through his actions, Lie accepted a reduction in the secretary-general's autonomy in the administration of the Secretariat – a contraction of his role from that envisioned in articles 100 and 101 of the UN Charter. Others argue that the secretary-general did not have much choice in the matter.[134] He could probably have gained support in the General Assembly if he had opposed the FBI's entry into the Secretariat and had defended his staff's judicial rights, but this would have lost him the support of the US, and he had already lost support of the Soviet Union over the Korean War and his re-election in 1950. Lie has not been the only secretary-general to discover that it is difficult to function effectively without the support of the great powers on the Security Council.

In addition to his desire to retain the support of the US in difficult circumstances, Lie truly believed he was doing the right thing by cooperating with the FBI. As noted previously, Lie believed it was contrary to article 100 for any Secretariat staff to spy for another government, whether their own or not.[135] Furthermore, by cooperating with the FBI the secretary-general hoped to speed up the process and allow conditions in the Secretariat to return to normal as soon as possible. Lie welcomed the presidential decree and the FBI investigation as it offered the accused staff members of a procedure by which they could clear their name, and also gave Lie the help he had asked for all along, by providing him the information he needed 'to make the right decisions in the building of a strong and independent Secretariat of the highest competence and integrity'.[136] In Lie's opinion, therefore, he sought information from the US regarding American staff members in the interest of building up a strong and independent Secretariat.

The British UN delegation supported Lie's decision,[137] as did several other states. The General Assembly in an April 1953 resolution endorsing Lie's report on the situation, '*expresse[d] its confidence* that the Secretary-General will conduct personnel policy with these considerations in mind', and asked the member states 'to assist the Secretary-General in the discharge of his responsibilities as chief administrative officer of the United Nations'.[138] The Assembly thus supported the actions Lie had taken in seeking information about the staff from the national governments in the interest of the integrity of the Secretariat. Despite widespread support for Lie's activities in the

General Assembly after the fact, the episode still left a lingering stain on Lie's legacy. It also poisoned the secretary-general's relationship with his staff in the Secretariat, and provided the immediate context for his decision to resign from office in November 1952

Lie's resignation from office, 1952

From an apparent highpoint of Lie's career as secretary-general when the General Assembly extended his term for a further three years in November 1950, discussed in the previous chapter, merely two years later in November 1952, Lie announced his resignation from office. At the time, Lie was under pressure from many quarters. The American process of McCarthyism caused tension in the secretary-general's relations with the UN's host state, and also lost Lie the support of the Secretariat staff as they resented him for not defending their interests. Eventually the steady loss of support from member states on both sides of the Cold War divide and from UN staff became too much for Lie to bear. On 10 November 1952, more than a year before the end of his term on 1 February 1954, Lie announced that he wished to resign, and asked the General Assembly to start the search for his replacement.[139]

Lie's announcement came as a surprise to most people, because although he had decided to resign as early as the summer of 1952, and had informed Lester Pearson of Canada, serving as President of the General Assembly, and a few others at the beginning of the Assembly session, those in the know had kept Lie's secret well.[140] Coming at the height of the Cold War, with UN forces still fighting in the Korean War, and with the UN Secretariat under tremendous pressure from the American search for communist spies, it would appear that Lie had decided to abandon his post and give up. In the opinion of the US State Department Lie's 'resignation could not have come at a worse time in the history of the United Nations'.[141] As one friend wrote to Lie in a letter of 12 November, in the interest of maintaining a firm stand on Korea, it was 'of the utmost importance that you continue in your position as secretary-general. This issue, in my opinion, is so vital that you're not allowed to take personal circumstances into account.'[142]

In Lie's opinion, however, by submitting his resignation at this time, he was doing exactly the opposite. He was not abandoning the UN, but giving it the best chance of survival and growth in a difficult situation: 'This is no desertion of the colors, and it doesn't mean that I'm leaving a sinking ship. I believe in the United Nations', he wrote to his daughter. 'But the Organization doesn't need me in order to continue its work for peace and security.'[143] The main reason behind his decision, Lie argued, was his earnest hope that it 'may help the United Nations to save the peace and to serve better the cause of freedom and progress for all mankind'.[144] A new secretary-general, with the support of all the P5, 'may be more helpful than I can be',[145] and might be in a position 'to achieve more than me in the political field … Even if his chances in this tense situation are slim, in my opinion even the smallest chance must be taken.'[146] Overall, Lie argued, the secretary-general of the UN 'was dispensable, and should be replaced by a new Secretary-General who could enter the work fresh and with fewer fixed ideas about persons and issues'.[147] Furthermore, Lie hoped his resignation might provide the 'shock treatment' necessary for the organization, 'to bring the member states to reflect on the situation'[148] and 'understand my difficult position'.[149] He argued that he had wanted to leave already in 1950, and although he had then accepted re-appointment in the interest of continuity in the UN's policies with regard to the Korean War, now that there was the prospect of a negotiated armistice in Korea, it would do no harm if the secretary-general resigned.[150] Likewise, 1952 was a better time to replace the secretary-general than 1950, because the new permanent headquarters were nearly completed, and the Secretariat was better organized and more experienced.[151]

In private Lie explained some of the more personal reasons why he wanted to resign and leave his exposed post at the head of the UN Secretariat. Ever since the start of his extended term in February 1951, the Soviet Union had insisted that he was occupying the office illegally and refused to have anything to do with him. Had these insults and rule-breaking from the Soviet Union and its allies been all, Lie claimed, he might have gone on until the end of his term in 1954: 'I should have been quite willing to stay until the end of my term had it been simply a question of continuing to bear with the many attacks upon me by the Soviet Union and its supporters.'[152] But the worse part was that 'for more than two years I've asked for solidarity from the member states, but they have always urged me not to make an issue out of the Russians' sidestepping of all rules and regulations for the various organs. My patience had to end one day.'[153] Furthermore, the secretary-general and Secretariat were under attack not only from the communist states, but also from 'conservative and reactionary isolationists in America'.[154] In a letter to the Norwegian prime minister in December 1952, Lie summed up the situation and his reasons for resigning. Lie felt alone in his struggle 'to keep a straight and constructive course to save what could be saved of the UN and trust in the UN', but it was difficult because 'never did anyone come to my defence or aid'. Between the communist states on the one hand and the American conservatives on the other it was an 'irreconcilable situation'. On top of this, Lie complained, 'it's no fun when people start discussing your replacement two years before the end of your contract. Perhaps I shouldn't let this get to me … But I am still only human.'[155]

Immediately following Lie's statement that he wanted to resign and return to Norway, rumours spread that Lie's actual motive was to obtain a fresh mandate and to be asked by the P5 to stay on.[156] Even so, this would have been a 'fresh start' for the UN, and would only have been possible if the P5 came together and agreed to prolong Lie's period – thus evidencing exactly the renewed East–West cooperation Lie was hoping to facilitate. Even in resigning, we can therefore see a consistency with Lie's earlier opinions on the role of the secretary-general as playing an important role in building bridges between the great powers, and in trying to overcome the Cold War.

Some contemporary observers did note the selfless aspects of Lie's resignation. During the General Assembly meeting where Hammarskjöld was elected secretary-general, many delegates offered their thanks and tribute to Lie's seven years of service to the UN. The Iranian delegate praised his decision to resign from office as 'a gesture of self-denial' which showed Lie's 'courage, honesty and devotion to the cause of peace and the United Nations'.[157] The Peruvian delegate further pointed out that Lie had 'crowned his career in an eminently honourable way' with his decision, because 'resignation from such a high, advantageous and influential position is in itself a mark of nobility of character, since power is a thing which men are most reluctant to give up'.[158] Despite such professions of thanks and goodwill, however, the fact remained that Lie had resigned from office because he had lost the support of the member states. This put a further stain on Lie's legacy as the only secretary-general ever to resign from office. Yet the circumstances also illustrate the impossibility of a secretary-general functioning properly in his role when he no longer enjoyed the trust or support of the UN member states.

Conclusion

In April 1953 when Hammarskjöld had been appointed, Lie wrote to a friend in Norway, that he and his wife were 'both happy and satisfied that I could finally be released from the position as secretary-general. None of us envy Dag Hammarskjöld … my successor will surely soon be faced with the same difficulties that I have faced over the past 2–3 years.'[159] This was also the sentiment Lie expressed when he famously welcomed Hammarskjöld at the airport with the warning that he was taking on 'the most impossible job in the world'.[160] The earlier chapters discussed the difficulties of balancing the competing interests of member states in different political crisis situations, while this chapter examined the challenges of establishing a functioning Secretariat and discussed the ways in which member states have either sought to interfere too much or not given enough support in the secretary-general's administrative tasks.

This chapter discussed the initial establishment and staffing of the UN Secretariat and headquarters, and the challenges faced in this period for the ICS concept. The initial build-up of the Secretariat was very rapid and hectic, and this caused problems further down the line. 'Staff were recruited in an enormous rush', argued one later study, and 'all this was done in a way that was less than ideal ... resulting in a very mixed quality staff'.[161] The initial frenzy and confusion left a geographically unbalanced staff and chaotic lines of organization and leadership. Not surprisingly, staff morale consequently suffered.

The large contingent of American nationals in the Secretariat created further problems a few years later when the McCarthy process descended on the UN. Initially, the secretary-general had requested help from the US government in running background checks on American applicants to the Secretariat – simply because the newly established Secretariat lacked the time and resources to take this process for itself – but Washington repeatedly turned down the request. When the McCarthy hearings started, the tables turned, and the US government turned its eyes with suspicion on the many unvetted American staff in the Secretariat. Lie's actions in response to the McCarthy process can be seen as a betrayal of the integrity and independence of the UN Secretariat. His actions in firing staff were also somewhat at odds with Lie's personal background as a trade union lawyer and champion of workers' rights in Norway during the 1920s and 1930s. Lie acted as he did because he argued that spies of any kind in the UN Secretariat would be contrary to the integrity of the ICS, and because he found himself under tremendous pressure from the US government to cooperate. At the time in 1950–53, a majority of UN member states supported Lie's actions, as evidenced in widespread support for Lie's activities in the General Assembly, yet the episode still left a stain on Lie's legacy. It also poisoned the secretary-general's relationship with the Secretariat staff, and provided the immediate context for his decision to resign in November 1952.

In a long-term perspective, Lie's attempts to cooperate with the US illustrated the difficulties of the secretary-general in managing the UN Secretariat, ostensibly the one task where the UN Charter gave him firm control by designating him 'chief administrative officer' in article 97 and by recognizing the independence of the Secretariat in articles 100 and 101. Ironically, the secretary-general has come to enjoy less autonomy in administrative matters than he does in many political areas. Javier Pérez de Cuéllar, secretary-general in the 1980s, lamented that it was 'ironic and unfortunate that, while there has been a dramatic rise in the Secretary-General's political responsibilities, his powers in the administrative field have been steadily eroded over the years'.[162] Lie's acquiescence to American screening of all US applicants to the Secretariat – later continued by Hammarskjöld and all following secretaries-general until 1986[163] – contributed to the position where member governments could exercise considerable influence over the appointments in the Secretariat. Combined with the control exercised over the organization's budget and finances through the General Assembly, this means that the secretary-general enjoys less autonomy in administration than his title would suggest.

Recent research has tended to emphasize continuities between the League of Nations and the UN. In the area of administration and the ICS, for example, scholars have argued that the ICS norms first developed by League secretary-general Drummond were essentially adopted by and continued into the UN Secretariat.[164] Karen Gram-Skjoldager and Haakon Ikonomou draw a direct link from the various reports on the League Secretariat in the interwar period and during WW2, to the establishment of the International Civil Service Advisory Board (ICSAB) in 1949 and its subsequent publication of the 'Report on Standards of Conduct in the International Civil Service' in 1954, through the role of League veterans such as Thanassis Aghnides, the inaugural ICSAB chair.[165] This chapter concurs that there are continuities between the UN and the League, yet upon closer examination of the initial establishment of the Secretariat under Lie it would be more accurate to view the ICS norms *re-established* in the UN. During the late 1940s, chaos, discontinuities, and changes, as much as continuities, characterized the administration of the UN Secretariat, as new staff and new administrative practices were brought in.

Lie's legacy on administrative matters holds up rather poorly to scrutiny. At the time complaints were raised that Lie was an 'inept' manager, and that 'although Lie was personally popular to a certain degree, he was neither a good leader nor a good administrator'.[166] But he was presented with an almost impossible task of getting the Secretariat up and running nearly from scratch in a very short period of time. It is unclear whether anyone else could have managed any differently, as part of Lie's troubles also stemmed from the limitations of General Assembly instructions and member states' simultaneous interference and lack of cooperation. Overall, with the exception of the headquarters issue which he followed throughout, Lie himself chose to focus his time and energy on political questions of peace and security, and sought to consolidate and expand the secretary-general's autonomy and toolbox of political and diplomatic practices. Perhaps if he had devoted more attention to the administration and leadership of the Secretariat, he could have prevented some of the administrative chaos that accumulated during his tenure.

Conclusion

The man does not count; the institution does.[1]
Dag Hammarskjöld (October 1960)

In the beginning of a new IGO's life it may develop in ways unintended or unanticipated by its state founders. When the organization faces unexpected crises in a situation where the rules are still fluid, surprising new precedents may emerge. The people involved during this phase when the IGO is first established have significant room for manoeuvre and flexibility in interpreting what rights and responsibilities their positions entail. Trygve Lie was determined that the UN organization, and the UN secretary-general in particular, should be 'a force for peace' in the world.[2] In the context of different political and security crises Lie took advantage of the ambiguity present in the UN Charter, and the vague but powerful potential of his own position, to insert the secretary-general's office into new areas of UN activity. Through these actions he secured acceptance for new procedural norms and a more public profile for the UN secretary-general than that envisioned by the UN's founders. The interplay of crisis decision-making, institutional constraints, and the individuals involved during this time thus built the foundations for the UN organization we know today.

In contrast to earlier scholarship on the role of the secretary-general which has tended to emphasize the contributions of Dag Hammarskjöld, the UN's second secretary-general, this book has uncovered and discussed the important foundations which were established during Lie's tenure from 1946 to 1953. Despite the many precedents set during his tenure and his strong principled activism on behalf of the UN and UN Charter values, Lie's contribution to the UN and the office of UN secretary-general remains largely overlooked and forgotten. Urquhart's blunt statement that 'Lie did not achieve any particularly notable political or diplomatic feats at the United Nations, nor at that time was he expected to do so',[3] represents the orthodox view on Lie's contribution. From this perspective, Lie's only significant contribution lay in ensuring the location of UN headquarters in

Manhattan, New York, and in bringing on board some of the world's top architects to design the new building.[4]

If we merely look at the apparent results of the initiatives undertaken by Lie, it becomes obvious why his tenure might be considered a failure. Nearly every time Lie tried to take an initiative or push his opinion on a political issue he would be ignored or opposed by the member states. In April 1946, the Security Council ignored his opinion that it was committing an error in keeping the Iranian question on the agenda. In 1947 Lie failed to ensure that Marshall Plan aid would be given through a UN framework which included both Western and Eastern Europe. The Security Council did not heed his advice to enforce the partition of Palestine, while the General Assembly declined his proposal to establish a UN armed guard. Britain and the US rejected Lie's suggestion of a currency study to seek a solution to the Berlin Blockade in 1948, and likewise resented his attempt to urge a solution of the blockade by issuing a public appeal with the president of the General Assembly. In 1950, the Chinese representation issue remained unresolved, and Lie would not live to see the Beijing government finally take its seat in the UN in 1971. Most importantly, despite Lie's continued attempts to mediate between East and West – by opposing the Truman Doctrine and the formation of NATO, by seeking to resolve problems in Berlin, by urging unity at every turn, and ultimately by proposing an ambitious 20-year peace plan in March 1950 – he was unable to prevent the Cold War from becoming the all-encompassing conflict that dominated international politics for the next four decades.

Arguably, the only instance where Lie's proposals and initiatives met with any success was in the Korean War, where the majority of the UN membership, led by the US, launched a military operation in aid of South Korea, just as Lie advised. Lie himself considered his 'stand on Korea the best justified act of seven years in the service of peace'.[5] When Lie left office in 1953, delegates to the General Assembly praised his work for the UN and particularly emphasized the role he had played in the Korean War.[6] But although his stand on Korea earned him praise from many member states, it also led to a whole new set of problems in his relationship with the Soviet Union, which ultimately motivated his resignation from office.

Despite the failure of the majority of Lie's specific proposals, he nonetheless succeeded in carving out space for an active political role for the secretary-general, and established a number of precedents for the relationship of the secretary-general with the organs of the UN and with the member states. The story of the development of the secretary-general's role in this period is therefore *not* merely a story about one person and what he wanted to achieve. Rather this is a story of how institutional forces allowed for an expansion of the role, and how the individual was able to take advantage of those forces to establish precedents for the future. What matters to this story is less the individual as such, but rather the individual in the role of secretary-general. As others have observed in relation to studies of IGO leadership: 'One has to make a distinction: the fact that the Secretary-General took initiatives and steps which enhanced his status and that of his office should be divorced from the success or failure of those initiatives.'[7] Thus the failure of the majority of Lie's specific initiatives does not automatically mean that he was a poor secretary-general, or that he did not make a contribution to the development of the secretary-general's role. The preceding chapters have shown that despite the disappointing success of Lie's various proposals and initiatives, he succeeded in establishing precedents for an expanded and politically activist role for the secretary-general.

Political expansion, administrative contraction

During Lie's tenure important precedents were established for the relationship between the secretary-general and the Security Council, as Lie explored his powers under article 99. As discussed in Chapter 2, Lie gained recognition that article 99 afforded the secretary-general the right to present her opinions on any matter under consideration by the Council. He would later avail himself of this right on numerous occasions, such as on questions of membership (Chapters 2 and 5), Palestine (Chapter 3), and the Berlin Blockade and Korea (Chapter 4). Lie furthermore interpreted his responsibilities under article 99 in broad terms, and frequently urged the Council to discuss questions and reach decisions, without formally invoking the article. This was seen most clearly in relation to Palestine and Berlin. Indeed, over time, applying pressure on states to take action has become the most common way of 'using' article 99, as the article itself has only formally been invoked twice; by Hammarskjöld on the Congo in 1960, and by Kurt Waldheim on the question of hostages in Iran in 1979.[8]

Lie also secured recognition from the Security Council that article 99 implies that the secretary-general has as an independent right to appoint investigative committees or send her personal representatives to investigate situations of conflict. Lie stated this right during discussions of the Greek Civil War in 1946 (Chapter 2), and although he himself never appointed a formal investigative committee, he did send his representatives to talk to member states, or offered to send such representatives, during the UN's consideration of Palestine (Chapter 3) and Berlin (Chapter 4). Later secretaries-general would frequently avail themselves of this independent right of investigation and information-seeking.

The right to appoint special representatives (SRSGs), as separate from a general right of fact-finding, deserves further mention. Today the secretary-general's use of SRSGs is one of the main tools at her disposal both for conflict resolution or conflict prevention and to highlight particular issues.

Lie appointed the first SRSGs mainly as a matter of expediency or necessity to perform a task he was unable to do himself. This was the case with the first SRSG, Wlodzimierz Moderow of Poland, director of the UN office in Geneva, whom Lie appointed 'Representative of the Secretary-General in Geneva' in 1946 to negotiate the transfer of assets from the League of Nations to the UN.[9] Lie's appointment of Ralph Bunche as 'Representative of the Secretary-General in Palestine' (Chapter 3), foreshadow the later development of SRSGs with more substantial political mandates, as Bunche became 'Acting Mediator for Palestine' and resumed responsibility for negotiating armistice agreements between the conflicting parties.[10] Although some legal scholars argue the first 'real' SRSG was appointed by U Thant in 1966 to negotiate between Cambodia and Thailand,[11] the development of appointing such representatives was instigated by Lie.

The last implied power under article 99 first explored by Lie and later expanded by other secretaries-general, was the right to present draft resolutions to the Security Council. As discussed in Chapter 4, Lie drafted a resolution proposing the establishment of a coordination committee for Korea. Although the Council in this instance chose to proceed with another resolution drafted by the US, none of the states on the Council objected to Lie's drafting of a resolution. Thus by 1950 the majority of states on the Council recognized the position of the secretary-general as a near-equal in the work of the organization for peace and security and accepted that she had broad rights to participate in the Council's work. Of course, this did not mean that they would not resent the secretary-general for 'interfering' if her opinions on a case should happen to diverge from their own.

Other important paths were forged for the role of the secretary-general as a 'guardian' of the UN Charter and a spokesman for world interest, as Lie boldly presented his ideas for a UN armed guard (Chapter 3) or suggestions for a peace plan to solve the Cold War (Chapter 5). Lie started the tradition of using the introduction to the secretary-general's annual report to the General Assembly as a means of highlighting global issues and suggesting areas of future work. He built the first foundations for the formation of an alliance between the secretary-general and the world's peoples and smaller member states, in opposition to the great powers. In this role as the foremost representative of the UN, the secretary-general seeks to enlist the support of world public opinion and the media to further the UN's mission. Through his actions Lie confirmed that the secretary-general was to be a 'guardian' of the UN Charter, and that she had a duty to protect and defend the organization. In this way, Lie set precedents for the overall goals and purposes of the role of UN secretary-general.

Building on the earlier work of the League of Nations secretary-general, still other precedents were established for the role of the UN secretary-general as a mediator or negotiator between the member states, including among the great powers. Lie worked tirelessly to forge cooperation and unity among the great powers and to ensure consistent policies across UN organs. Lie's concern for the coherence of the UN was evident in his activities in relation to the Palestine problem, as discussed in Chapter 3, while his attempts to seek unity among the great powers on the Security Council provided the main driver behind his actions in relation to the Cold War, as discussed in Chapters 4 and 5.

Also building on the work of the League secretary-general, Lie confirmed the central position of the UN secretary-general as a channel of communications between different member states and between the member states and UN organs. Yet Lie went further than the League secretary-general in also seeking to actively coordinate policies and policy responses of the UN and its member states. This was evident in his activities upon the outbreak of the Korean War in 1950, when Lie took the initiative to send telegrams to all member states to ask for assistance to South Korea, and when he proposed establishing a coordination committee to deal with incoming offers. In this sense he saw himself performing the task of an 'executive' of the UN, because the Security Council and other organs of the UN did not possess executive powers or the ability to implement their decisions themselves.[12]

Lastly, important precedents were established for the international status of the UN secretary-general and in her relationship with the member states. Through his active and direct diplomacy, Lie gained recognition that the secretary-general can contact heads of government directly, rather than having to go through the member states' delegations in New York. This reflects a higher position for the secretary-general than being a mere administrator of the UN Secretariat and signifies that she enjoys a status equal to politically appointed heads of government.

In these ways important precedents amounting to an expansion of the political role of the secretary-general were establishes under Lie. In many cases Lie himself actively pushed for this development, determined that the secretary-general should be a 'force for peace'.[13] In other cases the institution seemingly pulled the secretary-general into assuming more tasks and greater autonomy. As conflicts between the member states increased and the Security Council became unable to reach agreement, the secretary-general had to step up and act in the interest of preserving the organization. The mechanism of a vacuum effect helps explain why the role of the secretary-general expanded during the first few decades of UN history.

This book has thus charted the expansion of the political role of the UN secretary-general under Lie. As the final chapter of the book discussed, there is also a second way to explain how a role can be transformed from being administrative to becoming political – in addition to becoming *more* political, the role can also become *less* administrative. Both processes can be observed during Lie's tenure. As the discussion in Chapter 6 illustrated, the secretary-general actually lost autonomy in administrative matters as the member states assigned to themselves more control over the Secretariat than what the UN Charter had intended. Thus, the UN secretary-general today, somewhat ironically given the Charter's designation of her as 'the chief administrative officer of the Organization', actually enjoys less autonomy in many administrative matters than she does in political questions. In administrative matters, the secretary-general's role *contracted* under Lie, a development that continued under the following secretaries-general. This process, too, helps explain why the UN secretary-general today is seen as primarily political.

Beyond Lie: the later development of the office

Since Lie left the office in 1953, eight other men have held the position of UN secretary-general: Dag Hammarskjöld from Sweden (1953–61), U Thant from Burma (1961–71), Kurt Waldheim from Austria (1972–81), Javier Pérez de Cuéllar from Peru (1982–91), Boutros Boutros-Ghali from Egypt (1992–96), Kofi Annan from Ghana (1997–2006), Ban Ki-moon from South Korea (2007–16), and today António Guterres from Portugal (since 2017). Despite their differences in personality and background, they have ended up acting in fairly similar ways while UN secretary-general due to the institutional expectations that come with this role. These similarities underscore the importance of studying not just the personalities of the individual officeholders, but also the institutional context to understand the development of the UN secretary-general's role over time.

Ever since he left office, Lie has been overshadowed by his more celebrated immediate successor Dag Hammarskjöld. For the next 15 years until Lie's death in December 1968, we can detect his resentment at being outshone by Hammarskjöld. Already in 1953 before he left New York, Lie spread a rumour that Hammarskjöld was gay. At this time homosexuality was widely despised, and in many states a criminal offence. It is unclear why Lie chose to repeat these smears against Hammarskjöld, and the episode left a stain on Lie's legacy among UN staff and diplomats.[14] Upon Hammarskjöld's death in 1961, Lie registered his annoyance that newspapers were portraying Hammarskjöld as the founder of the office of UN secretary-general, writing in a letter: 'Since Hammarskjöld's death, I have almost had the feeling that everything that's been done in the UN has been done by him, and that my 7 years and 3 months in the UN have been forgotten.'[15] As the previous chapters of this book demonstrated, Lie had indeed made important contributions to the establishment of the UN and the development of the role of secretary-general. Yet his contribution has frequently been overshadowed by that of Hammarskjöld.

Hammarskjöld is often portrayed as the model of a UN secretary-general. 'Hammarskjöld did most to shape and define the institution, by his own intellectual appreciation of its possibilities and by his conduct in office', Tharoor stated matter-of-factly.[16] Urquhart called Hammarskjöld 'undeniably the most remarkable of the Secretaries-General so far appointed',[17] while Stahn and Melber praised his unique combination of vision and realism.[18] If we compare the tenures of Lie and Hammarskjöld, we find that the two men shared a similar ideal and vision for the UN and the role of secretary-general, but that they used different tactics to reach this shared goal. Lie and Hammarskjöld were both activist secretaries-general who believed that it was necessary for the secretary-general to play a central role in political questions if the ideals of the UN for a more peaceful world were to be realized.[19] Coming into office after Lie, Hammarskjöld could build on and refine the foundations Lie had established.

Hammarskjöld is well known and celebrated for his role in establishing the principles of UN peacekeeping after Suez in 1956, when he played a central role in setting up the United Nations Emergency Force (UNEF). At Hammarskjöld's insistence, the mission would be under the command of the UN directly and would not include troops from any of the P5 or from states closely connected to the conflict. Furthermore, the troops would be impartial, would not interfere in the internal affairs of the countries, and would use force only in self-defence.[20] These principles remain the benchmark for UN peacekeeping missions to this day. UNEF also established the important role of the UN secretary-general in negotiating and organizing UN peacekeeping missions.[21] Hammarskjöld is also credited with formulating the so-called 'Peking formula' when he sought the release of a group of American airmen who sat imprisoned in communist China in the aftermath of the Korean War. The 'Peking formula' 'allow[s] the Secretary-General a free hand in the implementation of a peace and security mandate, once called in by a political organ'.[22] It has later come to represent the secretary-general's independent right to engage in negotiations with the member states, and is seen as the foremost example of Hammarskjöld's 'quiet diplomacy'.[23] Overall, Hammarskjöld presented the appearance of a more intellectual and sophisticated diplomat compared with Lie. Although his actions on the face of it were similar to Lie's earlier responses, Hammarskjöld accompanied his initiatives with justifications built on the UN Charter and moral principles as an international civil servant, which remain of vital importance to understanding the position of the UN secretary-general today.

The other seven secretaries-general have mixed legacies. Like Lie, U Thant has largely been overlooked although he played important roles trying to defuse tension in the Cold War in relation to the Cuban Missile Crisis and the Vietnam War.[24] U Thant took office amid a crisis for the office of secretary-general after the Soviet 'troika' proposal and Hammarskjöld's untimely death. Throughout Thant's tenure great powers sought to limit the autonomy of the secretary-general and reclaim some of the powers the office had accumulated under Lie and Hammarskjöld, but Thant successfully protected the office against these trends.[25] Kurt Waldheim has widely been seen as passive and too much beholden to the P5. 'Pliancy was surely his hallmark', Meisler notes. The press used to call him 'the headwaiter', because 'he always stood there as if he were wringing his hands on a towel, asking what he could do for the powerful countries'.[26] Waldheim, perhaps more than his predecessors, saw the limitations of the office and felt himself bound by them, yet this did not necessarily make him an unsuitable secretary-general. One theory of executive leadership of IGOs finds that 'a constrained IO head should develop a vision that effectively positions the organization within its environment rather than one preoccupied with changing that environment'.[27] Urquhart, too, has noted that Waldheim 'was very much the limited and cautious, but reasonably effective, civil servant that the permanent members of the Security Council probably preferred'.[28] Indeed, Waldheim came close to achieving an unprecedented third term in office, but this was not to be as China insisted it was time for a secretary-general from the developing world.

In office during the 1980s, Javier Pérez de Cuéllar, like Waldheim, is largely seen as a pliant manager more than an activist. Where UN staff and journalists joked that Waldheim was a 'headwaiter', the joke about Pérez de Cuéllar was that he 'wouldn't make waves if he fell out of a boat'.[29] But with Pérez de Cuéllar these remarks were not meant to indicate that he possessed no opinions of his own, rather that he acted quietly and diplomatically correct. Meisler writes that Pérez de Cuéllar 'is probably the most underestimated secretary-general of all'.[30] With the easing of tensions as the Cold War came to an end, Pérez de Cuéllar was able to use his diplomatic skills to mediate an end to conflicts, and he successfully managed the transition of the UN as the Soviet Union dissolved.[31] Boutros Boutros-Ghali was an activist secretary-general who took office at a time of high hopes following the end of the Cold War. A professor of International Law, Boutros-Ghali was a brilliant analyst who, during his first year, wrote and published *An Agenda for Peace*, a wide-ranging review of UN peacemaking, peacekeeping, and peacebuilding practices which 'remains an indispensable guide to the tools and techniques employed by the United Nations'.[32] He has also been recognized for his role as a norm entrepreneur and a tireless promoter of democracy,[33] but his arrogant, 'autocratic and secretive style … caused difficulties within the UN, alienating large numbers of staff and diplomats',[34] and he was not re-elected for a second term.

Kofi Annan was a widely celebrated secretary-general, and if anything, his popularity increased after he left office. The European media and public still remembered that Annan received the Nobel Peace Prize in 2001 and that he stood up to the US and called the 2003 invasion of Iraq 'illegal'. Until his death in 2018, he was regarded as a wise and kind grandfather-like figure in the vein of Nelson Mandela, and indeed he succeeded Mandela as chairman of The Elders, a group of independent statesmen that lend their support to various global causes.[35] Annan exploited to the full the secretary-general's role as a norm entrepreneur. Determined that the organization should work for the peoples of the world and not just the governments, he was instrumental in promoting the new norm of 'responsibility to protect' (R2P).[36] One observer noted that Annan was 'perhaps the most moralistic and proselytizing' of all the UN secretaries-general.[37] Annan's immediate successor, Ban Ki-moon, by contrast, proved less popular among those looking for a strong and independent secretary-general. Rather in the vein of Waldheim, Ban was seen as passive and submissive to the member states, although he played a key role in facilitating and moving forwards the negotiation process on climate change, one of the most pressing issue on the UN's agenda in the 21st century, and also tried to strengthen the UN's work on R2P and human rights.[38]

At time of writing in 2022, the current occupant of the secretary-general's office is António Guterres, who by background and appearance is somewhat similar to Lie. They both came from small European states, and had been active labour party politicians and trade unionists with a firm home in the social democratic tradition. Looking at photos of the two men also reveals a similarity of physical appearance, and they both speak heavily accented English. Guterres was elected amid high hopes in 2016 following an unusually transparent and inclusive election process.[39] Although the campaign to elect a woman had failed,[40] many considered Guterres the 'best of the declared candidates for the job'.[41] Still serving, it is unclear what Guterres' final legacy will become. At time of writing in April 2022, Guterres and the UN are struggling to respond to the Russian invasion of Ukraine. Within Europe, millions of Ukrainians have left their homes to seek safety away from the war. They come in addition to more than 80 million people globally who were already forcibly displaced, the largest number ever recorded.[42] It is safe to assume that the war in Ukraine will come to define much of Guterres' second term in office. Perhaps the renewed deadlock in the Security Council will usher in a similar dynamic to that observed during the Cold War, when a vacuum effect led both the secretary-general and the General Assembly to assume greater responsibilities. The General Assembly has already dusted off the 1950 'Uniting for Peace' resolution, using it on 2 March 2022 to pass a resolution condemning the Russian invasion of Ukraine with 141 votes in favour, 5 against, and 35 abstentions.[43]

Institutions and individuals

The brief overview in the previous section illustrated that despite their differences in personality and individual preferences, once elected secretary-general the individual becomes socialized into the position. The role of secretary-general comes with established expectations. Today, in the 21st century, many observers from academia and civil society expect the secretary-general to perform a visible and politically activist role. The '1 for 7 billion'-campaign illustrates this trend in its call for 'a highly-qualified and visionary leader, equipped to deal with the world's crises' to hold the post of secretary-general.[44] Civil society, and a large number of the world's states besides, expects the secretary-general to be a 'spokeswoman' for world interest and a 'guardian' of the UN Charter and its values. Faced with the latest crisis situation or pressing global issue these constituencies expect the secretary-general to take a stand and to urge member states to action. Looking back through history they condemn those secretaries-general who have been too passive or too submissive to state interests.

On the other hand, a significant group of UN member states would prefer a secretary-general who is more accommodating of their views and who concentrates primarily on the administrative side of the job, but who can be called upon when needed to mediate conflicts where their interests are not at stake. The secretary-general's relationship with the Security Council, and in particular with the P5, have been and continue to be of central importance to understand her room for manoeuvre. Angering one or more of the P5, as Lie and others found out to their detriment, would make the job nearly impossible.

Both of these two constituencies, those who prefer a pliant and passive secretary-general and those who wish to see an activist and visionary secretary-general, contribute to setting the expectations for the role of the secretary-general today. An individual who is elected to this post will have autonomy in deciding where along this spectrum she wishes to orient herself during her tenure. From the beginning, the role of the secretary-general came equipped with both formal and informal expectations, but also a large measure of ambiguity and flexibility. Over time, as successive secretaries-general have been socialized into the role and added their interpretations and performances to the role, the ambiguity and flexibility has been somewhat reduced. The UN today is a well-established institution, and the secretary-general will find herself in fewer completely new situations without relevant precedents. This institutionalization may have limited the secretary-general's room for autonomy because as the institution becomes more established there is less room for the individual to innovate. Yet the very fact that two contradictory ideals for the secretary-general continue to coexist, also means that the holder of the office will possess autonomy in interpreting which ideal should take precedence in different situations. The secretary-general today, as during earlier UN history, will always be able to find allies among civil society and the small- and medium-sized states, who recognize her role as a 'guardian' of the Charter and wish to strengthen her independence from the control of the (great power) states.

Claims that the secretary-general should represent a broader constituency in her role as a 'guardian' of the UN Charter are not new. Indeed, the UN Preparatory Commission in 1945 recognized that 'the Secretary-General, more than anyone else, will stand for the United Nations as a whole. In the eyes of the world, no less than in the eyes of his own staff, he must embody the principles and ideals of the Charter to which the Organization seeks to give effect.'[45] Today the UN website describes the secretary-general as 'a symbol of United Nations ideals and a spokesman for the interests of the world's peoples, in particular the poor and vulnerable among them'.[46] The secretary-general occupies a symbolically important role within the UN as a 'guardian' of the UN Charter. This position has provided the office with authority that has enabled the office to expand its political and diplomatic activities. The position also brings heavy responsibilities and challenges for the secretary-general. Because the secretary-general, more than anyone else within the UN system, represents the UN overall, the office will often be called on to act when other UN organs are unable or unwilling. And when things go wrong, the secretary-general takes the blame. Furthermore, there is an inherent tension in the concept of a 'guardian' of the Charter. Who or what is the secretary-general supposed to be 'guarding', the member states or the peoples of the world? The two conflicting ideals of an activist and visionary or a pliant and passive secretary-general could be seen as different expressions of this conflict. On the one hand the option of a submissive secretary-general who places the emphasis on the states' interests, on the other an activist secretary-general who puts the premium on the interests of 'we the peoples' even when these may conflict with state interests.

This tension remains unresolved today. The secretary-general still faces conflicting demands from different constituencies and from different visions of what the secretary-general's role should be. This inherent tension continues to provide the role with autonomy. This book has argued that the UN can best be understood as an institution within which different actors occupy different roles that provide rules and expectations for how an individual in that role is supposed to act in different situations. That is, the secretary-general does not act as a private individual but as the holder of the Office of Secretary-General. This is not to say that the personalities of different officeholders are irrelevant. This book explored in detail the process whereby Lie was able to take advantage of institutional flexibility and ambiguity to expand the mandate of the office of UN secretary-general. The interplay of crisis decision-making, institutional constraints, and the individuals involved during Lie's tenure from 1946 to 1953 built the foundations for the UN organization we know today. As the past 75 years give ample illustration, secretaries-general have considerable autonomy in interpreting what their roles are, what rules and expectations apply in different situations, and what action to take given conflicting expectations or limited options. This provides the secretary-general – as a 'guardian' of the Charter – a wide array of tools at her disposal, and gives the individual holder of the office great potential to act as a force for good in the world, should she be so inclined.

APPENDIX

UN Charter, Chapter XV: The Secretariat

Article 97

The Secretariat shall comprise a Secretary-General and such staff as the Organization may require. The Secretary-General shall be appointed by the General Assembly upon the recommendation of the Security Council. He shall be the chief administrative officer of the Organization.

Article 98

The Secretary-General shall act in that capacity in all meetings of the General Assembly, of the Security Council, of the Economic and Social Council, and of the Trusteeship Council, and shall perform such other functions as are entrusted to him by these organs. The Secretary-General shall make an annual report to the General Assembly on the work of the Organization.

Article 99

The Secretary-General may bring to the attention of the Security Council any matter which in his opinion may threaten the maintenance of international peace and security.

Article 100

1. In the performance of their duties the Secretary-General and the staff shall not seek or receive instructions from any government or from any other authority external to the Organization. They shall refrain from any action which might reflect on their position as international officials responsible only to the Organization.

2. Each Member of the United Nations undertakes to respect the exclusively international character of the responsibilities of the Secretary-General and the staff and not to seek to influence them in the discharge of their responsibilities.

Article 101

1. The staff shall be appointed by the Secretary-General under regulations established by the General Assembly.
2. Appropriate staffs shall be permanently assigned to the Economic and Social Council, the Trusteeship Council, and, as required, to other organs of the United Nations. These staffs shall form a part of the Secretariat.
3. The paramount consideration in the employment of the staff and in the determination of the conditions of service shall be the necessity of securing the highest standards of efficiency, competence, and integrity. Due regard shall be paid to the importance of recruiting the staff on as wide a geographical basis as possible.

Notes

Introduction

1. UN Charter, article 97. Author's emphasis.
2. So far, all nine UN secretaries-general have been men, despite a strong campaign to elect a woman in 2016. The UN Charter (art. 8) states that all positions within the UN are open to men and women equally. The main historical case study of this book focuses on Trygve Lie, and for readability those chapters will use 'he' and 'his' to refer both to Lie directly and to the office of secretary-general in the abstract. For better balance in the book overall, I have therefore chosen to use 'she' and 'her' to refer to the office of secretary-general in the introduction and conclusion.
3. Annan, 'Foreword', xi.
4. 'The role of the secretary-general', https://www.un.org/sg/en/content/the-role-of-the-secretary-general (accessed 21 December 2021).
5. Whitfield, 'Good offices and groups of friends'; Franck and Nolte, 'Good Offices Function'; Ravndal, 'Secretaries-General and Crisis Management'; Skjelsbæk and Fermann, 'UN Secretary-General and the Mediation of International Disputes'.
6. Chesterman, 'Article 99'; Bourloyannis, 'Fact-finding by the Secretary-General'.
7. Rushton, 'UN Secretary-General and Norm Entrepreneurship'; Johnstone, 'Secretary-General as norm entrepreneur'; Ravndal, 'A Force for Peace'; Johnstone, 'Power of Persuasion Based on Law'.
8. Trinh, 'The bully pulpit'.
9. Lie, *In the Cause of Peace*, 88.
10. 'The role of the secretary-general', https://www.un.org/sg/en/content/the-role-of-the-secretary-general (accessed 21 December 2021).
11. Kille, 'Moral Authority', 11.
12. Rovine, *The First Fifty Years*, 204.
13. Haack, 'UN Secretary-General, role expansion and narratives of representation'.
14. Ravndal, 'A Guardian of the UN Charter', 298.
15. The text of the UN Charter is available at https://www.un.org/en/about-us/un-charter (accessed 21 December 2021). See also Tharoor, 'The most impossible job description', 33.
16. UN Charter, article 99. As argued by Schwebel, 'Article 99'; Fiedler, 'Article 99', 1044; Kennedy, *Parliament of Man*, 44; Traub, 'The Secretary-General's political space'.
17. Schwebel, 'Article 99'.
18. By Dag Hammarskjöld during the Congo Crisis in 1960, and by Kurt Waldheim over the occupation of the US Embassy in Teheran in 1979. Chesterman, 'Article 99', 2013–14.
19. 'Minutes of the Meeting of the United States Delegation (Executive Session)', 26 January 1946, FRUS, *1946*, I, 172–82.
20. 'Summary Report of the Eleventh Meeting of Committee I/2', 23 May 1945, UNCIO, VII, 96.

21 Urquhart, 'The Evolution of the Secretary-General', 19.
22 Kofi A. Annan, 'Dag Hammarskjöld and the 21st Century', The Fourth Dag Hammarskjöld Lecture, Uppsala, Sweden, 6 September 2001, www.dhf.uu.se/pdffiler/Kofi%20Annan.pdf
23 For example, Jordan (ed) *Dag Hammarskjöld Revisited*; Urquhart, *Hammarskjöld*; Ask and Mark-Jungkvist (eds) *The Adventure of Peace*; Fröhlich, *Political Ethics and the United Nations*; Stahn and Melber (eds) *Peace Diplomacy, Global Justice and International Agency*; Lipsey, *Hammarskjöld*.
24 For the exceptions, see two earlier books which provide detailed discussions of Trygve Lie's tenure: Barros, *Trygve Lie*; and Gaglione, *The United Nations under Trygve Lie*. These books are both now several decades old and they are written in a more biographical style. Neither makes any broader claims about the establishment of institutional precedents, restricting themselves to a largely descriptive narrative of the historical developments during this time. A recent Norwegian-language book for a general audience also discusses Lie's tenure, but not related to other scholarship on the UN secretary-general: Tveit, *Gudfaren*. Furthermore, some articles and chapters from recent years provide details of certain key events from Lie's period in office: Muldoon, 'The House That Trygve Lie Built'; Ravndal, 'The First Major Test'; Ravndal, 'La mission la plus impossible au monde'; Ravndal, 'A Force for Peace'; Ravndal, 'Trygve Lie'; Barnes, 'Chief Administrator or Political "Moderator"?'
25 For example, Kille and Scully, 'Executive Heads and the Role of Intergovernmental Organizations'; Harman, 'Searching for an Executive Head?'; Schroeder, 'Executive Leadership'; Hall and Woods, 'Theorizing the role of executive heads in international organizations'; Heinzel, 'Mediating power?'
26 Important general studies include Newman, *The UN Secretary-General From the Cold War to the New Era*; Kille, *From Manager to Visionary*; Chesterman (ed) *Secretary or General?*; Fröhlich and Williams (eds) *UN Secretary-General and the Security Council*.
27 For example, Egeberg, 'Executive politics as usual'; Kille and Hendrickson, 'Secretary-General Leadership Across the United Nations and NATO'; Nugent and Rhinard, 'The "political" roles of the European Commission'; Schuette, 'Why NATO survived Trump'.
28 This literature is too large to explain in detail here, but for some recent examples see: Bauer and Ege, 'Bureaucratic autonomy of international organizations' secretariats'; Ege, 'What International Bureaucrats (Really) Want'; Copelovitch and Rickard, 'Partisan Technocrats'; Eckhard and Steinebach, 'Staff recruitment and geographical representation'; Liese et al, 'The heart of bureaucratic power'.
29 North, *Institutions*; Koremenos, Lipson and Snidal (eds) *Rational Design*.
30 Johnson, *Organizational Progeny*.
31 Jinnah, *Post-Treaty Politics*.
32 Hall, *Displacement, Development, and Climate Change*.
33 For example, Gray, 'Life, Death, or Zombie'; Eilstrup-Sangiovanni, 'Death of international organizations'; Eilstrup-Sangiovanni, 'What kills international organisations?'; Debre and Dijkstra, 'Institutional design for a post-liberal order'.
34 MacMillan, *Peacemakers*, chapter 7.
35 Ravndal, 'International Organisations in Historical Perspective'.
36 Pedersen, *Guardians*; Clavin, *Securing the World Economy*; Jackson and O'Malley (eds) *The Institution of International Order*.
37 Sluga, *Internationalism in the Age of Nationalism*; Sluga and Clavin (eds) *Internationalisms*.
38 Eisenberg, 'The Status of Women'; Adami and Plesch (eds) *Women and the UN*; Pedersen, 'Women at work in the League of Nations Secretariat'; Herren, 'Gender and International Relations'.

39. Mazower, *No Enchanted Palace*; Pedersen, *Guardians*; Yao, 'Conquest From Barbarism'.
40. Getachew, *Worldmaking after Empire*; O'Malley, *Diplomacy of Decolonisation*.
41. Plesch, *America, Hitler and the UN*; Plesch and Weiss (eds) *Wartime Origins and the Future United Nations*; Hilderbrand, *Dumbarton Oaks*.
42. Schlesinger, *Act of Creation*; Rofe, 'Pre-war Post-war Planning'; Wertheim, 'Instrumental Internationalism'; Wertheim, *Tomorrow, the World*; Roberts, 'A League of Their Own'.
43. Gaiduk, *Divided Together*.
44. Ravndal, 'A Force for Peace,' 444–7.
45. Ravndal, 'A Guardian of the UN Charter'.
46. Scott, *Institutions and Organizations*, 56.
47. Ibid, 64.
48. March and Olsen, 'Institutional Perspectives on Political Institutions', 251–2.
49. Sewell, 'A Theory of Structure', 19.
50. Berger and Luckmann, *Social Construction of Reality*, 93–4.
51. Kille, 'Moral Authority', 11.
52. Rovine, *The First Fifty Years*, 204.
53. Lie, *In the Cause of Peace*, 88.
54. Waldheim, *In the Eye of the Storm*, 38.
55. Meisler, *Kofi Annan*, 149.
56. See similar argument in Johnstone, 'Power of Persuasion Based on Law', 444–6.
57. Lie, *In the Cause of Peace*, 85.

Chapter 1

1. Report of the Preparatory Commission of the United Nations, UN Doc. PC/20, 23 December 1945, 87.
2. UN Charter, article 97.
3. Urquhart, 'Evolution of the Secretary-General', 17.
4. See, for example, Schwebel, *The Secretary-General of the United Nations*; Gordenker, *UN Secretary-General and the Maintenance of Peace*; Barros, *Trygve Lie*; Luck, 'The Secretary-General in a unipolar world'; Gordenker, *The UN Secretary-General and Secretariat*.
5. UN Charter, article 99.
6. Russell, *History of the UN Charter*, 371.
7. Schlesinger, *Act of Creation*, 240.
8. See US Department of State, *PFPP*, 109, 175, 250, 298.
9. Walters, *A History of the League of Nations*, vol. 1, 75–6; Ranshofen-Wertheimer, *International Secretariat*. See also Newman and Ravndal, 'International Civil Service'; Gram-Skjoldager and Ikonomou, 'Making of the International Civil Servant'.
10. UN Charter, articles 100 and 101.
11. Chesterman, 'Introduction', 8.
12. Steiner, *The Lights That Failed*, 354. See also Barros, 'The Importance of Secretaries-General of the United Nations', 34–6; Walters, *A History of the League of Nations*, vol. 2, 559.
13. Gordenker, *UN Secretary-General and Maintenance of Peace*, 11.
14. The Covenant of the League of Nations, article 6.
15. The Covenant of the League of Nations, article 11.
16. Barros, *Betrayal from Within*, vii; Steiner, *The Lights That Failed*, 355; Barros, *Office without Power*.

17 Ramcharan, *Preventive Diplomacy*, 15; Rovine, *The First Fifty Years*, 59, 72; Walters, *League of Nations*, 1, 311.
18 Steiner, *The Triumph of the Dark*, 107; Gordenker, *UN Secretary-General and Maintenance of Peace*, 10.
19 Kunz, 'The Legal Position of the Secretary General of the United Nations'; Gordenker, *UN Secretary-General and Maintenance of Peace*, 11; Ranshofen-Wertheimer, *International Secretariat*, 38.
20 As reflected in the title of Barros' book; Barros, *Betrayal From Within*.
21 Rovine, *The First Fifty Years*, 203.
22 Gordenker, *UN Secretary-General and Secretariat*, 6; Kennedy, 'Leader, clerk, or policy entrepreneur?', 158.
23 'How the ILO works', http://www.ilo.org/global/about-the-ilo/how-the-ilo-works/lang--en/index.htm (accessed 22 October 2021).
24 Eden memo, 'Future World Organisation – Memorandum A', 3 July 1944, WP(44)370, CAB 66/52, UKNA.
25 Phelan, *Yes and Albert Thomas*, 249–50.
26 Russell, *History of the UN Charter*, 371.
27 Mazower, *Governing the World*, 148.
28 Russell, *History of the UN Charter*, 371.
29 Barros, *Trygve Lie*, 3–4.
30 'The [Staff] Charter of the United Nations', 14 August 1943, art. 8(2). Available as appendix 23 in US Department of State, *PFPP*, 526–34. See also 'Draft Constitution of International Organization', 14 July 1943, appendix 13, in ibid, 472–83.
31 Russell, *History of the UN Charter*, 372.
32 Ibid, 374.
33 'Memorandum for the President', 29 December 1943, and 'Plan for the Establishment of an International Organization for the Maintenance of International Peace and Security', 23 December 1943, appendix 33 in US Department of State, *PFPP*, 576–81, and appendix F in Russell, *History of the UN Charter*, 990–5.
34 Russell, *History of the UN Charter*, 373–4.
35 'Possible Plan for a General International Organization', 29 April 1944, art. VI(B)2, appendix 35 in US Department of State, *PFPP*, 582–91.
36 Ibid, art. X(B)2.
37 Russell, *History of the UN Charter*, 375.
38 Plesch, *America, Hitler and the UN*, 85, 91.
39 Russell, *History of the UN Charter*, 376.
40 '[United States] Tentative Proposals for a General International Organization', 18 July 1944, appendix 38 in US Department of State, *PFPP*, 595–606.
41 Russell, *History of the UN Charter*, 377.
42 See *UN Yearbook 1946–47*, 4.
43 Meisler, *United Nations*, 10–13.
44 Russell, *History of the UN Charter*, 431–2.
45 '[Dumbarton Oaks] Proposals for the Establishment of a General International Organization', 7 October 1944, appendix 43 in US Department of State, *PFPP*, 611–19, and appendix I in Russell, *History of the UN Charter*, 1019–28.
46 Ibid, art. X(3).
47 Eden memo, 'Future World Organisation: Memorandum A', 3 July 1944, WP(44)370, CAB 66/52, UKNA.
48 'Tentative Chinese Proposals for a General International Organization', 23 August 1944, art. XVI(4), in *FRUS 1944*, I, 718–28. Author's emphasis.
49 Russell, *History of the UN Charter*, 432.

50 Ibid, 854.
51 Rovine, *The First Fifty Years*, 206.
52 Russell, *History of the UN Charter*, 854–60.
53 'Summary Report of Seventeenth Meeting of Committee I/2', 1 June 1945, *UNCIO*, VII, 161–3. Underlined in original.
54 'Summary Report of Eighteenth Meeting of Committee I/2', 2 June 1945, *UNCIO*, VII, 168–170.
55 'Summary Report of Seventeenth Meeting of Committee I/2', 1 June 1945, *UNCIO*, VII, 161–3.
56 'Summary Report of Seventeenth Meeting of Committee I/2', 1 June 1945, and 'Summary Report of Eighteenth Meeting of Committee I/2', 2 June 1945, *UNCIO*, VII, 161–3, 168–70.
57 Russell, *History of the UN Charter*, n. 26, 608.
58 'Summary Report of Eighteenth Meeting of Committee I/2', 2 June 1945, *UNCIO*, VII, 168–70.
59 'Summary Report of the Eleventh Meeting of Committee I/2', 23 May 1945, *UNCIO*, VII, 96.
60 'Summary Report of Seventeenth Meeting of Committee I/2', 1 June 1945, *UNCIO*, VII, 161–3.
61 'Summary Report of Twenty-Ninth Meeting of Committee I/2', 17 June 1945, *UNCIO*, VII, 277–81.
62 Ibid.
63 The commission consisted of one representative from each of the 50 states that signed the UN Charter in June 1945. In the interest of effectiveness, the commission delegated powers to a 14-member Executive Committee. Its members were the representatives of Australia, Brazil, Canada, Chile, China, Czechoslovakia, France, Iran, Mexico, the Netherlands, the Soviet Union, the UK, the US, and Yugoslavia.
64 As also argued by Rovine, *The First Fifty Years*, 205.
65 Report of the Preparatory Commission of the United Nations, UN Doc. PC/20, 23 December 1945, 87. Author's emphasis.
66 Schwebel, 'Article 99', 376. Emphasis in original.
67 Goodrich, Hambro and Anne Simons, *Charter of the United Nations*, 576; Kennedy, *Parliament of Man*, 44; Ramcharan, *Preventive Diplomacy*, 17.
68 Brian E. Urquhart, 'Character Sketches: Gladwyn Jebb', in *UN News* (n.d.), https://news.un.org/en/spotlight/character-sketches-gladwyn-jebb-brian-urquhart (accessed 28 March 2022).
69 Urquhart, *A Life in Peace and War*, 92.
70 Transcript of oral history interview with Lord Gladwyn Jebb, 21 June 1983, UNOH.
71 Ibid.
72 Jebb, *The Memoirs of Lord Gladwyn*, 183.
73 Rovine, *The First Fifty Years*, 206.
74 Report of the Preparatory Commission of the United Nations, UN Doc. PC/20, 23 December 1945, 87.
75 Urquhart, 'Evolution of the Secretary-General', 15. See also Gordenker, *UN Secretary-General and Secretariat*, 6.
76 Muldoon and Ravndal, 'Lie, Trygve Halvdan'.
77 Lie, *In the Cause of Peace*, 17.
78 Ravndal, 'The appointment of Trygve Lie as the first UN Secretary-General: One World Trust background briefs for the 1 for 7 billion campaign, Brief no. 3', May 2016, https://www.1for7billion.org/s/3_Ravndal.pdf

79 Stettinius to Acheson, 19/20 September 1945, *FRUS 1945*, I, 1449–50; James Reston, 'UNO Council Picks Lie, a Norwegian, for Secretaryship: Security Body Is Unanimous after Russia Vetoes Lester Pearson of Canada: Geography Plays Part: Fact That Headquarters Will Be in North America Militated against Dominion Man', *New York Times*, 30 January 1946.
80 Rovine, *The First Fifty Years*, 206.
81 Lie, *Syv år for freden*, 14–15.
82 Barros, *Trygve Lie*, 10–11.
83 Acheson to Stettinius, 18 September 1945, *FRUS 1945*, I, 1448–9.
84 General Assembly resolution 11(I), 24 January 1946.
85 'Minutes of the First Meeting of the US Delegation on Board the Queen Elizabeth', 2 January 1946, *FRUS 1946*, I, 117–26.
86 Lie himself hoped to see the job go to Eden. Lie, *In the Cause of Peace*, 12–13; Urquhart, 'Evolution of the Secretary-General', 16; 'Minutes by the United States Delegation of the Five-Power Informal Meeting', 23 January 1946, *FRUS 1946*, I, 166–9.
87 Barros, *Trygve Lie*, 23.
88 Ibid, 17–18.
89 Ibid, 19.
90 'Minutes by the United States Delegation of the Five-Power Informal Meeting', 23 January and 28 January, 1946, *FRUS 1946*, I, 166–9, 183–4; Foote to Stevenson, 21 January 1946; Stevenson to the Secretary of State, 15 January 1946; Hiss to the Secretary of State, 18 January 1946, with 'Memorandum regarding selection of Secretary General', 18 January 1946, all in RG 84, 1030E, box 16, folder 7, NARA.
91 See Acheson to Stettinius, 18 September 1945, *FRUS 1945*, I, 1448–9. This did not prevent the continued mention of French and Chinese names at later stages of the debate. See, for example, 'Minutes by the United States Delegation of the Five-Power Informal Meeting', 23 January 1946, and 'Minutes of the Meeting of the United States Delegation (Executive Session)', 26 January 1946, *FRUS 1946*, I, 166–9, 172–82.
92 Urquhart, 'Evolution of the Secretary-General', 25.
93 'Minutes by the United States Delegation of the Five-Power Informal Meeting', 23 January 1946, *FRUS 1946*, I, 166–9.
94 See also 'Minutes of the First Meeting of the US Delegation on Board the Queen Elizabeth,' 2 January 1946, *FRUS 1946*, I, 117–26.
95 GAOR, 1st session, 1st mtg, 10 January 1946.
96 *UN Yearbook 1946–47*, 56; Barros, *Trygve Lie*, 21–2; Lie, *In the Cause of Peace*, 8–10.
97 Lie, *In the Cause of Peace*, 9–10.
98 The general understanding seems to be that Pearson was the forerunner for the post of UN secretary-general. Thus his Wikipedia entry stated: 'Pearson nearly became the first Secretary-General of the United Nations in 1945, but this move was vetoed by the Soviet Union' (http://en.wikipedia.org/wiki/Lester_Pearson, accessed 6 May 2014). Barros also goes far towards arguing that Pearson would have been elected if only the Soviet Union hadn't vetoed him. See Barros, *Trygve Lie*, 5–25; James Barros, 'Pearson or Lie'. However, as Gaiduk points out, British support for Pearson was lukewarm, while both the French and the Latin Americans would have preferred someone else. Gaiduk, *Divided Together*, 53–4.
99 'Minutes by the United States Delegation of the Five-Power Informal Meeting', 28 January 1946, *FRUS 1946*, I, 183–4. See also Barros, *Trygve Lie*, 25.
100 SCOR, 1st year, 4th mtg, 29 January 1946.
101 GAOR, 1st session, 20th plenary mtg, 1 February 1946.
102 Latin America, the Dominions, and Western European countries were unacceptable to the Soviet Union, and any Eastern European country was unacceptable to the West. The

secretary-general could obviously not come from a former enemy country (like Finland or Austria), and Sweden was not yet a member of the UN. No-one ever considered any candidates from the few independent African or Asian countries. This effectively left Denmark and Norway, but no candidate from Denmark was as well known as Lie, because Lie and the Norwegian government-in-exile had been in London during the war, while the Danish government had stayed in Copenhagen.

103 Lie, *In the Cause of Peace*, 17–20, 22–4.
104 UN Charter, article 97.
105 Barros, *Betrayal from Within*; Barros, *Office without Power*.
106 Rovine, *The First Fifty Years*, 203.
107 'Minutes by the United States Delegation of the Five-Power Informal Meeting', 23 January 1946, *FRUS 1946*, I, 166–9.
108 Lie, *In the Cause of Peace*, 42.
109 By Dag Hammarskjöld during the Congo Crisis in 1960, and by Kurt Waldheim over the occupation of the US Embassy in Teheran in 1979. Chesterman, 'Article 99', 2013–14.
110 Schwebel, 'Article 99'.
111 'Minutes of the Meeting of the United States Delegation (Executive Session)', 26 January 1946, *FRUS 1946*, I, 172–82.
112 See 'Minutes of the First Meeting of the US Delegation on Board the Queen Elizabeth', 2 January 1946, *FRUS 1946*, I, 117–26.
113 General Assembly resolution 11(I), 24 January 1946.
114 Such as the Greek Prime Minister Eleftherios Venizelos, President Tomas Masaryk of Czechoslovakia, or General Jan Smuts of South Africa. See Steiner, *The Lights That Failed*, 354; Barros, *Office without Power*, 2–5.

Chapter 2

1 Lie to Halvard Lange, 29 April 1946, Brevs. 410, NLN. Author's translation from Norwegian.
2 UN Charter, article 99.
3 Lie, *In the Cause of Peace*, 42.
4 For more on the relationship between the secretary-general and the Security Council, see also Fröhlich and Williams, *The UN Secretary-General and the Security Council*.
5 Good accounts of the background and developments of the crisis can be found in Fawcett, *Iran and the Cold War*; Kuniholm, *The Origins of the Cold War in the Near East*; Hasanli, *At the Dawn of the Cold War*; Fawcett, 'Revisiting the Iranian Crisis'.
6 Letter reproduced in *FRUS* 1946, VII, 304.
7 Security Council resolution 2, 30 January 1946.
8 Murray (Teheran) to Secretary of State, 14 March 1946, *FRUS 1946*, VII, 354–6; Kuniholm, *Origins of the Cold War*, 313–14, 23–4.
9 Gromyko to Lie, 19 March 1946, *FRUS 1946*, VII, 366–7.
10 Lie, *In the Cause of Peace*, 76.
11 Kuniholm, *Origins of the Cold War*, 328.
12 SCOR, 1st year, 26th mtg, 26 March 1946.
13 SCOR, 1st year, 30th mtg, 4 April 1946.
14 Murray to Byrnes, 4 April 1946, *FRUS 1946*, VII, 405–7.
15 *UN Yearbook 1946–47*, 332.
16 SCOR, 1st year, 32nd mtg, 15 April 1946.
17 Lie, *In the Cause of Peace*, 79–80.
18 Quote reproduced in Barros, *Trygve Lie*, 72.

19. Letter from the Secretary-General to the President of the Security Council concerning the question of the retention of the Iranian case on the agenda of the Security Council, UN doc. S/39, 19 April 1946.
20. Lie to Halvard Lange, 29 April 1946, Brevs. 410, NLN.
21. The Committee of Experts is a subsidiary organ of the Security Council which was set up at the Council's first meeting to examine and report on the provisional rules of procedure drafted by the Preparatory Commission. Until 1953 the Security Council would occasionally refer other constitutional and procedural matters for consideration by the Committee of Experts. The Committee was seen as a working body, not a political organ, and debates in the Committee of Experts were generally less heated compared with its parent organ. Its membership consisted of the same states as the Council, and the meetings were usually attended by the delegations' legal advisers. Although the committee has been largely inactive since 1953, only being called into action once in 1987 to examine the question of membership of the Republic of Nauru in the International Court of Justice, the committee still formally exists as one of the standing committees of the Security Council. *UN Yearbook 1946–47*, 327, 410; Bailey and Daws, *Procedure of the UN Security Council*, 334; Sievers and Daws, *Procedure of the UN Security Council*, 479–80.
22. SCOR, 1st year, 33rd mtg, 16 April 1946.
23. Ibid.
24. Ibid.
25. Lie, *In the Cause of Peace*, 84.
26. Ibid, 85.
27. Stettinius to Byrnes, 16 April 1946, 501.BC/4-1646, NARA.
28. 'Envoy Shifts Declared Out As U.S. Gestures of Protest', *New York Times*, 20 April 1946.
29. Lie, *In the Cause of Peace*, 85.
30. Fitzmaurice minute, 17 April 1946; FO to New York, 17 April 1946, FO 371/52673, UKNA.
31. Ward minute, 25 April 1946, FO 371/52673, UKNA.
32. SCOR, 1st year, 36th mtg, 23 April 1946.
33. Dølvik, 'Sovjetunionen og FNs første generalsekretær', 70–1.
34. Lie, *In the Cause of Peace*, 85–6.
35. Dølvik, 'Sovjetunionen og FNs første generalsekretær', 71.
36. Committee of Experts, 28th mtg, 16 April 1946, S/Procedure/60, 18 April 1946; Committee of Experts, 29th mtg, 17 April 1946, S/Procedure/62, 3 April 1946, UNDHL.
37. Report of chairman of Committee of Experts, S/Procedure/59, 17 April 1946, UNDHL.
38. Lie, *In the Cause of Peace*, 84–5.
39. SCOR, 1st year, 36th mtg, 23 April 1946.
40. SCOR, 1st year, 43rd mtg, 22 May 1946.
41. Bailey and Daws, *Procedure of the UN Security Council*, 80.
42. Fawcett, 'Revisiting the Iranian Crisis', 384.
43. Lie to Halvard Lange, 29 April 1946, Brevs. 410, NLN.
44. Lie, *In the Cause of Peace*, 83.
45. Lie to Halvard Lange, 29 April 1946, Brevs. 410, NLN.
46. James Reston, 'Trygve Lie's Precedent: U.N. Secretary General Won Right to Intervene in Council – At a Cost', *New York Times*, 19 April 1946.
47. Transcript of SG press conference, 6 May 1946, UNDHL.
48. SCOR, 1st year, 1st mtg, 17 January 1946.
49. At the time these were rules 20–3 of the rules of procedure. SCOR, 1st year, 31st mtg, 9 April 1946.
50. Lie to Halvard Lange, 29 April 1946, Brevs. 410, NLN.
51. Committee of Experts, 47th mtg, 15 May 1946, S/Procedure/100, 23 May 1946, UNDHL.

NOTES

52 Memorandum of conversation (Johnson, Hiss), 10 May 1946, 501.BC/5–1046; Stettinius to the Secretary of State, 11 May 1946, 501.BC/5–1146, NARA.
53 Committee of Experts, 47th mtg, 15 May 1946, S/Procedure/100, 23 May 1946, UNDHL.
54 Stettinius to the Secretary of State, 15 May 1946, 501.BC/5-1546, NARA.
55 Committee of Experts, 47th mtg, 15 May 1946, S/Procedure/100, 23 May 1946, UNDHL.
56 Lie, *In the Cause of Peace*, 87.
57 Stettinius to the Secretary of State, 15 May 1946, 501.BC/5–1546, NARA.
58 Committee of Experts, 47th mtg, 15 May 1946, S/Procedure/100, 23 May 1946, UNDHL.
59 Committee of Experts, 47th mtg, 15 May 1946, S/Procedure/100, 23 May 1946; Committee of Experts, 48th mtg, 20 May 1946, S/Procedure/103, 5 June 1946; Committee of Experts, 49th mtg, 21 May 1946, S/Procedure/104, 3 June 1946; Draft report of chairman of Committee of Experts on the secretary-general's right to make communications to the Security Council, S/Procedure/97, 23 May 1946, UNDHL.
60 Stettinius to the Secretary of State, 15 May 1946, 501.BC/5–1546; Stettinius to Secretary of State, 17 May 1946, 501.BC/5–1746; Stettinius to Secretary of State, 21 May 1946, 501.BC/5–2146, NARA.
61 Committee of Experts, 48th mtg, 20 May 1946, S/Procedure/103, 5 June 1946, UNDHL.
62 Committee of Experts, 48th mtg, 20 May 1946, S/Procedure/103, 5 June 1946, UNDHL; Byrnes to US UN delegation, 24 May 1946, 501. BC/5–2346, NARA.
63 Committee of Experts, 49th mtg, 21 May 1946, S/Procedure/104, 3 June 1946, UNDHL.
64 Stettinius to Secretary of State, no. 212, 21 May 1946, 501.BC/5–2146, NARA.
65 Noel-Baker minute, [n.d.], on Cadogan to FO, 15 May 1946, FO 371/57247, UKNA. Emphasis in original.
66 Ward minute, 21 May 1946, FO 371/57247, UKNA.
67 FO to UK UN delegation, 22 May 1946, FO 371/57247, UKNA.
68 Committee of Experts, 50th mtg, 23 May 1946, S/Procedure/105, 31 May 1946, UNDHL.
69 Committee of Experts, 51st mtg, 27 May 1946, S/Procedure/106, 6 June 1946, UNDHL.
70 SCOR, 1st year, 44th mtg, 6 June 1946.
71 Lie, *In the Cause of Peace*, 87.
72 *UN Yearbook, 1947–48*, 326.
73 *UN Yearbook, 1948–49*, 98, 103.
74 Daily report to the secretary-general from the Legal Department, 15 March 1949, S-0188-0002-01, UNA.
75 ECOSOC resolution 217(VIII), 18 March 1949.
76 Memorandum of conversation (Hiss, Dennison, Claxton), 12 June 1946, 501.BC/6-1246, NARA; Committee of Experts, 71st mtg, 9 September 1946, S/Procedure/133, 12 September 1946; Committee of Experts, 72nd mtg, 10 September 1946, S/Procedure/134, 11 September 1946; Committee of Experts, 74th mtg, 16 September 1946, S/Procedure/137, 17 September 1946, UNDHL.
77 Lie, *In the Cause of Peace*, 88.
78 UN Charter, article 4.
79 Security Council resolution 6 (1946), 17 May 1946.
80 Johnson to the Secretary of State, 23 August 1946, *FRUS 1946*, I, 432–4.
81 SCOR, 1st year, 54th mtg, 28 August 1946.
82 SCOR, 1st year, 55th mtg, 28 August 1946.
83 SCOR, 1st year, 55th mtg, 28 August 1946.
84 SCOR, 1st year, 56th and 57th mtgs, 29 August 1946.
85 Security Council resolution 8, 29 August 1946.
86 Cordier and Foote, *Public Papers, vol. 1: Trygve Lie*, 44.
87 Security Council resolution 109, 14 December 1955.
88 Cordier and Foote, *Public Papers, vol. 1: Trygve Lie*, 44.

[89] Cadogan to FO, 30 August 1946, FO 371/59733, UKNA.
[90] Beckett minute, 18 September 1946, FO 371/59733, UKNA.
[91] Jebb to Gore-Booth, 1 October 1946, FO 371/59718, UKNA.
[92] For accounts of the background and development of the Greek civil war, see Rajak, 'The Cold War in the Balkans'; Close, *Origins of the Greek Civil War*; Gerolymatos, *Red Acropolis, Black Terror*.
[93] SCOR, 1st year, 6th mtg, 1 February 1946.
[94] SCOR, 1st year, 10th mtg, 6 February 1946.
[95] *UN Yearbook 1946–47*, 351.
[96] SCOR, 1st year, 70th meeting, 20 September 1946.
[97] Memorandum of telephone conversations (Hiss), 18 September 1946, *FRUS 1946*, VII, 219–220.
[98] Ibid.
[99] Quoted in *FRUS 1946*, VII, 220n.
[100] SCOR, 1st year, 70th mtg, 20 September 1946. Also quoted in Cordier and Foote, *Public Papers, vol. 1: Trygve Lie*, 46–7.
[101] SCOR, 1st year, 70th mtg, 20 September 1946.
[102] Cordier and Foote, *Public Papers, vol. 1: Trygve Lie*, 47.
[103] Goodrich, Hambro, and Simons, *Charter of the United Nations*, 576; Ramcharan, *Preventive Diplomacy*, 17.
[104] Peck minute, 24 October 1946, FO 371/59719, UKNA.
[105] Lie, *In the Cause of Peace*, 88.

Chapter 3

[1] Bunche to Lie with 'Draft Statement on the Palestine Question', 23 February 1948, PA-1407/D/L0013, NAN.
[2] An earlier version of this chapter was published as Ravndal, 'The First Major Test'.
[3] Statement by Haakon Lie in TV documentary by Lasse Solberg and Herbjørn Sørebø, 'Trygve Lie – mannen som bygde opp FN' (Oslo: NRK, 1985). Author's translation from Norwegian.
[4] Ralph Bunche was a director in the trusteeship division of the UN Secretariat who played a central role in every phase of the UN's involvement with Palestine. He travelled to Palestine as principal secretary or as the secretary-general's representative with UNSCOP, the Palestine Commission, the Palestine Conciliation Commission, and the UN mediator, and in the spring of 1949 he negotiated armistice agreements between Israel and four Arab states as acting UN mediator. Urquhart, *Ralph Bunche*; Ben-Dror, 'Ralph Bunche'.
[5] Bunche diary note, 4 May 1949, box 2, folder 13, UCB. Underlined in original.
[6] Waage, 'The Winner Takes All', 289–90; Lie, *In the Cause of Peace*, 162.
[7] Waage, *Da staten Israel ble til*, 213–18.
[8] The strongest proponent of these arguments today is Waage; Waage, 'The Winner Takes All'; Waage, *Da staten Israel ble til*; Jensehaugen, Heian-Engdal, and Waage, 'Securing the State'; Heian-Engdal, Jensehaugen, and Waage, 'Finishing the Enterprise'. See also Barros, *Trygve Lie*; Urquhart, *Ralph Bunche*; Tveit, *Alt for Israel: Oslo – Jerusalem 1948–78*; Tveit, *Gudfaren*.
[9] Ravndal, 'Exit Britain'.
[10] In his Norwegian memoirs Lie titled the chapter on Palestine 'Den første store prøven'; that is, 'The first major test'. Lie, *Syv år for freden*, 126.
[11] Bunche to Lie with 'Draft Statement on the Palestine Question', 23 February 1948, PA-1407/D/L0013, NAN.

12 The 'iron wall' was a concept first used by the revisionist Zionist Ze'ev Jabotinsky in the 1920s to describe the strategy that the Zionists, in his opinion, would have to follow in Palestine. He argued that the Arabs would never accept the Zionist state-building project, and that the Zionists therefore had to build an 'iron wall' to be strong enough militarily to defeat the Arabs again and again until they accepted the existence of the Jewish state. Later researchers have used this concept to describe the actual policy of Israel toward the Arab states. See Jabotinsky, 'The Iron Wall'; Jabotinsky, 'The Ethics of the Iron Wall'; Lustick, 'To Build and to Be Built By'; Shlaim, *The Iron Wall*; Lustick, 'Abandoning the Iron Wall'; Shlaim, 'The Iron Wall Revisited'.

13 See, for example, 'Address by Secretary-General Trygve Lie at Annual Convention of Rotary International', 14 June 1949, and 'Tale av Generalsekretær Trygve Lie, Bergen, Norway', 8 August 1949, both in PA-1407/D/L0017, NAN.

14 Lie to Gerhardsen, 9 March 1948, in PA-1407/D/L0019, NAN. Author's translation from Norwegian.

15 Lie, *In the Cause of Peace*, 159.

16 Bosco, *Five to Rule Them All*; Mazower, *No Enchanted Palace*; Plesch, *America, Hitler and the UN*.

17 Minutes of meeting in Mr Lie's office, Lake Success, 20 February 1947, S-0194-0003-04, UNA. See also Ben-Dror, 'Ralph Bunche', 519.

18 See note 4 in this chapter.

19 Bunche memorandum to Cordier, 'Suggested procedural arrangements for a Secretariat work-program on the Palestine question', 3 March 1947, S-0159-0001-07, UNA.

20 How to relate to Spain, under the leadership of Franco, was a difficult and controversial question for the UN at this time. In December 1946 the General Assembly recommended that all member states withdraw their ambassadors or ministers plenipotentiary from Madrid. Argentina did not. (Only three states withdrew their ambassadors, the large majority had no diplomatic presence or only representation at a lower level.) See *UN Yearbook 1946–47*, 126–30.

21 South Africa faced opposition against its proposal to annex the mandated territory of South West Africa, and the General Assembly in December 1946 requested that it submit a trusteeship agreement for the territory, but South Africa never did. This became one of the many cases against South Africa in the following decades, and South West Africa only gained independence in 1990 as Namibia.

22 Minutes of meeting in Mr Lie's office, Lake Success, 4 March 1947, S-0194-0003-04, UNA.

23 Minutes of meeting in Mr Lie's office, Lake Success, 19 March 1947, S-0194-0003-04, UNA.

24 The 11 members of UNSCOP were Australia, Canada, Czechoslovakia, Guatemala, India, Iran, the Netherlands, Peru, Sweden, Uruguay, and Yugoslavia. See Ben-Dror, 'The Arab Struggle against Partition'; Ben-Dror, 'The success of the Zionist strategy vis-à-vis UNSCOP'; Morris, *1948*, 37–51; Cohen, *Palestine and the Great Powers*.

25 Lie, 'Opening Address to Special Committee on Palestine, New York', 26 May 1947, PA-1407/D/L0015, NAN.

26 Lie, *In the Cause of Peace*, 161. I have not found any evidence to suggest otherwise, and neither did Barros in his thorough study of Lie as secretary-general. See Barros, *Trygve Lie*, 180–1.

27 The majority of UNSCOP recommended partitioning Palestine into two independent states, one Arab and one Jewish, with an international regime for Jerusalem, and economic union among all three parts. The minority, consisting of India, Iran, and Yugoslavia, proposed a federal state with local autonomy. See UNSCOP, 'Report to the General

28. Lie, *In the Cause of Peace*, 162. Italic in original.
29. UN Press Release, GA/PAL/12, 11 October 1947, and Statement by Tsarapkin (USSR) in General Assembly Ad Hoc Committee on the Palestine Question, 12th mtg, 13 October 1947, A/AC.14/SR.12, UNISPAL.
30. Gaiduk, *Divided Together*, 137.
31. Anne O'Hare McCormick, 'Glimpse of What Might Have Been, and What Might Be', *New York Times*, 12 November 1947.
32. General Assembly resolution 181(II), 29 November 1947.
33. The members of the Palestine Commission were Bolivia, Czechoslovakia, Denmark, Panama, and the Philippines.
34. Thomas J. Hamilton, 'Small-Nation View on Palestine Asked: Lie Inquires of Several Whether They Would Send Troops to Maintain Order', *New York Times*, 8 January 1948; Thomas J. Hamilton, 'UN Palestine Unit Will Meet Today: Commission Gathering Amid Uncertainty on Force to Protect Partition', *New York Times*, 9 January 1948; Thomas J. Hamilton, 'Palestine Board Reassured by Lie: U.N. Secretary General Tells Commission It Should Expect Security Council Backing: Absence of Force Feared: British and Zionists Accept, Arabs Reject Liaison Roles – Czech Named Chairman', *New York Times*, 10 January 1948.
35. This meeting was mentioned in a 'first rough draft' letter from the secretary-general to the Security Council [early March 1948], PA-1407/D/L0013, NAN.
36. See the two papers attached to the memo of conversation (Lie, Feller, Ross), 8 January 1948, RG 59, Rusk-McClintok Papers, box 1, NARA.
37. Cadogan to FO, 19 December 1947, FO 371/61893, UKNA; Shertok report, 26 December 1947, in Yogev et al (eds) *Political and Diplomatic Documents*, 110–12.
38. Lie was supposed to have consulted with Belgium, the Netherlands, Sweden, Norway, Denmark, Brazil, Mexico, and one other Latin American country. Thomas J. Hamilton, 'Small-Nation View on Palestine Asked: Lie Inquires of Several Whether They Would Send Troops to Maintain Order', *New York Times*, 8 January 1948; Memo of conversation (Lie, Feller, Ross), 8 January 1948, RG 59, Rusk-McClintok Papers, box 1, NARA.
39. Lie opening statement at the first meeting of the Palestine Commission, 9 January 1948, PA-1407/D/L0025, NAN.
40. Bunche diary note, 12 January 1948, box 5, folder 6, UCB.
41. SCOR, 3rd year, 253rd mtg, 24 February 1948.
42. See different draft statements from the secretary-general to the Security Council in PA-1407/D/L0013, NAN.
43. Lie, *In the Cause of Peace*, 166.
44. Bunche to Lie with 'Draft Statement on the Palestine Question', 23 February 1948, PA-1407/D/L0013, NAN.
45. Minutes of 110th private mtg, 1 March 1948, box 112, folder 5, CCC.
46. Austin to Secretary of State, 10 February 1948, *FRUS, 1948*, V, 614–16.
47. SCOR, 3rd year, 253rd mtg, 24 February 1948.
48. Lie, *In the Cause of Peace*, 167–8.
49. 'Relations between the United Nations Commission and the Security Council', working paper prepared by the Secretariat, A/AC.21/13, 9 February 1948, UNISPAL. [The paper was first published on 3 February as A/AC.21/W.25.]
50. *New York Times*, 'Partition Powers of U.N. Affirmed: Palestine Action by Security Council in Event of Arab Balk Declared Legal', 9 March 1948.
51. Barros, *Trygve Lie*, 188.
52. Memorandum by McClintock to Lovett, 9 March 1948, *FRUS* 1948, V, 700–1.

53 Lie, *In the Cause of Peace*, 168.
54 SCOR, 3rd year, 265th mtg, 9 March 1948.
55 Security Council resolution 42 (1948), 5 March 1948.
56 Lie to Gerhardsen, 5 April 1948, PA-1407/D/L0013, NAN; Lie, *Syv år for freden*, 137.
57 Austin to the Secretary of State, 13 March 1948, *FRUS 1948*, V, 712–719.
58 'Corrigendum', 19 March, PA-1407/D/L0024, NAN.
59 SCOR, 3rd year, 270th and 271st mtgs, 19 March 1948.
60 Lie, *Syv år for freden*, 138. Author's translation from Norwegian.
61 See Cadogan to Jebb, 27 May 1948, FO371/72676, UKNA and Barros, *Trygve Lie*, 130.
62 Security Council resolution 44 (1948), 1 April 1948.
63 Security Council resolution 43 (1948), 1 April 1948.
64 Lie to Gerhardsen, 5 April 1948, PA-1407/D/L0013, NAN.
65 The story is recounted in Waage, *Da staten Israel ble til*, 142–3.
66 Lie to Stoneman, 22 June 1948, PA-1407-D-L0013, NAN.
67 General Assembly resolution 186 (S-2), 14 May 1948.
68 Lie letter to the permanent members of Security Council, 16 May 1948, reprinted in Lie, *In the Cause of Peace*, 178–79.
69 Feller to Lie with attached memorandum by Stavropoluos, 'Powers of the Secretary-General under Article 99', 3 May 1948, and Stavropoulos to Lie with draft letter by Feller, 5 May 1948, both in PA-1407/D/L0013, NAN.
70 Lie, *In the Cause of Peace*, 174–5.
71 Jackson memo, 'Notes on a conversation with Sir Alexander Cadogan at 6:45 p.m., 16th May 1948', PA-1407/D/L0014, NAN; Cadogan to FO, 17 May 1948, FO 371/68553, UKNA; Lie, *Syv år for freden*, 159–62.
72 SCOR, 3rd year, 293rd mtg, 17 May 1948.
73 'Contacts made by Mr. Cordier with State Department officials with regard to the Palestine issue 15–17 May 1948', PA-1407/D/L0014, NAN, and box 130, folder 7, CCC.
74 Cadogan to FO, 19 May 1948, FO371/72676, UKNA.
75 [Jackson] memo, [21 May] 1948, FO 371/72676, UKNA.
76 Jebb minute, 21 May 1948, FO371/72676, UKNA.
77 Cadogan to Jebb, 27 May 1948, FO 371/72676, UKNA.
78 See Marshall to Lie, 21 May 1948, and Henderson memo to Marshall, 25 May 1948, *FRUS 1948*, V, 1018, 1044–5, and Urquhart, 'Points from Commander Jackson', [25] May 1948, PA-1407/D/L0014, NAN.
79 Britain and the US decided to work together later in the summer in response to the UN mediator's first proposal, and there were rumours at the time that Bernadotte's second plan had been drafted by, or at least heavily influenced by, the two Western powers, which later turned out to be unfounded. See Gazit, 'American and British Diplomacy and the Bernadotte Mission'.
80 The members of the Truce Commission were the US, France, and Belgium; the three states (apart from Britain) that had consulates in Jerusalem.
81 Security Council resolution 50 (1948), 29 May 1948.
82 Lie to Bernadotte, 21 May 1948, box 5, folder 4, UCB.
83 Lie, *In the Cause of Peace*, 98. For more on Lie's reactions to the Marshall Plan, see also chapter 4 in this book.
84 See text of speech in pamphlet 'Call for a United Nations Force: by Trygve Lie, Secretary General: Text of the Secretary-General's address to the Harvard Alumni Association on June 10, 1948', PA-1407/D/L0018, NAN.
85 Feller memo, 'United Nations Guard', 3 June 1948, PA-1407/D/L0018, NAN.

86. 'Proposed United Nations Guard: Memorandum by the Secretary-General', 21 June 1948. Several copies of this memo (and its attachments) can be found in PA-1407/D/L0018, NAN, and in box 111, folder 6, CCC.
87. McClintok memo to Rusk, 1 July 1948; Marshall to Jessup, 23 June 1948, *FRUS 1948*, V, 1171–1179, 1138–9.
88. Security Council resolution 50 (1948), 29 May 1948.
89. See https://www.un.org/en/peacekeeping/missions/untso/ (accessed 15 August 2022). See also Pelcovits, *The Long Armistice*.
90. Bernadotte to Lie, 19 June 1948, PA-1407/D/L0024, NAN. The editors of FRUS claimed the request was made on 20 June. See Editorial note, *FRUS 1948*, V, 1138.
91. Jackson to Lie, 10 June 1948, PA-1407/D/L0014, NAN.
92. Lie to Bernadotte, 22–4 June 1948, S-0615-0001-01, UNA; Marshall to Jessup, 23 June 1948, *FRUS 1948*, V, 1138–9.
93. Marshall to Jessup, 23 June 1948; Marshall to Jessup, 28 June 1948, *FRUS 1948*, V, 1138–9, 1155–6.
94. Jackson to Bernadotte, 22 July 1948, S-0615-0001-02, UNA, and box 130, folder 7, CCC.
95. Lie, *In the Cause of Peace*, 187–8.
96. General Assembly resolution 194(III), 11 December 1948. The three members of this commission were France, Turkey, and the US. See also Caplan, *Futile Diplomacy, Volume 3*; Tiller and Waage, 'Powerful State, Powerless Mediator'.
97. Lie, *In the Cause of Peace*, 192–3.
98. See https://operationalsupport.un.org/en (accessed 15 November 2021).
99. See Caplan, 'A Tale of Two Cities'; Waage, 'The Winner Takes All'; Jensehaugen and Waage, 'Coercive Diplomacy'; Ben-Dror, 'The Armistice Talks between Israel and Jordan'.
100. See Heian-Engdal, Jensehaugen, and Waage, 'Finishing the Enterprise'.
101. 'Address by Secretary-General Trygve Lie at the American Association for the United Nations Dinner in Honour of Dr. Ralph J. Bunche', 9 May 1949, PA-1407/D/L0017, NAN.
102. Lie draft, 'Palestine challenge – and my response', PA-1407/D/L0020, NAN.
103. See, for example, 'Address by Secretary-General Trygve Lie at Annual Convention of Rotary International', 14 June 1949, and 'Tale av Generalsekretær Trygve Lie, Bergen, Norway', 8 August 1949, PA-1407/D/L0017, NAN.
104. See https://www.nobelprize.org/prizes/peace/1950/summary/ (accessed 11 August 2022).
105. Lie to Johan Falkberget, 30 November 1947, Brevs. 434, NLN. Author's translation from Norwegian.
106. Lie to Johan Bech-Friis, 18 February 1947, Brevs. 410, NLN. Author's translation from Norwegian.
107. All numbers on Security Council resolutions taken from https://www.un.org/security council/content/resolutions-0 (accessed 22 December 2021).
108. Transcript of secretary-general's press conference, 25 February 1949, UNDHL. Lie also quoted from this press conference in his memoirs, Lie, *In the Cause of Peace*, 192.

Chapter 4

1. Lie to Johan Falkberget, 30 November 1947, Brevs. 434, NLN. Author's translation from Norwegian.
2. Lie, *In the Cause of Peace*, 28.
3. Johnstone, 'Secretary-General as norm entrepreneur'; Rushton, 'UN Secretary-General and Norm Entrepreneurship'.

NOTES

4 Newman, 'Secretary-General'; Chesterman, 'Introduction'; Cockayne and Malone, 'Relations with the Security Council'.
5 Lie to Johan Falkberget, 30 November 1947, Brevs. 434, NLN. Author's translation from Norwegian.
6 Lie to Rolf Andvord, 7 June 1946, PA-1407-D-L0006, NAN. Author's translation from Norwegian.
7 Lie, Introduction, 'Report of the Secretary-General on the Work of the Organization', UN doc. A/65, 30 June 1946.
8 Trygve Lie, 'A Community of Nations – Plans for a Lasting Peace after Victory – The Bankruptcy of Neutrality', *The Times* (London), 14 November 1941.
9 *UNCIO*, verbatim minutes, 8th plenary session, 2 May 1945. Reprinted in Cordier and Foote, *Public Papers, Vol. 1: Trygve Lie*, 25–8.; GAOR, 1st session, 9th plenary mtg, 16 January 1946.
10 Lie to Johan Bech-Friis, 18 February 1947, Brevs. 410, NLN. Author's translation from Norwegian.
11 Lie to Hans Amundsen, 23 November 1946, Brevs. 410, NLN. Author's translation from Norwegian.
12 Lie to Rolf Andvord, 7 June 1946, PA-1407-D-L0006, NAN. Author's translation from Norwegian.
13 Lie to Arthur Guinness, 7 June 1946, Brevs. 410, NLN.
14 Lie to Thormod Knutsen, 20 June 1946, Brevs. 410, NLN. Author's translation from Norwegian.
15 Lie, Introduction, 'Report of the Secretary-General on the Work of the Organization', UN doc. A/65, 30 June 1946.
16 Lie to Johan Bech-Friis, 18 February 1947, Brevs. 410, NLN. Author's translation from Norwegian.
17 GAOR, 1st session, 9th plenary mtg, 16 January 1946.
18 Lie to Arthur Guinness, 7 June 1946, Brevs. 410, NLN.
19 Lie address to the Norwegian Students' Association in Oslo, 27 February 1946, PA-1407/D/L0024, NAN. Lie used the same quote in his memoirs to describe the momentous task of setting up the Secretariat, which this book discusses in Chapter 6. See Lie, *In the Cause of Peace*, 54.
20 Lie to Johan Falkberget, 17 September 1946, Brevs. 434, NLN.
21 Lie to Rolf Andvord, 7 June 1946, PA-1407-D-L0006, NAN. Author's translation from Norwegian.
22 Lie to Johan Falkberget, 30 November 1947, Brevs. 434, NLN. Author's translation from Norwegian.
23 Lie to Johan Falkberget, 8 December 1948, Brevs. 434, NLN. Author's translation from Norwegian.
24 Gaddis, *United States and the Origins of the Cold War*, 317–18.
25 President Harry S. Truman's address before a Joint Session of Congress, 12 March 1947, http://avalon.law.yale.edu/20th_century/trudoc.asp (accessed 21 December 2021).
26 Lie, *In the Cause of Peace*, 104–5.
27 Minutes of meeting, 19 March 1947, S-0194-0003-04, UNA.
28 President Harry S. Truman's address before a Joint Session of Congress, 12 March 1947, http://avalon.law.yale.edu/20th_century/trudoc.asp (accessed 21 December 2021).
29 Minutes of meeting, 19 March 1947, S-0194-0003-04, UNA.
30 'The Marshall Plan Speech', 5 June 1947, http://marshallfoundation.org/marshall/the-marshall-plan/marshall-plan-speech/ (accessed 21 December 2021).

31 *UN Yearbook 1946–47*, 483–4. The members of ECE in May 1947 were Belgium, Byelorussian SSR, Czechoslovakia, Denmark, France, Greece, Luxembourg, Netherlands, Norway, Poland, Sweden, Turkey, Ukrainian SSR, USSR, the UK, the US, and Yugoslavia.
32 Transcript of SG press conference, 13 June 1947, UNDHL.
33 Transcript of SG press conference, 19 June 1947, UNDHL.
34 Barros, *Trygve Lie*, 124.
35 Kennan to Acheson, with recommendation of the policy planning staff, 23 May 1947, *FRUS 1947*, III, 227–8.
36 'Summary of discussion on problems of relief, rehabilitation and reconstruction of Europe', 29 May 1947, *FRUS 1947*, III, 234–6.
37 Kennan to Acheson, with recommendation of the policy planning staff, 23 May 1947, and 'Summary of discussion on problems of relief, rehabilitation and reconstruction of Europe', 29 May 1947, *FRUS 1947*, III, 227–8, 234–6.
38 Hitchcock, 'Marshall Plan', 157.
39 Eisenberg, *Drawing the Line*, 323.
40 Leffler, *For the Soul of Mankind*, 65–6; Hopf, *Reconstructing the Cold War*, 3.
41 Naimark, 'Sovietization of Eastern Europe', 189.
42 Transcript of SG press conference, 25 June 1947, UNDHL.
43 Cadogan to FO, 3 July 1947, FO 371/62405, UKNA.
44 Barros, *Trygve Lie*, 128; Dølvik, 'Sovjetunionen og FNs første generalsekretær', 78–9.
45 Lie, Introduction, 'Annual report of the Secretary-General on the Work of the Organization', UN doc. A/565, 5 July 1948.
46 Lie, 'Trygve Lie Appraises the Future of the U.N. – It is strained by the East-West conflict but it remains the essential agency for peace', *New York Times*, 9 May 1948.
47 Lie to Jens Halvard Bratz, [30 November] 1947. Letter in the Bratz family's possession. Copy provided by Guri Hjeltnes. Author's translation from Norwegian.
48 Lie, Introduction, 'Annual report of the Secretary-General on the Work of the Organization', UN doc. A/565, 5 July 1948.
49 Lie to Jens Halvard Bratz, [30 November] 1947. Letter in the Bratz family's possession. Copy provided by Guri Hjeltnes. Author's translation from Norwegian.
50 For more on Lie's opposition to the formation of NATO, see Barros, *Trygve Lie*, 156–65.
51 Minutes of mtg, 28 June 1948, S-0194-0003-06, UNA.
52 UN Charter, Article 107: 'Nothing in the present Charter shall invalidate or preclude action, in relation to any state which during the Second World War has been an enemy of any signatory to the present Charter, taken or authorized as a result of that war by the Governments having responsibility for such action.'
53 Minutes of mtg, 29 June 1948, S-0194-0003-06, UNA.
54 FO to Cadogan, 30 June 1948, FO 371/70497, UKNA.
55 Transcript of UNSG press conference, 15 July 1948, UNDHL.
56 Sargent note on conversation with Lie, 4 August 1948, FO 371/72677, UKNA.
57 'Identical notification from the governments of the French Republic, the United States of America and the United Kingdom to the Secretary-General', UN doc. S/1020, 29 September 1948.
58 Jessup, 'Berlin Blockade', 168. See also Jessup memo of conversation with Marshall, Douglas and Rusk, 27 September 1948, *FRUS 1948*, II, 1193–4.
59 Lie, *In the Cause of Peace*, 202.
60 SCOR, 3rd year, 362nd mtg, 5 October 1948.
61 The six 'neutrals' were the states on the Council that were not directly involved in Berlin: Argentina, Belgium, Canada, China, Colombia, and Syria.
62 SCOR, 3rd year, 370th mtg, 22 October 1948.
63 Harrington, *Berlin on the Brink*, 197–8.

NOTES

64. Jessup, 'Berlin Blockade', 170; Harrington, *Berlin on the Brink*, 1989.
65. SCOR, 3rd year, 372nd mtg, 25 October 1948.
66. Lie to Sissel Bratz, 27 October 1948. Letter in the Bratz family's possession. Copy provided by Guri Hjeltnes. Author's translation from Norwegian.
67. For more on the secretary-general's use of special representatives in general, see Fröhlich, 'Special Representatives'.
68. Lie, Berlin note #1, 29 October 1948, PA-1407/D/L0014, NAN.
69. Jessup, 'Berlin Blockade', 172.
70. Lie, Berlin note #1, 29 October 1948, PA-1407/D/L0014, NAN.
71. Lie, Berlin note #3, 29 October 1948, PA-1407/D/L0014, NAN.
72. Lie, Berlin note #4, 31 October 1948, PA-1407/D/L0014, NAN.
73. Lie, Berlin note #5, 2 November 1948, PA-1407/D/L0014, NAN.
74. Lie, *In the Cause of Peace*, 211.
75. Lie, Berlin note #5, 2 November 1948, PA-1407/D/L0014, NAN; FO telegram to Cadogan, 4 November 1948, FO 371/70520, UKNA.
76. Cadogan to FO, 3 November 1948, FO 371/70520, UKNA.
77. FO telegram to Cadogan, 4 November 1948, FO 371/70520, UKNA. See also Harrington, *Berlin on the Brink*; Jessup, 'Berlin Blockade'.
78. Lie, Berlin note #7, 10 November 1948, PA-1407/D/L0014, NAN.
79. Lie, Berlin note #8, 11 November 1948, PA-1407/D/L0014, NAN.
80. Thomas J. Hamilton, 'New Compromises Drafted to Settle the Berlin Crisis – Lie and Bramuglia Preparing Proposals as Time Grows Short for Getting the Issue before the U.N. Assembly', *New York Times*, 9 November 1948.
81. UN press release P/PM/142, 9 November 1948, PA-1407/D/L0014, NAN.
82. Lie, *In the Cause of Peace*, 212.
83. Lie, Berlin note #7, 10 November 1948, PA-1407/D/L0014, NAN.
84. Lie to Hjørdis and Mette, 10 November 1948, PA-1407/D/L0014, NAN.
85. Simultaneously Evatt also sent the appeal directly to the four heads of government. See Evatt identical telegrams to Truman, Attlee, Queueille, and Stalin, 13 November 1948, box 129, folder 7, CCC.
86. General Assembly resolution 190 (III), 3 November 1948.
87. Lie and Evatt to Marshall, 13 November 1948, PA-1407/D/L0014, NAN.
88. Shlaim, *United States and the Berlin Blockade*, 371.
89. Harrington, *Berlin on the Brink*, 200–1.
90. Lie to Hjørdis and Mette, 15 November 1949, PA-1407/D/L0014, NAN.
91. Dons to MFA, 15 November 1948, RA/S-2259/Dye/L10917, NAN. Author's translation from Norwegian.
92. Lie, Berlin note #9, 16 November 1948, PA-1407/D/L0014, NAN.
93. Camille M. Cianfarra, 'Parlay Soon Asked – Letter Asserts Failure to Reach Agreement Will Endanger Peace – Marshall Plans Reply – British Cool to Proposal – French are Noncommittal – Bramuglia Hails Move', *New York Times*, 14 November 1948.
94. Vyshinsky to Evatt and Lie, 16 November 1948, box 129, folder 7, CCC.
95. Lie to Hjørdis and Mette, 19 November 1948, PA-1407/D/L0014, NAN.
96. Lie, *In the Cause of Peace*, 88.
97. Paus to MFA, 14 February 1949, RA/S-2259/Dye/L10917, NAN.
98. Harrington, *Berlin on the Brink*, 209.
99. See Jessup's own account in Jessup, 'Park Avenue Diplomacy'.
100. The value of the UN as a 'concert' is explored in detail by Bosco, *Five to Rule Them All*.
101. Bosco, 'Assessing the UN Security Council', 554.
102. Harrington, *Berlin on the Brink*, 185.

103 For more on the secretary-general's actions in Korea, see also Barnes, 'Chief Administrator or Political Moderator'.
104 Oral history interview with John D. Hickerson, 1972–3, TPL.
105 Lie, *In the Cause of Peace*, 327–8.
106 SCOR, 5th year, 473rd mtg, 25 June 1950.
107 Cordier and Foote, *Public papers, vol. 1: Trygve Lie*, 20.
108 Chesterman, 'Article 99', 2016.
109 Lie, *In the Cause of Peace*, 333.
110 Reminiscences of Ernest A. Gross (13 January 1965), 569–72, CCOHC.
111 Lie, *In the Cause of Peace*, 329.
112 Security Council resolution 83, 27 June 1950.
113 Text reprinted in *FRUS 1950*, VII, 221n.
114 Memorandum of conversation (Holmes, Ordonneau, Ross, Hyde), 18 July 1950, *FRUS 1950*, VII, 416.
115 Memorandum of conversation (Ross, Hickerson), 28 June 1950, *FRUS 1950*, VII, 221–2.
116 Cordier to Gross, Sunde, Jebb, and Chauvel, 3 July 1950, PA-1407/D/L0030, NAN.
117 Security Council resolution 84, 7 July 1950.
118 Lie, *In the Cause of Peace*, 329.
119 Gaiduk, *Divided Together*, 166.
120 Reminiscences of Ernest A. Gross (13 January 1965), 569, CCOHC.
121 Lie, *In the Cause of Peace*, 323.
122 Lie to Johan Falkberget, 30 November 1947, Brevs. 434, NLN. Author's translation from Norwegian.

Chapter 5

1 Prepared statement before SG press conference, 10 February 1950, UNDHL.
2 Rushton, 'UN Secretary-General and Norm Entrepreneurship'; Johnstone, 'Secretary-General as norm entrepreneur'; Ravndal, 'A Force for Peace'.
3 United Nations, 'The role of the Secretary-General', https://www.un.org/sg/en/content/the-role-of-the-secretary-general (accessed 13 December 2021).
4 1 for 7 billion, 'This is important', https://www.1for7billion.org/why (accessed 7 April 2022).
5 Ravndal, 'A Force for Peace'.
6 Lie, *In the Cause of Peace*, 88.
7 Holloway, 'Nuclear weapons'; Krepon, *Winning and Losing*.
8 General Assembly resolution 494(V), 20 November 1950.
9 Ravndal, 'A Force for Peace'; Ravndal, 'A Guardian of the UN Charter'; Trinh, 'The bully pulpit'.
10 Weart, *Rise of Nuclear Fear*, 57.
11 Holloway, 'Nuclear weapons'.
12 Kearn, 'Baruch Plan', 43–4.
13 Krepon, *Winning and Losing*, 17.
14 Goedde, *Politics of Peace*, 68.
15 Bartel, 'Surviving the Years of Grace'; Goedde, *Politics of Peace*; Krepon, *Winning and Losing*; Kearn, 'Baruch Plan'.
16 *UN Yearbook 1946–47*, 445.
17 General Assembly resolution 1(I), 24 January 1946.
18 Krepon, *Winning and Losing*, 28–9; Roehrlich, 'Negotiating Verification'.

NOTES

[19] 'The Baruch Plan', text available at https://www.atomicarchive.com/resources/documents/deterrence/baruch-plan.html (accessed 20 December 2021).
[20] *UN Yearbook 1946–47*, 445.
[21] Prepared statement attached to transcript of SG press conference, 3 February 1950, UNDHL.
[22] On 15 November 1949 the Peking government sent a letter to the president of the General Assembly to protest that the Nationalist Chinese delegation at the Assembly did not legally represent the Chinese people. The Soviet Union gave its support to the Peking government's letter in the plenary debate on 23 November. See GAOR, 4th session, 253rd plenary mtg, 23 November 1949.
[23] SCOR, 4th year, 458th mtg, 29 December 1949.
[24] SCOR, 5th year, 461st mtg, 13 January 1950.
[25] Price memorandum conversation Lie, Acheson, Webb, Rusk, Hickerson, 21 January 1950, PA-1407/D/L0029, NAN.
[26] The five states which had recognized the PRC were Britain, India, Norway, the USSR, and Yugoslavia. The fact that Britain and Norway had recognized the PRC indicates that this was not a straightforward East–West conflict.
[27] 'Legal aspects of problems of representation in the United Nations', February 1950, S/1466, 9 March 1950.
[28] Lie, *In the Cause of Peace*, 253–4.
[29] Lie focused his efforts on France, and also hoped to be able to persuade Egypt or one of the Latin American states to vote in favour of seating the communist Chinese.
[30] Lie, *In the Cause of Peace*, 258.
[31] Ibid, 262.
[32] Ibid, 272.
[33] 'The resumption of East-West Negotiations in the United Nations', 7 March 1950, PA-1407/D/L0029, NAN.
[34] Ibid.
[35] Lie, *In the Cause of Peace*, 262.
[36] Address by Secretary-General Trygve Lie at the National Convention of B'nai B'rith, Hotel Statler, Washington DC, 21 March 1950, PA-1407/D/L0025, NAN.
[37] 'Memorandum of Points for Consideration in the Development of a Twenty-Year Program for Achieving Peace Through the United Nations', available in Cordier and Foote, *Public Papers, vol. 1: Trygve Lie*, 296–303.
[38] Ibid.
[39] 'The Resumption of East-West Negotiations in the United Nations', 7 March 1950, PA-1407/D/L0029, NAN.
[40] Gjesdal to Lie, 29 March 1950, PA-1407/D/L0029, NAN.
[41] Cordier and Foote, *Public Papers, vol. 1: Trygve Lie*, 296.
[42] Lie, *In the Cause of Peace*, 283–316.
[43] The ACC was set up by ECOSOC in 1946. The Committee is chaired by the secretary-general and brings together the directors of the UN's funds, programmes, and specialized agencies. Its first task was to supervise the implementation of relationship agreements with the specialized agencies, some of which like the ILO and ITU had been in operation for decades before the UN was founded, and then to coordinate the policies and programmes of the various UN organizations. In 2001 the ACC was renamed the UN System Chief Executives Board for Coordination (CEB). See http://www.unsceb.org/ (accessed 21 December 2021).
[44] Gjesdal to Lie, 29 March 1950, PA-1407/D/L0029, NAN.
[45] Ibid.
[46] Cordier and Foote, *Public Papers, Vol. 1: Trygve Lie*, 281–2.

47 UN press release ORG/135, 4 May 1950, PA-1407/D/L0029, NAN.
48 Lie letter to Hjørdis, Guri, and Mette Lie, and Sissel, Jens-Halvard, and Ragnvald Bratz, 6 May 1950. Letter in the Bratz family's possession. Copy provided by Guri Hjeltnes. Author's translation from Norwegian.
49 General Assembly resolution 494 (V), 20 November 1950.
50 Cordier and Foote, *Public Papers, vol. 1: Trygve Lie*, 362. The nine sponsoring countries were Canada, Chile, Colombia, Haiti, Lebanon, Pakistan, the Philippines, Sweden, and Yugoslavia. Individual votes were not recorded, but the five opposing votes are likely to have been the Soviet bloc (the USSR, Ukraine, Belarus, Czechoslovakia, and Poland), while the abstaining state was likely Nationalist China in protest against Lie's position on the Chinese representation issue.
51 'Brief on Mr. Trygve Lie's proposal for a special meeting of the Security Council', 24 April 1950, FO 371/88391, UKNA.
52 Lie letter to Hjørdis, Guri, and Mette Lie, and Sissel, Jens-Halvard, and Ragnvald Bratz, 6 May 1950. Letter in the Bratz family's possession. Copy provided by Guri Hjeltnes; Lie letter to Halvard Lange, 3 May 1950, PA-1407/D/L0029, NAN.
53 Lie to Halvard Lange, 3 May 1950, PA-1407/D/L0029, NAN.
54 Lie letter to Hjørdis, Guri, and Mette Lie, and Sissel, Jens-Halvard, and Ragnvald Bratz, 6 May 1950. Letter in the Bratz family's possession. Copy provided by Guri Hjeltnes.
55 Neal to Hickerson, 14 June 1950, with attached memo on Lie's visit Paris, 10 May 1950, folder 11, box 1, RG 59 Bureau of UN Affairs, NARA.
56 Lie note on meeting with Schuman, 20 May 1950, PA-1407/D/L0029, NAN.
57 Acheson memo conversation Truman and Lie, 20 April 1950, *FRUS 1950*, II, 371–3; Price note on Lie's meeting with Truman and Acheson, 20 April 1950, PA-1407/D/L0029, NAN; Price note on Lie's meeting with Truman, Acheson, and Hickerson, 29 May 1950, PA-1407/D/L0029, NAN; Hickerson memo conversation Acheson, Lie and Price, 29 May 1950, *FRUS 1950*, II, 379–83.
58 Acheson statement on Lie's report, US State Dept press release no. 599, 7 June 1950, FO 371/88939, UKNA.
59 Ibid.
60 Lie note on meeting with Stalin, Molotov, and Vyshinsky, 15 May 1950, PA-1407/D/L0029, NAN; Lie, *In the Cause of Peace*, 297–303.
61 GAOR, 5th session, 309th plenary mtg, 18 November 1950.
62 ' "United or Not?" Transcript of Radio-Press Conference on the Korean Crisis and Twenty-Year Peace Program', 26 June 1950, Cordier and Foote, *Public Papers, vol. 1: Trygve Lie*, 315–22.
63 Lie, *In the Cause of Peace*, 319.
64 Lie letter to Hjørdis, Guri, and Mette Lie, and Sissel, Jens-Halvard, and Ragnvald Bratz, 6 May 1950. Letter in the Bratz family's possession. Copy provided by Guri Hjeltnes. Author's translation from Norwegian.
65 Einstein to Lie, 18 April 1950, PA-1407/D/L0029, NAN.
66 Lie letter to Hjørdis, Guri, and Mette Lie, and Sissel, Jens-Halvard, and Ragnvald Bratz, 6 May 1950. Letter in the Bratz family's possession. Copy provided by Guri Hjeltnes.
67 UN press release SG/102, 23 June 1950, PA-1407/D/L0029, NAN.
68 General Assembly resolution 11 (I), 24 January 1946. See also Report of the Preparatory Commission of the United Nations, PC/20, 23 December 1945, 81.
69 Quoted in Gaiduk, *Divided Together*, 178.
70 Lie, *In the Cause of Peace*, 370–1.
71 As indicated by two memorandums written by Arkadij Sobolev and Aleksej Rostsjin in April 1950 referred to by Dølvik, ' Sovjetunionen og FNs første generalsekretær', 194–6; and Gaiduk, *Divided Together*, 177. Lie also reports that Vyshinksy confirmed to him

during their meeting in May 1950 that the Soviet Union would support his re-election. See Mrs Berntzen's note of lunch between Lie and Vyshinsky, 15 May 1950, PA-1407/D/L0029, NAN; Lie, *In the Cause of Peace*, 368.
72. Cadogan to Jebb, 11 August 1949, FO 371/78794, UKNA.
73. McNeill minute, 1 September 1949, FO 371/78794, UKNA.
74. Hall comment on memorandum of conversation with Aghnides, 23 May 1949, folder 7, box 16, USUN 1030E, NARA.
75. Salt to Jebb, 1 October 1949, FO 371/78794, UKNA.
76. UN Press Release SG/29, 16 December 1949, UNDHL.
77. Jebb to Dixon, 10 July 1950, FO 371/88448, UKNA.
78. Parrott minute, 2 June 1950, FO 371/88391, UKNA.
79. General Assembly resolution 492 (V), 1 November 1950.
80. Draft position paper, 18 April 1950, *FRUS 1950*, II, 87–9.
81. Lie note, 'The appointment as Secretary-General', November 1950, PA-1407/D/L0013, NAN.
82. 'Minutes of meeting on President Truman's Train, New York', 24 October 1950, *FRUS 1950*, III, 158–9.
83. Lie, *In the Cause of Peace*, 375, 85.
84. Summary record of 510th mtg of the Security Council, 12 October 1950, PA-1407/D/L0013, NAN.
85. 'Minutes of meeting on President Truman's Train, New York', 24 October 1950, *FRUS 1950*, III, 158–9. Italic in original.
86. General Assembly resolution 492 (V), 1 November 1950.
87. Lie, *In the Cause of Peace*, 385.
88. General Assembly resolution 377 (V), 3 November 1950.
89. Austin letter to Lie, 7 November 1950, PA-1407/D/L0013, NAN.
90. Gaiduk, *Divided Together*, 197.
91. Memcon (Meade, Hickerson, Allen), 26 February 1952, *FRUS 1952–54*, III, 1.
92. GAOR, 5th session, 296th mtg, 31 October 1950.
93. Lie, *In the Cause of Peace*, 408.
94. Ibid, 385.
95. Ravndal, 'A Force for Peace', 452–4.
96. Johnstone, 'Secretary-General as norm entrepreneur'.
97. Ravndal, 'A Guardian of the UN Charter'.
98. Lie, *In the Cause of Peace*, 88.
99. Kille, 'Moral Authority', 11.

Chapter 6
1. Report of the Preparatory Commission of the United Nations, UN Doc. PC/20, 23 December 1945, 87.
2. Newman and Ravndal, 'International Civil Service', 165–6.
3. Ibid, 166–9.
4. Thant and Scott, *UN Secretariat*, 6.
5. Gram-Skjoldager and Ikonomou, 'Making of the International Civil Servant', 226.
6. Muldoon and Ravndal, 'Lie, Trygve Halvdan'.
7. Lie, *Oslo – Moskva – London*, 46–47; Amundsen, *Trygve Lie*, 60–70.
8. Lie and Hansteen, *Den nye arbeidstvistlov*.
9. Furre, *Norsk Historie 1914–2000*, 54–8.
10. Lie, *In the Cause of Peace*, 44.

11. Ibid, 52–3.
12. Urquhart, 'Evolution of the Secretary-General', 18.
13. SCOR, 1st year, 24th mtg, 25 March 1946.
14. Lie letter to Halvard Lange, 29 April 1946, Brevs. 410, NLN.
15. Thant and Scott, *UN Secretariat*, 16.
16. Lie, *In the Cause of Peace*, 42.
17. Thant and Scott, *UN Secretariat*, 3.
18. Lie, *In the Cause of Peace*, 43.
19. Report of the Preparatory Commission of the United Nations, UN Doc. PC/20, 23 December 1945, 81–94. See also Thant and Scott, *UN Secretariat*, 5.
20. Report of the Preparatory Commission of the United Nations, UN Doc. PC/20, 23 December 1945, 81.
21. Lie, *In the Cause of Peace*, 42–3.
22. Ibid, 54.
23. Gordenker, *UN Secretary-General and Secretariat*, 14.
24. Hjeltnes, 'McCarthyismens inntog i FN', 43.
25. Barros, *Trygve Lie*, 311.
26. 'Statement by the Assistant Secretary-General for Administrative and Financial Services', 23 December 1952, annex 1 to 'Report of the Secretary-General on Personnel Policy', UN Doc. A/2364, 30 January 1953.
27. Barros, *Trygve Lie*, 312.
28. Quoted in ibid, 58.
29. Lie, *In the Cause of Peace*, 54.
30. Laugier to Lie and ASGs, 8 April 1946, S-0184-0001-09, UN ARMS.
31. Ibid.
32. Ibid.
33. Jordan, 'Fluctuating fortunes'.
34. Lie letter to Rolf Andvord, 7 June 1946, PA-1407/D/L0006, NAN.
35. Lie, *In the Cause of Peace*, 65–7.
36. SCOR, 1st year, 24th mtg, 25 March 1946.
37. Lie, *In the Cause of Peace*, 68–9.
38. Mires, *Capital of the World*, 179–80.
39. Barros, *Trygve Lie*, 59.
40. Lie letters to Thormod Knutsen, 20 June 1946, and to Sven Arntzen, 16 September 1946, both in Brevs. 410, NLN.
41. Lie letter to Arthur Guinness, 7 June 1946, Brevs. 410, NLN.
42. Lie, *In the Cause of Peace*, 108.
43. Lie letter to Thormod Knutson, 20 June 1946, Brevs. 410, NLN. Author's translation from Norwegian.
44. 'Summary Report of Twenty-Ninth Meeting of Committee I/2', 17 June 1945, *UNCIO*, VII, 277–81. See also discussion of the San Francisco conference in Chapter 1 of this book.
45. General Assembly resolution 13 (I), 13 February 1946.
46. Gordenker, *UN Secretary-General and Secretariat*, 14.
47. Lie, *In the Cause of Peace*, 45.
48. Barros, *Trygve Lie*, 64.
49. Urquhart, *A Life in Peace and War*, 103.
50. Lie, *In the Cause of Peace*, 51.
51. Ibid, 48–50.
52. Ibid, 47.
53. Ibid, 48.
54. Ibid, 46–7.

55 Ibid, 47.
56 Gladwyn Jebb, quoted in Barros, *Trygve Lie*, 59.
57 Brian E. Urquhart, 'Character Sketches: Trygve Lie', in *UN News* (n.d.) https://news.un.org/en/spotlight/character-sketches-trygve-lie-brian-urquhart (accessed 28 March 2022).
58 Lie to Johan Bech-Friis, 18 February 1947, Brevs. 410, NLN. Author's translation from Norwegian.
59 Lie, *In the Cause of Peace*, 51.
60 'Summary Report of Twenty-Ninth Meeting of Committee I/2', 17 June 1945, *UNCIO*, VII, 277–81.
61 Lie, *In the Cause of Peace*, 51.
62 Urquhart, 'Character Sketches: Trygve Lie'.
63 Lie letter to Halvard Lange, 29 April 1946, Brevs. 410, NLN.
64 Lie, *In the Cause of Peace*, 48.
65 Urquhart, *A Life in Peace and War*, 104.
66 For more details about Bunche's long career at the UN, see Urquhart, *Ralph Bunche*.
67 General Assembly resolution 13 (I), 13 February 1946.
68 Stevenson to Stoneman, 3 February 1947, S-0184-0001-09, UNARMS.
69 Ibid.
70 Barros, *Trygve Lie*, 60.
71 Ibid, 60–1.
72 Thant and Scott, *UN Secretariat*, 16.
73 Barros, *Trygve Lie*, 203.
74 Lie, *In the Cause of Peace*, 52.
75 Thant and Scott, *UN Secretariat*, 27–30.
76 For a full account of these campaigns, see Mires, *Capital of the World*.
77 Lie, *In the Cause of Peace*, 62.
78 Ibid, 57–8.
79 Ibid, 64.
80 General Assembly resolution 25(I), 14 February 1946.
81 Quoted in Mires, *Capital of the World*, 145.
82 Lie, *In the Cause of Peace*, 62–3; Mires, *Capital of the World*.
83 General Assembly resolution 25(I), 14 February 1946.
84 Mires, *Capital of the World*, 185.
85 Statement by Arthur Vandenberg of US delegation, quoted in ibid, 171.
86 Hanlon, *A Worldly Affair*, 32–3; Mires, *Capital of the World*, 181–2.
87 Mires, *Capital of the World*, 182.
88 Lie, *In the Cause of Peace*, 71–3; Mires, *Capital of the World*, 182.
89 Lie, *In the Cause of Peace*, 72.
90 Lie, *In the Cause of Peace*, 109–10; Mires, *Capital of the World*, 185–203.
91 Mires, *Capital of the World*, 208.
92 Dudley, *Workshop for Peace*, 21.
93 Lie, *In the Cause of Peace*, 111–14; Dudley, *Workshop for Peace*, 22–3; Mires, *Capital of the World*, 210–18; Hanlon, *A Worldly Affair*, 45–51.
94 Mires, *Capital of the World*, 210–11; Hanlon, *A Worldly Affair*, 47–48.
95 Hanlon, *A Worldly Affair*, 51; Mires, *Capital of the World*, 217–18; Lie, *In the Cause of Peace*, 113–14.
96 General Assembly resolution 100 (I), 14 December 1946.
97 GAOR, 1st session, 65th mtg, 14 December 1946.
98 General Assembly resolution 100 (I), 14 December 1946.

99. Hanlon, *A Worldly Affair*, 54.
100. Lie, *In the Cause of Peace*, 115.
101. Dudley, *Workshop for Peace*, 3.
102. Lie, *In the Cause of Peace*, 115; Dudley, *Workshop for Peace*, 2–3.
103. Hanlon, *A Worldly Affair*, 54; Dudley, *Workshop for Peace*, 43.
104. Detailed accounts of these mtgs are available in Dudley, *Workshop for Peace*.
105. Quoted in Hanlon, *A Worldly Affair*, 59.
106. Hanlon, *A Worldly Affair*, 60; Dudley, *Workshop for Peace*.
107. All quoted in Dudley, *Workshop for Peace*, 117–18.
108. Ibid.
109. Ibid, 234–6.
110. Niemeyer quoted in ibid, 234.
111. Ibid, 251–2.
112. Hanlon, *A Worldly Affair*, 65.
113. Quoted in ibid, 69.
114. Quoted in ibid, 70.
115. Lie, *In the Cause of Peace*, 118.
116. General Assembly resolution 182 (II), 20 November 1947.
117. Lie, *In the Cause of Peace*, 120; Hanlon, *A Worldly Affair*, 67.
118. Lie, *In the Cause of Peace*, 120; Hanlon, *A Worldly Affair*, 67; Mires, *Capital of the World*, 1.
119. Lie, *In the Cause of Peace*, 120.
120. Ibid, 123.
121. Ibid, 119.
122. Ibid, 114–15.
123. Urquhart, 'Evolution of the Secretary-General', 18.
124. Urquhart, 'Character Sketches: Trygve Lie'.
125. Barros, *Trygve Lie*, 59.
126. Price memorandum for the files, 28 June 1949, PA-1407/D/L0014, NAN.
127. Barros, *Trygve Lie*, 315; Gaiduk, *Divided Together*, n. 28, 230; Hjeltnes, 'McCarthyismens inntog i FN', 37–8.
128. Meisler, *United Nations*, 82.
129. Hjeltnes, 'McCarthyismens inntog i FN', 39.
130. Ibid, 39–40.
131. Ibid, 38–39.
132. Ibid, 41.
133. Quoted in Hazzard, *Countenance of Truth*, 26. See also Luard, *History of the United Nations: Vol 1*, 356; Gaiduk, *Divided Together*, 202.
134. Barros, *Trygve Lie*, 320.
135. Price memorandum for the files, 28 June 1949, PA-1407/D/L0014, NAN.
136. Lie, 'Statement on Personnel Policy before the General Assembly', 10 March 1953, reprinted in Cordier and Foote, *Public Papers, Vol. 1: Trygve Lie*, 488–504.
137. Barros, *Trygve Lie*, 319.
138. General Assembly resolution 708 (VII), 1 April 1953. Italic in original.
139. Lie to Pearson, 10 November 1952. Letter quoted in full in GAOR, 7th session, 392nd plenary mtg, 10 November 1952.
140. Cordier and Foote, *Public Papers, vol. 1: Trygve Lie*, 483; Lie, *In the Cause of Peace*, 406–7, 12.
141. Memocon (Hickerson, Malik, Ludlow), 17 November 1952, *FRUS 1952–54*, III, 430.
142. Terje Wold to Lie, 12 November 1952, Brevs. 410, NLN. Author's translation from Norwegian.
143. Lie to Sissel Bratz, November 1952. Letter quoted in Lie, *In the Cause of Peace*, 414.

144 GAOR, 7th session, 392nd plenary mtg, 10 November 1952.
145 Ibid.
146 Lie to Sverre Iversen, 16 December 1952, Brevs. 410, NLN. Author's translation from Norwegian.
147 Lie, *In the Cause of Peace*, 411.
148 Lie to Johan Falkberget, 12 December 1952, Brevs. 434, NLN. Author's translation from Norwegian.
149 Lie to Sverre Iversen, 16 December 1952, Brevs. 410, NLN. Author's translation from Norwegian.
150 GAOR, 7th session, 392nd plenary mtg, 10 November 1952.
151 Ibid.
152 Lie, 'Statement on Personnel Policy before the General Assembly', 10 March 1953, reprinted in Cordier and Foote, *Public Papers, vol. 1: Trygve Lie*, 488–504.
153 Lie to Gunnar Jahn, 19 November 1952, Brevs. 410, NLN. Author's translation from Norwegian.
154 Lie to Sverre Iversen, 16 December 1952, Brevs. 410, NLN. Author's translation from Norwegian.
155 Lie to Oscar Torp, 16 December 1952, Brevs. 410, NLN. Author's translation from Norwegian.
156 Hjeltnes, 'McCarthyismens inntog i FN', 49.
157 Entezam (Iran), GAOR, 7th session, 423rd plenary mtg, 7 April 1953.
158 Belaunde (Peru), ibid.
159 Lie letter to Johan Falkberget, 22 April 1953, Brevs. 410, NLN. Author's translation from Norwegian.
160 As told by Hammarskjöld in 'Statement by Secretary-General Dag Hammarskjöld at a General Meeting of the Staff', UN Press Release SG/299, 1 May 1953, UNDHL.
161 Thant and Scott, *UN Secretariat*, 16–17.
162 Pérez de Cuéllar, 'Role of the UN Secretary-General', 137.
163 Hazzard, *Countenance of Truth*, 28.
164 Weiss, 'International Bureaucracy'; Udom, 'International Civil Service'; Newman, 'International Civil Service'; Sending, 'International Civil Servant'.
165 Gram-Skjoldager and Ikonomou, 'Making of the International Civil Servant', 226.
166 Barros, *Trygve Lie*, 59–60.

Conclusion

1 GAOR, 15th session, 883rd plenary mtg, 3 October 1960.
2 Lie, *In the Cause of Peace*, 42.
3 Urquhart, 'Evolution of the Secretary-General', 18.
4 Ibid.
5 Lie, *In the Cause of Peace*, 323.
6 GAOR, 7th session, 423rd plenary mtg, 7 April 1953.
7 Akinrade quoted in Kille and Scully, 'Executive Heads', 178.
8 Chesterman, 'Article 99,' 2014–15. For a more generous reading and slightly longer list, see Loraine Sievers and Sam Daws, 'How many times have Secretaries-General acted under Article 99 of the Charter?' *Update Website of the Procedure of the UN Security Council*, 4th edn, 4 September 2017, https://www.scprocedure.org/chapter-3-section-10b (accessed 11 April 2022).
9 Fröhlich, 'The John Holmes Memorial Lecture', 171–2.
10 Ibid, 172–4.
11 Chesterman, 'Article 99', 2012.

12 Lie, *In the Cause of Peace*, 333.
13 Ibid, 42.
14 Barros, *Trygve Lie*, 341; Urquhart, *Hammarskjöld*, 27.
15 Lie to Leif Kr. Tobiassen, 12 October 1961, Brevs. 410, NLN. Author's translation from Norwegian. See also the same sentiment expressed in letter to Hans Olav, 13 October 1961, ibid.
16 Tharoor, 'The Role of the Secretary-General', 147.
17 Urquhart, 'Evolution of the Secretary-General', 19.
18 Stahn and Melber, 'Human security and ethics', 2–3.
19 Ravndal, 'Secretaries-General and Crisis Management'.
20 Guéhenno, 'The Peacekeeper', 187.
21 Fröhlich, 'The Suez Story', 335. See also Skjelsbæk and Fermann, 'UN Secretary-General', 97–8.
22 Cockayne and Malone, 'Relations with the Security Council', 72. See also Urquhart, *Hammarskjöld*, 100–5.
23 Fröhlich, *Political Ethics*, 132.
24 Dorn and Pauk, 'Unsung Mediator'; Firestone, 'Failed Mediation'; Firestone, 'U Thant'.
25 Firestone, 'U Thant', 71.
26 Meisler, *United Nations*, 195.
27 Schroeder, 'Executive Leadership', 351.
28 Urquhart, 'Evolution of the Secretary-General', 26.
29 Meisler, *Kofi Annan*, 37–8.
30 Ibid, 38.
31 de Soto, 'Javier Pérez de Cuéllar'.
32 Adebajo, 'Pope, pharaoh, or prophet', 156.
33 Rushton, 'UN Secretary-General and Norm Entrepreneurship'.
34 Annan and Mousavizadeh, *Interventions*, 138.
35 The Elders, 'Kofi Annan', https://theelders.org/profile/kofi-annan (accessed 5 April 2022).
36 Johnstone, 'Secretary-General as norm entrepreneur', 131–7.
37 Adebajo, 'Pope, pharaoh, or prophet', 143.
38 Gowan, 'Ban Ki-moon', 195.
39 Terlingen, 'A Better Process, a Stronger UN Secretary-General'.
40 Anne Marie Goetz, 'Why Is There Still No Woman at the UN Helm?', *IPI Global Observatory*, 7 October 2016, https://theglobalobservatory.org/2016/10/antonio-guterres-united-nations-secretary-general-gender-equality/ (accessed 6 April 2022); Anna Samya Sri, 'A Huge Missed Opportunity: Putting a Woman at the Top of the UN', *PassBlue*, 9 June 2021, https://www.passblue.com/2021/06/09/a-missed-opportunity-putting-a-woman-at-the-top-of-the-un/ (accessed 6 April 2022).
41 Weiss and Carayannis, 'Windows of opportunity for UN reform', 310.
42 According to the UN High Commissioner for Refugees, 82.4 million people were forcibly displaced at the end of 2020. UNHCR, 'Figures at a glance', https://www.unhcr.org/figures-at-a-glance.html (accessed 6 April 2022).
43 General Assembly resolution ES-11/1, 2 March 2022.
44 1 for 7 billion, 'This is important', https://www.1for7billion.org/why (accessed 7 April 2022).
45 Report of the Preparatory Commission of the United Nations, UN Doc. PC/20, 23 December 1945, 87.
46 United Nations (n.d.), 'The role of the secretary-general', https://www.un.org/sg/en/content/the-role-of-the-secretary-general (accessed 9 September 2022).

References

Archival collections
A collection of letters from Trygve Lie to his daughter Sissel Bratz, now in the possession of Ragnvald Bratz, Oslo. Copies provided by Guri Hjeltnes.

Columbia University, New York
Andrew W. Cordier Collection (CCC)
The Columbia Center for Oral History Collection (CCOHC)

The National Archives of Norway, Oslo (NAN)
PA-1407: Trygve Lie
RA/S-2259: The Ministry of Foreign Affairs

The National Library of Norway, Oslo (NLN)
Brevsamling 410: Trygve Lie
Brevsamling 434: Johan Falkberget

The United Kingdom National Archives, Kew Gardens (UKNA)
CAB: Cabinet papers
FO 371: Foreign Office: Political Departments: General Correspondence, 1906–1966

United Nations Archives and Records Management Section, New York (UNA)
S-0159: Middle East Missions and Commissions, 1948–1960
S-0184: Personnel administration issues, 1946–1961
S-0194: Executive Assistant to the SG (1946–1961: Cordier): Top Official's Meetings – agendas and minutes
S-0615: Palestine Mediator, Dr. Ralph Bunche, 1948–1949

United Nations Dag Hammarskjöld Library, New York (UNDHL)
Minutes of meetings of Security Council's Committee of Experts, 1946
Transcripts of the secretary-general's press conferences, 1946–1953
UN Press releases, 1946–1953

United States National Archive and Records Administration, College Park, MD (NARA)
  RG 59, Department of State, Decimal Files 1945–49, 501.BC, UN Security Council
  RG 59, Bureau of UN Affairs
  RG 59, Rusk-McClintok Papers
  RG 84, United States Mission to the UN:
    1030 E, International organization, subject files
    1030 F, Telegrams

University of California, Los Angeles
  Collection 364: The Brian Urquhart Collection of Material on Ralph Bunche (UCB)

Published primary sources
  US Department of State. *Foreign Relations of the United States*. Washington, DC: US Government Printing Office (FRUS)
  US Department of State. *Postwar Foreign Policy Preparation, 1939–1945*. Washington DC: Government Printing Office, 1950 (PFPP)
  Yogev, Gedalia, Yehoshua Freundlich, Michal Engel, and Yemima Rosenthal, eds. *Political and Diplomatic Documents: December 1947 – May 1948*, Israel State Archives and Central Zionist Archives. Jerusalem, 1979.

United Nations
  Documents of the United Nations Conference of International Organization (UNCIO)
  Economic and Social Council (ECOSOC) resolutions
  General Assembly resolutions
  Official records of the General Assembly (GAOR)
  Official records of the Security Council (SCOR)
  Security Council resolutions
  UN Department of Public Information, *Yearbook of the United Nations* (UN Yearbook)
  UN Oral History Collection (UNOH)
  United Nations Information System on the Question of Palestine (UNISPAL)
  Various documents available through the UN databases on https://digitallibrary.un.org/ and https://documents.un.org/

Harry S. Truman Presidential Library, Independence, Missouri (TPL)
  Oral history interview transcripts, http://www.trumanlibrary.org/oralhist/oral_his.htm

References

Newspapers
Aftenposten (Oslo)
The Guardian
The New York Times
The Times (London)
The Washington Post

Articles and books

Adami, Rebecca and Dan Plesch (eds) (2021) *Women and the UN: A New History of Women's International Human Rights*, London: Routledge.

Adebajo, Adekeye (2007) 'Pope, Pharaoh, or Prophet? The Secretary-General after the Cold War', in Simon Chesterman (ed) *Secretary or General? The UN Secretary-General in World Politics*, Cambridge: Cambridge University Press, pp 139–57.

Amundsen, Hans (1946) *Trygve Lie: Gutten fra Grorud som ble generalsekretær i FN*, Oslo: Tiden Norsk Forlag.

Annan, Kofi A. (2007) 'Foreword', in Simon Chesterman (ed) *Secretary or General? The UN Secretary-General in World Politics*, Cambridge: Cambridge University Press, pp xi–xiii.

Annan, Kofi A. and Nader Mousavizadeh (2012) *Interventions: A Life in War and Peace*, London: Allen Lane.

Ask, Sten and Anna Mark-Jungkvist (eds) (2005) *The Adventure of Peace: Dag Hammarskjöld and the Future of the UN*, Basingstoke: Palgrave Macmillan.

Bailey, Sydney D. and Sam Daws (1998) *The Procedure of the UN Security Council* (3rd edn), Oxford: Oxford University Press.

Barnes, Robert (2019) 'Chief Administrator or Political "Moderator"? Dumbarton Oaks, the Secretary-General and the Korean War', *Journal of Contemporary History* 54(2): 347–67.

Barros, James (1969) *Betrayal from Within: Joseph Avenol, Secretary-General of the League of Nations, 1933–1940*, New Haven and London: Yale University Press.

Barros, James (1977) 'Pearson or Lie: The Politics of the Secretary-General's Selection, 1946', *Canadian Journal of Political Science*, 10(1): 65–92.

Barros, James (1979) *Office without Power: Secretary-General Sir Eric Drummond, 1919–1933*, Oxford: Clarendon Press.

Barros, James (1983) 'The Importance of Secretaries-General of the United Nations', in Robert S. Jordan (ed) *Dag Hammarskjöld Revisited: The UN Secretary-General as a Force in World Politics*, Durham, NC: Carolina Academic Press, pp 25–37.

Barros, James (1989) *Trygve Lie and the Cold War: The UN Secretary-General Pursues Peace, 1946–1953*, DeKalb, IL: Northern Illinois University Press.

Bartel, Fritz (2015) 'Surviving the Years of Grace: The Atomic Bomb and the Specter of World Government, 1945–1950', *Diplomatic History*, 39(2): 275–302.

Bauer, Michael W. and Jörn Ege (2016) 'Bureaucratic Autonomy of International Organizations' Secretariats', *Journal of European Public Policy*, 23(7): 1019–37.

Ben-Dror, Elad (2007) 'The Arab Struggle against Partition: The International Arena of Summer 1947', *Middle Eastern Studies*, 43(2): 259–93.

Ben-Dror, Elad (2008) 'Ralph Bunche and the Establishment of Israel', *Israel Affairs*, 14(3): 519–37.

Ben-Dror, Elad (2012) 'The Armistice Talks between Israel and Jordan, 1949: The View from Rhodes', *Middle Eastern Studies*, 48(6): 879–902.

Ben-Dror, Elad (2014) 'The Success of the Zionist Strategy vis-à-vis UNSCOP', *Israel Affairs*, 20(1): 19–39.

Berger, Peter L. and Thomas Luckmann (1967) *The Social Construction of Reality: A Treatise in the Sociology of Knowledge*, London: Allen Lane.

Bosco, David L. (2009) *Five to Rule Them All: The UN Security Council and the Making of the Modern World*, Oxford: Oxford University Press.

Bosco, David L. (2014) 'Assessing the UN Security Council: A Concert Perspective', *Global Governance*, 20(4): 545–61.

Bourloyannis, M. Christiane (1990) 'Fact-Finding by the Secretary-General of the United Nations', *New York University Journal of International Law and Politics*, 22(4): 641–69.

Caplan, Neil (1997) *Futile Diplomacy, Volume 3: The United Nations, the Great Powers and Middle East Peacemaking, 1948–1954*, London: Frank Cass.

Caplan, Neil (1992) 'A Tale of Two Cities: The Rhodes and Lausanne Conferences, 1949', *Journal of Palestine Studies*, 21(3): 5–34.

Chesterman, Simon (2007) 'Introduction: Secretary or General?', in Simon Chesterman (ed) *Secretary or General? The UN Secretary-General in World Politics*, Cambridge: Cambridge University Press, pp 1–11.

Chesterman, Simon (ed) (2007) *Secretary or General? The UN Secretary-General in World Politics*, Cambridge: Cambridge University Press.

Chesterman, Simon (2012) 'Article 99', in Bruno Simma, Daniel-Erasmus Khan, Georg Nolte, Andreas Paulus, and Nikolai Wessendorf (eds) *The Charter of the United Nations: A Commentary, Volume 2*, Oxford: Oxford University Press, pp 2009–21.

Clavin, Patricia (2013) *Securing the World Economy: The Reinvention of the League of Nations, 1920–1946*, Oxford: Oxford University Press.

Close, David H. (1995) *The Origins of the Greek Civil War*, London: Longman.

Cockayne, James and David M. Malone (2007) 'Relations with the Security Council', in Simon Chesterman (ed) *Secretary or General? The UN Secretary-General in World Politics*, Cambridge: Cambridge University Press, pp 69–85.

Cohen, Michael J. (1982) *Palestine and the Great Powers, 1945–1948*, Princeton: Princeton University Press.

Copelovitch, Mark and Stephanie Rickard (2021) 'Partisan Technocrats: How Leaders Matter in International Organizations', *Global Studies Quarterly*, 1(3): 1–14.

Cordier, Andrew W. and Wilder Foote (eds) (1969) *Public Papers of the Secretaries-General of the United Nations: Vol. 1: Trygve Lie, 1946–1953*, New York: Columbia University Press.

de Soto, Álvaro (2018) 'Javier Pérez de Cuéllar, 1982–1991', in Manuel Fröhlich and Abiodun Williams (eds) *The UN Secretary-General and the Security Council: A Dynamic Relationship*, Oxford: Oxford University Press, pp 116–37.

Debre, Maria Josepha and Hylke Dijkstra (2021) 'Institutional Design for a Post-Liberal Order: Why Some International Organizations Live Longer Than Others', *European Journal of International Relations*, 27(1): 311–39.

Dølvik, Sverre Olav (2002) 'Sovjetunionen og FNs første generalsekretær Trygve Lie, 1946–1951', Hovedoppgave/ MPhil dissertation, University of Oslo.

Dorn, A. Walter and Robert Pauk (2009) 'Unsung Mediator: U Thant and the Cuban Missile Crisis', *Diplomatic History*, 33(2): 261–92.

Dudley, George A. (1994) *A Workshop for Peace: Designing the United Nations Headquarters*, New York and Cambridge, MA: The Architectural History Foundation and the MIT Press.

Eckhard, Steffen and Yves Steinebach (2021) 'Staff Recruitment and Geographical Representation in International Organizations', *International Review of Administrative Sciences*, OnlineFirst.

Ege, Jörn (2020) 'What International Bureaucrats (Really) Want: Administrative Preferences in International Organization Research', *Global Governance*, 26(4): 577–600.

Egeberg, Morten (2006) 'Executive Politics as Usual: Role Behaviour and Conflict Dimensions in the College of European Commissioners', *Journal of European Public Policy*, 13(1): 1–15.

Eilstrup-Sangiovanni, Mette (2018) 'Death of International Organizations: The Organizational Ecology of Intergovernmental Organizations, 1815–2015', *The Review of International Organizations*, 15(2): 339–70.

Eilstrup-Sangiovanni, Mette (2021) 'What Kills International Organisations? When and Why International Organisations Terminate', *European Journal of International Relations*, 27(1): 281–310.

Eisenberg, Carolyn Woods (1996) *Drawing the Line: The American Decision to Divide Germany, 1944–1949*, Cambridge: Cambridge University Press.

Eisenberg, Jaci (2013) 'The Status of Women: A Bridge from the League of Nations to the United Nations', *Journal of International Organizations Studies*, 4(2): 8–24.

Fawcett, Louise (1992) *Iran and the Cold War: The Azerbaijan Crisis of 1946*, Cambridge: Cambridge University Press.
Fawcett, Louise (2014) 'Revisiting the Iranian Crisis of 1946: How Much More Do We Know?', *Iranian Studies*, 47(3): 379–99.
Fiedler, Wilfried (1995) 'Article 99', in Bruno Simma (ed) *The Charter of the United Nations: A Commentary*, München: C.H. Beck, pp 1044–57.
Firestone, Bernard J. (2013) 'Failed Mediation: U Thant, the Johnson Administration, and the Vietnam War', *Diplomatic History*, 37(5): 1060–89.
Firestone, Bernard J. (2018) 'U Thant, 1961–1971', in Manuel Fröhlich and Abiodun Williams (eds) *The UN Secretary-General and the Security Council: A Dynamic Relationship*, Oxford: Oxford University Press, pp 71–93.
Franck, Thomas M. and Georg Nolte (1993) 'The Good Offices Function of the UN Secretary-General', in Adam Roberts and Benedict Kingsbury (eds) *United Nations, Divided World: The UN's Roles in International Relations*, Oxford: Oxford University Press, pp 143–82.
Fröhlich, Manuel (2008) *Political Ethics and the United Nations: Dag Hammarskjöld as Secretary-General*, London and New York: Routledge.
Fröhlich, Manuel (2013) 'The Special Representatives of the United Nations Secretary-General', in Bob Reinalda (ed) *Routledge Handbook of International Organization*, London: Routledge, pp 231–43.
Fröhlich, Manuel (2014) 'The John Holmes Memorial Lecture: Representing the United Nations – Individual Actors, International Agency, and Leadership', *Global Governance*, 20(2): 169–93.
Fröhlich, Manuel (2014) 'The "Suez Story"', in Carsten Stahn and Henning Melber (eds) *Peace Diplomacy, Global Justice and International Agency: Rethinking Human Security and Ethics in the Spirit of Dag Hammarskjöld*, Cambridge: Cambridge University Press, pp 305–40.
Fröhlich, Manuel and Abiodun Williams (eds) (2018) *The UN Secretary-General and the Security Council: A Dynamic Relationship*, Oxford: Oxford University Press.
Furre, Berge (2000) *Norsk historie 1914–2000: Industrisamfunnet – frå vokstervisse til framtidstvil*, Oslo: Det Norske Samlaget.
Gaddis, John Lewis (1972) *The United States and the Origins of the Cold War, 1941–1947*, New York: Columbia University Press.
Gaglione, Anthony (2001) *The United Nations under Trygve Lie, 1945–1953*, Lanham, MD, and London: Scarecrow Press.
Gaiduk, Ilya V. (2012) *Divided Together: The United States and the Soviet Union in the United Nations, 1945–1965*, Washington, DC, and Stanford, CA: Woodrow Wilson Center Press and Stanford University Press.
Gazit, Mordechai (1986) 'American and British Diplomacy and the Bernadotte Mission', *The Historical Journal*, 29(3): 677–96.
Gerolymatos, André (2004) *Red Acropolis, Black Terror: The Greek Civil War and the Origins of Soviet-American Rivalry, 1943–1949*, New York: Basic Books.

Getachew, Adom (2019) *Worldmaking after Empire: The Rise and Fall of Self-Determination*, Princeton: Princeton University Press.

Goedde, Petra (2019) *The Politics of Peace: A Global Cold War History*, Oxford: Oxford University Press.

Goodrich, Leland M., Edvard Hambro, and Anne Patricia Simons (1969) *Charter of the United Nations: Commentary and Documents* (3rd edn), New York and London: Columbia University Press.

Gordenker, Leon (1967) *The UN Secretary-General and the Maintenance of Peace*, New York: Columbia University Press.

Gordenker, Leon (2010) *The UN Secretary-General and Secretariat* (2nd edn), London and New York: Routledge.

Gowan, Richard (2018) 'Ban Ki-moon, 2007–2016', in Manuel Fröhlich and Abiodun Williams (eds) *The UN Secretary-General and the Security Council: A Dynamic Relationship*, Oxford: Oxford University Press, pp 188–210.

Gram-Skjoldager, Karen and Haakon A. Ikonomou (2020) 'The Making of the International Civil Servant c. 1920–60: Establishing the Profession', in Karen Gram-Skjoldager, Haakon A. Ikonomou, and Torsten Kahlert (eds) *Organizing the 20th-Century World: International Organization and the Emergence of International Public Administration, 1920–60s*, London: Bloomsbury Academic, pp 215–30.

Gray, Julia (2018) 'Life, Death, or Zombie? The Vitality of International Organizations', *International Studies Quarterly*, 62(1): 1–13.

Guéhenno, Jean-Marie (2005) 'The Peacekeeper', in Sten Ask and Anna Mark-Jungkvist (eds) *The Adventure of Peace: Dag Hammarskjöld and the Future of the UN*, Basingstoke: Palgrave Macmillan, pp 180–91.

Haack, Kirsten (2018) 'The UN Secretary-General, Role Expansion and Narratives of Representation in the 2016 Campaign', *The British Journal of Politics and International Relations*, 20(4): 898–912.

Hall, Nina (2016) *Displacement, Development, and Climate Change: International Organizations Moving Beyond Their Mandates*, London and New York: Routledge.

Hall, Nina and Ngaire Woods (2018) 'Theorizing the Role of Executive Heads in International Organizations', *European Journal of International Relations*, 24(4): 865–86.

Hanlon, Pamela (2017) *A Worldly Affair: New York, the United Nations, and the Story Behind Their Unlikely Bond*, New York: Fordham University Press.

Harman, Sophie (2011) 'Searching for an Executive Head? Leadership and UNAIDS', *Global Governance*, 17(4): 429–46.

Harrington, Daniel F. (2012) *Berlin on the Brink: The Blockade, the Airlift, and the Early Cold War*, Lexington, KY: University Press of Kentucky.

Hasanli, Jamil (2006) *At the Dawn of the Cold War: The Soviet-American Crisis over Iranian Azerbaijan, 1941–1946*, Lanham, MD: Rowman & Littlefield Publishers.

Hazzard, Shirley (1990) *Countenance of Truth: The United Nations and the Waldheim Case*, New York: Viking Penguin.

Heian-Engdal, Marte, Jørgen Jensehaugen, and Hilde Henriksen Waage (2013) '"Finishing the Enterprise": Israel's Admission to the United Nations', *The International History Review*, 35 (3): 465–85.

Heinzel, Mirko (2022) 'Mediating Power? Delegation, Pooling and Leadership Selection at International Organisations', *The British Journal of Politics and International Relations*, 24 (1): 153–170.

Herren, Madeleine (2016) 'Gender and International Relations through the Lens of the League of Nations', in Glenda Sluga and Carolyn James (eds) *Women, Diplomacy and International Politics since 1500*, London and New York: Routledge, pp 182–201.

Hilderbrand, Robert C. (1990) *Dumbarton Oaks: The Origins of the United Nations and the Search for Postwar Security*, Chapel Hill: University of North Carolina Press.

Hitchcock, William I. (2010) 'The Marshall Plan and the Creation of the West', in Melvyn P. Leffler and Odd Arne Westad (eds) *The Cambridge History of the Cold War: Volume 1: Origins*, Cambridge: Cambridge University Press, pp 154–74.

Hjeltnes, Guri (2004) 'McCarthyismens inntog i FN', *Arbeiderhistorie*: 32–53.

Holloway, David (2010) 'Nuclear Weapons and the Escalation of the Cold War, 1945–1962', in Melvyn P. Leffler and Odd Arne Westad (eds) *The Cambridge History of the Cold War: Volume 1: Origins*, Cambridge: Cambridge University Press, pp 376–97.

Hopf, Ted (2012) *Reconstructing the Cold War: The Early Years, 1945–1958*, Oxford: Oxford University Press.

Jabotinsky, Ze'ev (1923) 'The Ethics of the Iron Wall', *Razsviet*.

Jabotinsky, Ze'ev (1923) 'The Iron Wall', *Razsviet*.

Jackson, Simon and Alanna O'Malley (eds) (2018) *The Institution of International Order: From the League of Nations to the United Nations*, London and New York: Routledge.

Jebb, Gladwyn (1972) *The Memoirs of Lord Gladwyn*, London: Weidenfeld and Nicolson.

Jensehaugen, Jørgen and Hilde Henriksen Waage (2012) 'Coercive Diplomacy: Israel, Transjordan and the UN – a Triangular Drama Revisited', *British Journal of Middle Eastern Studies*, 39(1): 79–100.

Jensehaugen, Jørgen, Marte Heian-Engdal, and Hilde Henriksen Waage (2012) 'Securing the State: From Zionist Ideology to Israeli Statehood', *Diplomacy & Statecraft*, 23(2): 280–302.

Jessup, Philip C. (1971) 'The Berlin Blockade and the Use of the United Nations', *Foreign Affairs*, 50(1): 163–73.

Jessup, Philip C. (1972) 'Park Avenue Diplomacy: Ending the Berlin Blockade', *Political Science Quarterly*, 87(3): 377–400.

Jinnah, Sikina (2014) *Post-Treaty Politics: Secretariat Influence in Global Environmental Governance*, Cambridge, MA: MIT Press.

Johnson, Tana (2014) *Organizational Progeny: Why Governments are Losing Control over the Proliferating Structures of Global Governance*, Oxford: Oxford University Press.

Johnstone, Ian (2003) 'The Role of the UN Secretary-General: The Power of Persuasion Based on Law', *Global Governance*, 9(4): 441–58.

Johnstone, Ian (2007) 'The Secretary-General as Norm Entrepreneur', in Simon Chesterman (ed) *Secretary or General? The UN Secretary-General in World Politics*, Cambridge: Cambridge University Press, pp 123–38.

Jordan, Robert S. (ed) (1983) *Dag Hammarskjöld Revisited: The UN Secretary-General as a Force in World Politics*, Durham, NC: Carolina Academic Press.

Jordan, Robert S. (1991) 'The Fluctuating Fortunes of the United Nations International Civil Service: Hostage to Politics or Undeservedly Criticized?', *Public Administration Review*, 51(4): 353–57.

Kearn, David W. (2010) 'The Baruch Plan and the Quest for Atomic Disarmament', *Diplomacy & Statecraft*, 21(1): 41–67.

Kennedy, David (2007) 'Leader, Clerk, or Policy Entrepreneur? The Secretary-General in a Complex World', in Simon Chesterman (ed) *Secretary or General? The UN Secretary-General in World Politics*, Cambridge: Cambridge University Press, pp 158–81.

Kennedy, Paul (2006) *The Parliament of Man: The United Nations and the Quest for World Government*, London: Penguin Books.

Kille, Kent J. (2006) *From Manager to Visionary: The Secretary-General of the United Nations*, New York and Basingstoke: Palgrave Macmillan.

Kille, Kent J. (2007) 'Moral Authority and the UN Secretary-General's Ethical Framework', in Kent J. Kille (ed) *The UN Secretary-General and Moral Authority: Ethics and Religion in International Leadership*, Washington, DC: Georgetown University Press, pp 7–37.

Kille, Kent J. and Ryan C. Hendrickson (2010) 'Secretary-General Leadership across the United Nations and NATO: Kofi Annan, Javier Solana, and Operation Allied Force', *Global Governance*, 16 (4): 505–23.

Kille, Kent J. and Roger M. Scully (2003) 'Executive Heads and the Role of Intergovernmental Organizations: Expansionist Leadership in the United Nations and the European Union', *Political Psychology*, 24(1): 175–98.

Koremenos, Barbara, Charles Lipson, and Duncan Snidal (eds) (2003) *The Rational Design of International Institutions*, Cambridge: Cambridge University Press.

Krepon, Michael (2021) *Winning and Losing the Nuclear Peace: The Rise, Demise, and Revival of Arms Control*, Stanford, CA: Stanford University Press.

Kuniholm, Bruce Robellet (1980) *The Origins of the Cold War in the Near East: Great Power Conflict and Diplomacy in Iran, Turkey, and Greece*, Princeton: Princeton University Press.

Kunz, Josef L. (1946) 'The Legal Position of the Secretary General of the United Nations', *The American Journal of International Law*, 40 (4): 786–92.

Leffler, Melvyn P. (2007) *For the Soul of Mankind: The United States, the Soviet Union, and the Cold War*, New York: Hill and Wang.

Lie, Trygve (1954) *In the Cause of Peace: Seven Years with the United Nations*, New York: Macmillan.

Lie, Trygve (1954) *Syv år for freden*, Oslo: Tiden Norsk Forlag.

Lie, Trygve (1968) *Oslo – Moskva – London*, Oslo: Tiden Norsk Forlag,.

Lie, Trygve and Viggo Hansteen (1933) *Den nye arbeidstvistlov: Boikottbestemmelsene*, Oslo: Det norske Arbeiderpartis Forlag.

Liese, Andrea, Jana Herold, Hauke Feil, and Per-Olof Busch (2021) 'The heart of bureaucratic power: Explaining international bureaucracies' expert authority', *Review of International Studies*, 47(3): 353–376.

Lipsey, Roger (2016) *Hammarskjöld: A Life*, Ann Arbor, MI: University of Michigan Press.

Luard, Evan (1982) *A History of the United Nations: Volume 1: The Years of Western Domination, 1945–1955*, London and Basingstoke: Macmillan Press.

Luck, Edward C. (2007) 'The Secretary-General in a Unipolar World', in Simon Chesterman (ed) *Secretary or General? The UN Secretary-General in World Politics*, Cambridge: Cambridge University Press, pp 202–31.

Lustick, Ian S. (1996) 'To Build and to Be Built By: Israel and the Hidden Logic of the Iron Wall', *Israel Studies*, 1(1): 196–223.

Lustick, Ian S. (2008) 'Abandoning the Iron Wall: Israel and "The Middle Eastern Muck"', *Middle East Policy*, 15(3): 30–56.

MacMillan, Margaret (2003) *Peacemakers: Six Months that Changed the World*, London: John Murray.

March, James G. and Johan P. Olsen (1996) 'Institutional Perspectives on Political Institutions', *Governance*, 9(3): 247–64.

Mazower, Mark (2009) *No Enchanted Palace: The End of Empire and the Ideological Origins of the United Nations*, Princeton and Oxford: Princeton University Press.

Mazower, Mark (2012) *Governing the World: The History of an Idea*, New York: The Penguin Press.

Meisler, Stanley (2007) *Kofi Annan: A Man of Peace in a World of War*, Hoboken, NJ: John Wiley & Sons.

Meisler, Stanley (2011) *United Nations: A History* (revised and updated edn), New York: Grove Press.

Mires, Charlene (2013) *Capital of the World: The Race to Host the United Nations*, New York: New York University Press.

Morris, Benny (2008) *1948: The First Arab-Israeli War*, New Haven and London: Yale University Press.

Muldoon, James P. (2007) 'The House That Trygve Lie Built: Ethical Challenges as the First UN Secretary-General', in Kent J. Kille (ed) *The UN Secretary-General and Moral Authority: Ethics and Religion in International Leadership*, Washington, DC: Georgetown University Press, pp 67–109.

Muldoon, James P. and Ellen J. Ravndal (2017) 'Lie, Trygve Halvdan', in Bob Reinalda, Kent J. Kille, and Jaci Eisenberg (eds) *IO BIO, Biographical Dictionary of Secretaries-General of International Organizations*, www.ru.nl/fm/iobio

Naimark, Norman (2010) 'The Sovietization of Eastern Europe, 1944–1953', in Melvyn P. Leffler and Odd Arne Westad (eds) *The Cambridge History of the Cold War: Volume 1: Origins*, Cambridge: Cambridge University Press, pp 175–97.

Newman, Edward (1998) *The UN Secretary-General from the Cold War to the New Era: A Global Peace and Security Mandate?*, Basingstoke: Palgrave.

Newman, Edward (2007) 'The International Civil Service: Still a Viable Concept?', *Global Society*, 21(3): 429–47.

Newman, Edward (2007) 'Secretary-General', in Sam Daws and Thomas G. Weiss (eds) *The Oxford Handbook on the United Nations*, Oxford: Oxford University Press.

Newman, Edward and Ellen J. Ravndal (2019) 'The International Civil Service', in Diane Stone and Kim Moloney (eds) *The Oxford Handbook of Global Policy and Transnational Administration*, Oxford: Oxford University Press, pp 165–81.

North, Douglass C. (1990) *Institutions, Institutional Change and Economic Performance*, Cambridge: Cambridge University Press.

Nugent, Neill and Mark Rhinard (2019) 'The "Political" Roles of the European Commission', *Journal of European Integration*, 41(2): 203–20.

O'Malley, Alanna (2018) *The Diplomacy of Decolonisation: America, Britain and the United Nations during the Congo Crisis 1960–1964*, Manchester: Manchester University Press.

Pedersen, Susan (2015) *The Guardians: The League of Nations and the Crisis of Empire*, Oxford: Oxford University Press.

Pedersen, Susan (2021) 'Women at Work in the League of Nations Secretariat', in Heidi Egginton and Zöe Thomas (eds) *Precarious Professionals: Gender, Identities and Social Change in Modern Britain*, London: University of London Press, Institute of Historical Research, pp 181–203.

Pelcovits, Nathan A. (1993) *The Long Armistice: UN Peacekeeping and the Arab-Israeli Conflict, 1948–1960*, Boulder, CO: Westview Press.

Pérez de Cuéllar, Javier (1993) 'The Role of the UN Secretary-General', in Adam Roberts and Benedict Kingsbury (eds) *United Nations, Divided World: The UN's Roles in International Relations*, Oxford: Oxford University Press, pp 125–42.

Phelan, Edward Joseph (1936) *Yes and Albert Thomas*, London: The Cresset Press.

Plesch, Dan (2010) *America, Hitler and the UN: How the Allies Won World War II and Forged a Peace*, London: I.B. Tauris.

Plesch, Dan and Thomas G. Weiss (eds) (2015) *Wartime Origins and the Future United Nations*, London and New York: Routledge.

Rajak, Svetozar (2010) 'The Cold War in the Balkans, 1945–1956', in Melvyn P. Leffler and Odd Arne Westad (eds) *The Cambridge History of the Cold War: Volume 1: Origins*, Cambridge: Cambridge University Press, pp 198–220.

Ramcharan, Bertrand G. (2008) *Preventive Diplomacy at the UN*, Bloomington and Indianapolis, IN: Indiana University Press.

Ranshofen-Wertheimer, Egon F. (1945) *The International Secretariat: A Great Experiment in International Administration*, Washington: Carnegie Endowment for International Peace.

Ravndal, Ellen J. (2010) 'Exit Britain: British Withdrawal from the Palestine Mandate in the Early Cold War, 1947–1948', *Diplomacy & Statecraft*, 21(3): 416–33.

Ravndal, Ellen J. (2016) 'The Appointment of Trygve Lie as the First UN Secretary-General: One World Trust Background Briefs for the 1 for 7 Billion Campaign, Brief No. 3', https://www.1for7billion.org/s/3_Ravndal.pdf

Ravndal, Ellen J. (2016) '"The First Major Test": The UN Secretary-General and the Palestine Problem, 1947–9', *The International History Review*, 38(1): 196–213.

Ravndal, Ellen J. (2016) 'La mission la plus impossible au monde: Le Secrétaire général Trygve Lie face à la Guerre froide, 1946–1953', *Revue d'histoire diplomatique*, 130(2): 145–61.

Ravndal, Ellen J. (2017) '"A Force for Peace": Expanding the Role of the UN Secretary-General under Trygve Lie, 1946–1953', *Global Governance*, 23(3): 443–59.

Ravndal, Ellen J. (2018) 'Trygve Lie (1946–1953)', in Manuel Fröhlich and Abiodun Williams (eds) *The UN Secretary-General and the Security Council: A Dynamic Relationship*, Oxford: Oxford University Press, pp 22–41.

Ravndal, Ellen J. (2020) 'A Guardian of the UN Charter: The UN Secretary-General at Seventy-Five', *Ethics & International Affairs*, 34(3): 297–304.

Ravndal, Ellen J. (2020) 'Secretaries-General and Crisis Management: Trygve Lie and Dag Hammarskjöld at the United Nations', in Karen Gram-Skjoldager, Haakon A. Ikonomou, and Torsten Kahlert (eds) *Organizing the 20th-Century World: International Organization and the Emergence of International Public Administration, 1920–60s*, London: Bloomsbury Academic, pp 183–97.

Ravndal, Ellen J. (2021) 'International Organisations in Historical Perspective', in Benjamin de Carvalho, Julia Costa Lopez, and Halvard Leira (eds) *Routledge Handbook on Historical International Relations*, London: Routledge, pp 330–40.

Roberts, Geoffrey (2019) 'A League of Their Own: The Soviet Origins of the United Nations', *Journal of Contemporary History*, 54(2): 303–27.

Roehrlich, Elisabeth (2018) 'Negotiating Verification: International Diplomacy and the Evolution of Nuclear Safeguards, 1945–1972', *Diplomacy & Statecraft*, 29(1): 29–50.

Rofe, J. Simon (2012) 'Pre-War Post-War Planning: The Phoney War, the Roosevelt Administration, and the Case of the Advisory Committee on Problems of Foreign Relations', *Diplomacy & Statecraft*, 23(2): 254–79.

Rovine, Arthur W. (1970) *The First Fifty Years: The Secretary-General in World Politics 1920–1970*, Leyden: A.W. Sijthoff.

Rushton, Simon (2008) 'The UN Secretary-General and Norm Entrepreneurship: Boutros Boutros-Ghali and Democracy Promotion', *Global Governance*, 14(1): 95–110.

Russell, Ruth B. (1958) *A History of the United Nations Charter: The Role of the United States 1940–1945*, Washington, DC: The Brookings Institution.

Schlesinger, Stephen C. (2003) *Act of Creation, The Founding of the United Nations: A Story of Superpowers, Secret Agents, Wartime Allies and Enemies, and Their Quest for a Peaceful World*, Boulder, CO: Westview Press.

Schroeder, Michael Bluman (2014) 'Executive Leadership in the Study of International Organization: A Framework for Analysis', *International Studies Review*, 16(3): 339–61.

Schuette, Leonard August (2021) 'Why NATO Survived Trump: The Neglected Role of Secretary-General Stoltenberg', *International Affairs*, 97(6): 1863–81.

Schwebel, Stephen M. (1951) 'The Origins and Development of Article 99 of the Charter: The Powers of the Secretary-General of the United Nations', *British Year Book of International Law*, 28(1951): 371–82.

Schwebel, Stephen M. (1952) *The Secretary-General of the United Nations: His Political Powers and Practice*, Cambridge, MA: Harvard University Press.

Scott, W. Richard (2014) *Institutions and Organizations: Ideas, Interests, and Identities* (4th edn), Thousand Oaks, CA: SAGE.

Sending, Ole Jacob (2014) 'The International Civil Servant', *International Political Sociology*, 8(3): 338–40.

Sewell, William H. Jr (1992) 'A Theory of Structure: Duality, Agency, and Transformation', *American Journal of Sociology*, 98(1): 1–29.

Shlaim, Avi (1983) *The United States and the Berlin Blockade, 1948–1949: A Study in Crisis Decision-Making*, Berkeley, CA: University of California Press.

Shlaim, Avi (2000) *The Iron Wall: Israel and the Arab World* (paperback edn), London: Penguin Books.

Shlaim, Avi (2012) 'The Iron Wall Revisited', *Journal of Palestine Studies*, 41(2): 80–98.

Sievers, Loraine and Sam Daws (2014) *The Procedure of the UN Security Council* (4th edn), Oxford: Oxford University Press.

Skjelsbæk, Kjell and Gunnar Fermann (1996) 'The UN Secretary-General and the Mediation of International Disputes', in Jacob Bercovitch (ed) *Resolving International Conflicts: The Theory and Practice of Mediation*, Boulder, CO: Lynne Rienner, pp 75–104.

Sluga, Glenda (2013) *Internationalism in the Age of Nationalism*, Philadelphia: University of Pennsylvania Press.

Sluga, Glenda and Patricia Clavin (eds) (2017) *Internationalisms: A Twentieth-Century History*, Cambridge: Cambridge University Press.

Stahn, Carsten and Henning Melber (2014) 'Human Security and Ethics in the Spirit of Dag Hammarskjöld: An Introduction', in Carsten Stahn and Henning Melber (eds) *Peace Diplomacy, Global Justice and International Agency: Rethinking Human Security and Ethics in the Spirit of Dag Hammarskjöld*, Cambridge: Cambridge University Press, pp 1–32.

Stahn, Carsten and Henning Melber (eds) (2014) *Peace Diplomacy, Global Justice and International Agency: Rethinking Human Security and Ethics in the Spirit of Dag Hammarskjöld*, Cambridge: Cambridge University Press.

Steiner, Zara (2005) *The Lights That Failed: European International History 1919–1933*, Oxford: Oxford University Press.

Steiner, Zara (2011) *The Triumph of the Dark: European International History 1933–1939*, Oxford: Oxford University Press.

Terlingen, Yvonne (2017) 'A Better Process, a Stronger UN Secretary-General: How Historic Change Was Forged and What Comes Next', *Ethics & International Affairs*, 31(2): 115–27.

Thant Myint-U and Amy Scott (2007) *The UN Secretariat: A Brief History (1945–2006)*, New York: International Peace Academy.

Tharoor, Shashi (2005) 'The Role of the Secretary-General', in Sten Ask and Anna Mark-Jungkvist (eds) *The Adventure of Peace: Dag Hammarskjöld and the Future of the UN*, Basingstoke: Palgrave Macmillan, pp 146–60.

Tharoor, Shashi (2007) '"The Most Impossible Job" Description', in Simon Chesterman (ed) *Secretary or General? The UN Secretary-General in World Politics*, Cambridge: Cambridge University Press, pp 33–46.

Tiller, Stian Johansen and Hilde Henriksen Waage (2011) 'Powerful State, Powerless Mediator: The United States and the Peace Efforts of the Palestine Conciliation Commission, 1949–51', *The International History Review*, 33(3): 501–24.

Traub, James (2007) 'The Secretary-General's political space', in Simon Chesterman (ed) *Secretary or General? The UN Secretary-General in World Politics*, Cambridge: Cambridge University Press, pp 185–201.

Trinh, Quang (2007) 'The Bully Pulpit', in Simon Chesterman (ed) *Secretary or General? The UN Secretary-General in World Politics*, Cambridge: Cambridge University Press, pp 102–20.

Tveit, Odd Karsten (1996) *Alt for Israel: Oslo – Jerusalem 1948–78*, Oslo: J.W. Cappelen.

Tveit, Odd Karsten (2018) *Gudfaren: Trygve Lie: Generalsekretæren som sviktet FN*, Oslo: Kagge Forlag.

Udom, Udoh Elijah (2003) 'The International Civil Service: Historical Development and Potential for the 21st Century', *Public Personnel Management*, 32(1): 99–124.

Urquhart, Brian E. (1987) *A Life in Peace and War*, London: Weidenfeld and Nicolson.

Urquhart, Brian E. (1993) *Ralph Bunche: An American Life*, New York and London: W.W. Norton.

Urquhart, Brian E. (1994) *Hammarskjöld* (paperback edn), New York: W.W. Norton.

Urquhart, Brian E. (2007) 'The Evolution of the Secretary-General', in Simon Chesterman (ed) *Secretary or General? The UN Secretary-General in World Politics*, Cambridge: Cambridge University Press, pp 15–32.

Waage, Hilde Henriksen (1989) *Da staten Israel ble til: Et stridsspørsmål i norsk politikk, 1945–49*, Oslo: Gyldendal Norsk Forlag.

Waage, Hilde Henriksen (2011) 'The Winner Takes All: The 1949 Island of Rhodes Armistice Negotiations Revisited', *The Middle East Journal*, 65(2): 279–304.

Waldheim, Kurt (1985) *In the Eye of the Storm*, London: Weidenfeld and Nicolson.

Walters, Francis Paul (1952) *A History of the League of Nations*, Vol. 1, Oxford: Oxford University Press.

Walters, Francis Paul (1952) *A History of the League of Nations*, Vol. 2, Oxford: Oxford University Press.

Weart, Spencer R. (2012) *The Rise of Nuclear Fear*, Boston, MA: Harvard University Press.

Weiss, Thomas G. (1982) 'International Bureaucracy: The Myth and Reality of the International Civil Service', *International Affairs*, 58(2): 287–306.

Weiss, Thomas G. and Tatiana Carayannis (2017) 'Windows of Opportunity for UN Reform: Historical Insights for the Next Secretary-General', *International Affairs*, 93(2): 309–26.

Wertheim, Stephen (2019) 'Instrumental Internationalism: The American Origins of the United Nations, 1940–3', *Journal of Contemporary History*, 54(2): 265–83.

Wertheim, Stephen (2020) *Tomorrow, the World: The Birth of U.S. Global Supremacy*, Cambridge, MA: Harvard University Press.

Whitfield, Teresa (2007) 'Good Offices and "Groups of Friends"', in Simon Chesterman (ed) *Secretary or General? The UN Secretary-General in World Politics*, Cambridge: Cambridge University Press, pp 86–101.

Yao, Joanne (2019) '"Conquest from Barbarism": The Danube Commission, International Order and the Control of Nature as a Standard of Civilization', *European Journal of International Relations*, 25(2): 335–59.

Index

References to photographs appear in *italic* type.
References to endnotes show both the
page number and the note number (145n18).

A
Acheson, D. 24, 97, 99, 103
actors 4–6, 7
Afghanistan 41, 42
Aghnides, T. 130
Ala, H. 31
Albania 41, 42, 44
Aldrich, W. 118
Angel, E.Z. 120
Annan, K. 1, 3, 6, 70, 136, 138–9
architects 121
archives 5, 7–8, 171–2
Argentina 54, 79, 155n20, 160n61
armed guard 52–3, 54, 58–61, 64, *66*, 132, 134
  see also UN forces
armistice agreements 60, 62, 64, *67*, 134, 154n4
arms race 89, 90, 91, 94, 105
article 99 *see* UN Charter article 99
assistant secretaries-general 113–15, 116
atomic bombs 89, 90, 94, 95
  see also nuclear arms race
atomic energy 91, 95, 96
Atomic Energy Commission *see* UN Atomic Energy Commission
Attlee, C. 97
Auriol, V. 97
Austin, W. 53, 54, 55, 120
Australia 31, 38–9, 42, 85, 104, 155n24
Austria 42, 82
authority 5, 17, 19, 22, 34, 44, 57, 59–60, 64, 84, 89, 105, 107, 112, 115, 141
autonomy 3, 4, 5, 6–7, 8, 14, 21, 28, 30, 35, 43, 47, 49, 71–2, 80, 86, 89, 107, 125, 129–30, 135–6, 138, 140–1
Avenol, J. 14
Azerbaijan 31, 32, 35

B
Ban Ki-moon 136, 139

Barros, J. 26, 76, 110, 113
Baruch, B. 91
Baruch Plan 90–1
Belarus 164n50
Belgium 24, 28, 157n80, 160n61
Berlin Blockade 9, 61, 78–83, 132, 133
Bernadotte, F. 58, 59, 60
Bevin, E. 77, 97
Bidault, G. 77, 97
Black, E.R. 97
Blanchard, F. 97
Bolivia 156n33
Boutros-Ghali, B. 70, 136, 138
Bramuglia, J.A. 79, 80, 81–2
Bratz, R. *69*
Brazil 31, 41, 42
bridge-building policy 9, 71, 74, 94
Britain
  article 99 18, 78
  Berlin Blockade 78–81, 132
  Chinese representation conflict 93
  Dumbarton Oaks conference 18
  Greek civil war 44, 70
  International Labour Organization (ILO) 15
  Iranian crisis 1946 31, 32, 34
  League of Nations 16, 28
  Lie's election 24, 150n98
  Lie's peace plan 97, 98
  Lie's re-appointment 101, 103
  Marshall Plan 76, 77
  occupation of Iran 31
  Palestine problem 49, 51, 54, 57–8, 157n79
  People's Republic of China (PRC) 163n26
  post-war cooperation 72–3
  role of secretary-general 39, 42–3, 45, 46, 73, 78, 81
  UN Charter 15, 16, 18
  UN headquarters 119
  UN Secretariat 113, 116–17, 125
    McCarthyism 125

187

view on UN membership 43
Bulgaria 42, 44
Bunche, R. 67, 116
  Israel-Egypt armistice 60, 64
  Nobel Peace Prize 62
  Palestine problem 48, 51, 53, 58, 60, 154n4
  as Representative of the Secretary-General in Palestine 58, 134
  as secretary-general candidate 102
Burma 93
Byrnes, J. 34, 114

C
Cadogan, A. 42–3, 57, 77, 80, 101
Cambodia 42
Canada 79, 155n24, 160n61, 164n50
Ceylon 42
Chase National Bank 118
Chiang Kai-shek 92
Chile 113, 164n50
China
  article 99 18
  League of Nations 16
  Lie's election 24–5
  Lie's peace plan 96, 98, 164n50
  Lie's re-appointment 101–3
  as neutral member 160n61
  Peking formula 137
  post-war cooperation 73
  role of secretary-general 34, 39
  UN Charter 16, 18, 149n63
  UN membership 42
  UN Secretariat 113
  UN Security Council rules of procedure 38, 39
  veto of Waldheim third term 138
  see also People's Republic of China (PRC)
Chinese representation conflict 92–4, 132, 163n22
Chisholm, B. 97
Churchill, W. 17, 70
Cohen, B. 113
Cold War 9–10, 35, 62–3, 70–87, 137, 138
  Berlin Blockade 78–83
  Chinese representation conflict 92–4, 163n22
  consequences for UN organization 50, 52, 58, 62, 70–1, 86, 88–9, 90, 96
  Korean War 83–6
  Lie's Cold War strategy 72–4
  Lie's election as compromise 26, 150, 151n102
  Lie's re-election 100, 103–4
  Lie's resignation 126
  Marshall Plan 74, 75–8
  nuclear arms race 89, 90–2
  Truman Doctrine 74–5, 78
  UN membership 41
  and vacuum effect 71, 139
  see also peace plan

Colombia 160n61, 164n50
Committee of Experts 152n21
  Iranian crisis 1946 33, 34, 35
  UN Security Council rules of procedure 37, 38, 39, 40, 46
Cordier, A.W. 7, 37, 57, 96, 115–16
Czechoslovakia 53, 113, 155n24, 156n33, 164n50

D
Denmark 156n33
deputy secretary-general 116–17
Drummond, E. 14, 109, 130
Dudley, G.A. 119, 121
Dumbarton Oaks conference 17–18

E
economic aid programmes *see* Marshall Plan
Economic Commission for Europe (ECE) 76
Eden, A. 24, 25, 27
Egypt 31, 39, 56, 60, 64
Einstein, A. 100
Eisenhower, D. 24, 25, 27
Eisenhower, M. 114, 116
election of secretary-general 2, 17, 18–19, 20, 23–6, 27–8
  see also Lie's election
European Recovery Programme (ERP) *see* Marshall Plan
Evatt, H. 80–1, 82

F
Federal Bureau of Investigation (FBI) 10, 108, 124, 125
Feller, A. 79
Finland 42
Flushing Meadows 111, 119
Food and Agricultural Organization (FAO) 97
Foote, W. 96
France
  Berlin Blockade 78, 79, 80, 81
  Chinese representation conflict 93
  Iranian crisis 1946 32, 33
  Korean War 85
  Lie's election 24, 25
  Lie's peace plan 97, 98–9
  Lie's re-appointment 103
  Marshall Plan 77
  role of secretary-general 25, 27
  Truce Commission 157n80
  UN Secretariat 113

G
Gavrilovic, S. 118
Germany 31, 42, 82
Gjesdal, T. 97
Goedde, P. 90
Gram-Skjoldager, K. 130

great powers 5, 17, 19, 23, 26, 32, 50, 51, 52, 57, 61–3, 72–4, 80, 83, 89, 91, 96, 97, 103, 105, 115, 125, 128, 134–5, 138, 141
   and election of secretary-general 17, 18, 23–4, 27
   see also permanent members of the Security Council (P5); superpowers
Greece 75
Greek civil war 43–5
Gromyko, A. 25, 31, 32, 34, 35, 42, 45
Gross, E. 84
Gross, G.C. 97
Guatemala 155n24
Guterres, A. 136, 139

H
Haiti 164n50
Hammarskjöld, D. 3, *69*, 131
   Article 99 133, 145n18, 151n109
   election 128
   and International Civil Service 137
   legacy of 3, 136–7
   Lie's resentment of 136
   and peacekeeping 137
   and Peking formula 137
   screening of US applicants 129
   UN Secretariat 117, 129
Harrison, W.K. 119, 120, 121, 122
Hickerson, J.D. 83
Hiroshima 90
Ho Chi Minh 93
Hoo, V.C.T. 113, 116
housing 112, 118
Hungary 42
Hutson, J.B. 114, 116

I
IBM 118
Iceland 41, 42
Ikonomou, H. 130
India 85, 92, 155–6n27, 155n24, 163n26
individual push 1, 5, 6–7, 8, 63, 86, 92, 132, 135
   see also autonomy
institutional design 4
institutional factors 2–3, 4, 10, 29, 49, 71, 131, 132, 136, 139–40, 141
institutional history 4
institutional pull 5, 6, 7, 86, 135
   see also vacuum effect
institutionalism 4, 5
institutions 5–6, 7, 131, 141
intergovernmental organizations (IGOs) 1, 4, 29, 131, 138
International Atomic Development Authority 91
International Civil Aviation Organization 97
International Civil Service Advisory Board (ICSAB) 130

International Civil Service (ICS) 10, 107, 108, 123–6, 128, 129, 130
international cooperation 50, 52, 58, 71, 72–3, 91, 96, 128, 135
International Labour Organization (ILO) 15–16, 28, 97
International Refugee Organization 97
International Telecommunications Union (ITU) 97
International Trade Organization 97
investigative committees 1, 30, 43–5, 46, 133
Iran 155–6n27
Iranian crisis 1946 8–9, 31–2, 45–6, 155n24
   Lie's legal memorandum 33–5
   implications of 36–40
Iraq invasion 138
Ireland 41, 42
iron wall policy 50, 155n12
Israel 48–9, 56, 60–1
Italy 42

J
Jabotinsky, Z. 155n12
Jackson, R. 57, 59, 60, 117
Japan 82, 90
Jebb, G. 21–2, 43, 110, 114
Jerusalem 59, 60
Jessup, P. 80, 82–3
Johnson, H. 44
Jordan *see* Transjordan

K
Kennan, G. 26
Kerno, I. 113
Korean War 9, 10, 42, 83–6, 89, 132, 135
   and Lie's re-appointment 99–100, 102–3
   and Lie's resignation 126, 127

L
Lange, H. 36
Lange, O. 33
Laos 42
Laugier, H. 111, 113
Le Corbusier 121, 122
League of Nations 4, 13–15, 118, 134
   Covenant 14, 18
   International Civil Service (ICS) 10, 107, 109, 110, 130
   members 16
   secretary-general 12, 14–15, 26, 28, 30, 42, 43, 64, 68, 105, 130, 134–5
Lebanon 60, 164n50
Libya 42
Lie, T.
   article 99 29, 30, 36, 43, 45, 46, 47, 56–7, 78, 84, 133
   and Chinese representation conflict 92–4
   Cold War 70, 71–2, 86–7
      Berlin Blockade 78, 79–83
      conception of 62, 70, 72–4, 91–2

Korean War 83–6
Lie's election as compromise 26
Marshall Plan 75, 76, 77–8
Truman Doctrine 75, 78
contribution to role 3, 7, 9, 10, 30, 48, 63–4, 80, 82, 86, 89, 94, 105, 130, 131–6, 141
and D. Hammarskjöld 69, 128, 136
early life and background 23, 108
election 23–6, 65
with grandson 69
investigative committees 43–5
Iranian crisis 1946 31
  implications of legal memorandum 36–40
  legal memorandum 33–5
Israel 48–9
with J.D. Rockefeller and W. O'Dwyer 66
meditation between member states 57–8, 64, 71, 80, 86, 94, 99–100, 134–5
as Norwegian foreign minister 23, 25, 72, 74
Palestine problem 49–50, 61–4
  Lie's views on 9, 48–50, 51–2, 53, 54, 55, 56, 61–3
  partition implementation 52–6
  partition resolution 51–2
  UN armed guard 52–3, 58–61
  see also armed guard; UN forces
  UN Security Council involvement 56–8, 132
peace plan 9–10, 67, 88–105, 132, 134
  20-year peace program 94–6
  aftermath 99–105
  background 86–7, 90–4
  promotion and peace tour 96–9
  sponsoring v. opposing countries 164n50
personal papers 7–8
with R. Bunche 67
radio broadcast 67
re-appointment 68, 100–5
resignation 126–8
scholarly writings about 146n24
Soviet boycott boyott of second term 85, 100, 104–5, 127
statement on UN membership 40–3
successors 136–9
swearing in 11, 23
and Trusteeship Council 40
UN headquarters 66, 117–18, 119–20, 122–3
UN Secretariat 108, 109, 130
  assistant secretaries-general 113–14, 115
  deputy secretary-general 116
  McCarthyism 108, 123, 124–6, 129
  staffing 109, 110–11, 112
and UN Security Council 29, 36, 38, 53, 54, 57, 84, 133, 134
use of media 54, 55, 63–4, 67, 68, 88, 134

view of secretary-general's role 2, 6, 27, 30, 36–7, 42–3, 44, 46–7, 71, 73, 74, 84, 85, 87, 88, 105, 126–7
Lisicky, K. 53

M
MacMillan, M. 4
Malik, Y. 82–3, 92
Mao Zedong 92
Marshall, G. 58, 76
Marshall Plan 9, 74, 75–8, 87, 132
Maxwell, E. 119
McCarthyism 10, 110, 123–6, 129
McNeill, H. 101
media 12, 25, 63–4, 138
  Lie's use of 54, 55, 63–4, 67, 68, 88, 134
  see also public opinion
Mexico 31, 41
Mires, C. 119
Moderow, W. 134
Molotov, V. 77, 97
Mongolian People's Republic 41
Morse, D.A. 97
Moses, R. 119

N
Nagasaki 90
Nansen, F. 74
NATO 78, 132
Nepal 42
Netherlands 20, 31, 39, 42, 113, 155n24
New York 10, 65, 66, 83, 109, 110–11, 112, 117, 118–20, 122–3, 131–2
New York Times 34, 36, 52, 54, 77, 80, 82, 118
New Zealand 85
Niemeyer, O. 121
Nobel Peace Prize 62, 138
Noel-Baker, P. 39
norm entrepreneurs 1, 10, 88, 90, 105, 138, 139
normative institutionalism 5–6
Norway 85, 163n26
nuclear arms race 89, 90–2, 94, 95, 105
nuclear energy 91, 95
  see also atomic energy
nuclear weapons 91
  see also atomic bombs

O
O'Dwyer, W. 66, 118, 119
Oppenheimer, R. 91
Overby, A.N. 97
Owen, D. 109, 114

P
Pakistan 164n50
Palestine Commission 52, 53, 54, 156n33
Palestine Conciliation Commission 60, 61
Palestine problem 9, 48–64
  First Arab-Israeli War 56–8, 60–1

INDEX

Lie's views on 9, 48–50, 51–2, 53, 54, 55, 56, 61–3
partition implementation 52–6
partition resolution 51–2
UN armed guard 52–3, 58–61
  see also armed guard; UN forces
UN Security Council involvement 56–8, 132
UN truce observers 59, 61, 66
Panama 156n33
Paris Peace conference 14, 15
Parodi, A. 80
Pasvolsky, L. 2, 27
peace plan 9–10, 67, 88–105, 132, 134
  20-year peace program 94–6
  aftermath 99–105
  background 86–7, 90–4
  promotion and peace tour 96–9
  sponsoring v. opposing countries 164n50
Pearson, L. 24, 25, 126, 150n99
Peking formula 137
Pelt, A. 113
People's Republic of China (PRC) 92, 137, 138, 163n26
  and Korean war 93
  see also China
Pérez de Cuéllar, J. 129, 136, 138
permanent members of the Security Council (P5) 72–3, 87
  Chinese representation conflict 92, 94
  election of secretary-general 23, 25
  and Kurt Waldheim 138
  Lie's peace plan 96, 98–9
  Lie's resignation 126, 127–8
  Palestine problem 52, 53, 54
  and peacekeeping 137
  relations to secretary-general 72, 87, 92, 94, 140
  and UN membership 41
  UN Secretariat 113
  veto 41, 73
  voting procedures in Security Council 20
  see also great powers
Peru 155n24
Philippines 53, 156n33, 164n50
Poland 31, 33, 164n50
Portugal 41, 42
post-war cooperation 72–3
  see also international cooperation
Price, B. 114, 116, 122, 123, 124
primary sources 7–8
  see also archives
public opinion 1–2, 7, 9, 10, 11, 17, 23, 24, 49, 59, 63–4, 68, 75, 76, 86, 88, 90, 96, 100, 105, 124, 134, 138
  see also media

Q
Quo Tai-chi 33–4

R
Radice, F. 97
refugees 139, 170n42
Reston, J. 36
Robertson, H. 121
Rockefeller, J.D. 66, 120
Rockefeller, N.A. 118, 119
roles 5–6
  see also secretary-general
Romania 42
Roosevelt, E. 119
Roosevelt, F.D. 16, 17
Rose, B. 118
Rovine, A.W. 19
Rusk, D. 26
Russell, R.B. 12
Rzymowski, W. 24, 25

S
San Francisco conference 11, 18–21, 22, 23, 26, 27, 28, 73, 112, 115
Schlesinger, S.C. 12
Schuman, R. 97, 98–9
secretary-general 1–3, 8
  as advocate for global issues 1, 10, 64, 88, 90, 105
    see also secretary-general as guardian of UN Charter
  autonomy of role 4, 5, 6–7, 14, 21, 28, 30, 35, 43, 47, 49, 71, 80, 86, 89, 107, 125, 129, 130, 135, 136, 138, 140, 141
  bridge-building policy 9, 10, 50, 71, 73, 74, 79, 94, 128
    see also secretary-general as mediator
  early candidates 24–5, 28, 150–1n102
  election of 2, 17, 18–19, 20, 23–6, 27–8
  expectations of role 7, 8, 11–22, 26–8, 107
    in 1946 2, 11–13, 24, 26–8, 29, 47
    21st century 139–42
  first drafts of UN Charter 16–18, 26–7
  during Iranian crisis 1946 33–4, 45–6
  political by design 8, 12, 13, 21, 26, 28, 29, 47
  precedents set by earlier models 13–16, 26
  San Francisco conference 18–21, 26
  UN Preparatory Commission 11, 20–2
  as guardian of UN Charter 2, 5, 6, 22, 50, 61, 63, 67, 71, 85, 86, 105, 134, 140–2
  Lie's successors 136–9
  as mediator 14, 21, 28, 50, 57–8, 64, 71, 73, 78, 80, 83, 86, 132, 134–5, 138, 140
  as norm entrepreneur 1, 10, 88, 90, 105, 138, 139
  relationship between UN Security Council and 6, 21, 29–30, 34, 36–40, 44–5, 46–7, 54, 63, 64, 65, 80, 84, 85, 89, 92, 94, 133, 134, 135, 140

see also UN Charter article 99
  as scapegoat 6
  see also assistant secretaries-general; deputy secretary-general; Lie, T.
Siam 41
Simić, S. 24, 25
Sobolev, A. 37, 38–9, 79, 113
sociological institutionalism 5–6
South Africa 51, 155n21
South Korea 83, 84
Soviet Union
  Berlin Blockade 78, 79, 80, 81, 82–3
  boycott of Lie's second term 85, 100, 104–5, 127
  boycott of Security Council 32, 89, 92–3
  Chinese representation conflict 92–3
  Cold War 70, 71, 75
  Dumbarton Oaks conference 17, 18
  Greek civil war 43–4, 45
  Iranian crisis 1946 8, 31–5
  Korean War 85–6
  League of Nations 16
  Lie's election 24, 25
  Lie's peace plan 99
  Lie's re-appointment *68*, 101–5
  Lie's resignation 105, 127
  Marshall Plan 77–8
  nuclear arms race 89, 90, 91
  Palestine problem 52, 62–3
  post-war cooperation 73, 82
  role of secretary-general 20, 38, 44–5, 46, 80
  San Francisco conference 20
  UN Charter 16, 17, 18
  UN Secretariat 20, 110, 113
  view on UN membership 41, 42
Spaak, P.-H. 24, 25, 28
Spain 42, 51, 155n20
special representatives of secretary-general (SRSGs) 57, 58, 79, 133–4
Sri Lanka 42
Stalin, J. 77, 97
Stettinius, E. 34, 38, 114
Stevenson, A. 116
Sulzberger, A.H. 118
superpowers 70–1, 86, 89, 90, 91
Sweden 41, 42, 155n24, 164n50
Syria 60, 160n61

T
Thailand 41
Thant, U 116, 134, 136, 137–8
Thomas, A. 15
The Times 72
Torres-Bodet, J. 97
Transjordan 41, 60
Truce Commission 58, 157n80
Truman Doctrine 9, 74–5, 78, 132
Truman, H. 89, 91, 97, 103

Tsiang Ting-fu 92
Turkey 75

U
Ukraine 20, 25, 44, 79, 92, 139, 164n50
UN Administrative Committee on Coordination (ACC) 97–8, 163n43
UN archives 8
UN armed guard 58–61, 64, 132
  see also armed guard; UN forces
UN Atomic Energy Commission 38, 89, 91
UN Charter 1, 2, 5, 6, 10, 11, 12, 14, 26, 33, 39, 45, 47, 53, 54, 73, 75, 83–4, 85, 87, 93, 94–5, 104, 106, 107, 110, 131, 136, 137
  Article 4 41
  Article 7 6
  Article 28(2) 96
  Article 39 57
  Article 43 58, 95, 96
  Article 97 11, 34, 103, 129, 143
  Article 98 15, 21, 36, 38, 143
  Article 99 2, 8, 9, 12, 16, 18, 19, 21, 26, 27, 28, 29, 30, 34, 36, 39, 43, 45, 46, 47, 56, 78, 84, 133, 134, 143, 145n18
  Article 100 107, 110, 112, 124, 125, 143–4
  Article 101 107, 112, 144
  Article 107 78, 160n52
  Chapter VII 58
  first drafts 16–18
  negotiation of 18–20
  signing 11, 20
UN Economic and Social Council (ECOSOC) 30, 37, 38, 40, 46, 47, 76, 109, 114
UN Emergency Force (UNEF) 137
UN Field Service 60
UN forces 58, 95–6
  see also armed guard
UN General Assembly 6, 11, 17, 19, 23, *68*, 111
  Berlin Blockade 78, 80–1
  election of secretary-general 17, 19, 23
  Iranian crisis 1946 31
  Korean War 132
  Lie's election 24, 25, *65*
  Lie's peace plan 89, 98, 99
  Lie's re-appointment *68*, 85, 100–4
  Lie's resignation 128
  Palestine problem 51, 52, 55, 56, 60
  role of secretary general 15, 21, 27, 30, 64, 134
  rules of procedure 30, 37, 38, 40, 46–7
  South Africa 155n21
  Spain 155n20
  UN armed guard 59, 132
  UN headquarters 118, 120, 122
  UN membership 41
  UN Secretariat 109, 113, 116, 130

INDEX

McCarthyism 124, 125–6, 129
Uniting for Peace resolution 104, 139
UN headquarters 23, 66, 109, 117–23, 127, 131–2
UN High Commissioner for Refugees 170n42
UN Military Staff Committee 38, 40, 58, 89
UN peacekeeping 137
  see also UN forces
UN Preparatory Commission 149n63
  International Civil Service (ICS) 107
  role of secretary-general 11, 20–2, 27, 141
  UN headquarters 117–18
  UN Secretariat 106, 109, 113, 116
  UN Security Council rules of procedure 36
UN Relief and Works Agency (UNRWA) 61
UN Secretariat 2, 6, 10, 80, 83, 85, 106–8, 130, 135–6
  McCarthyism 123–6, 129
  office space 111
  organization and leadership 112–17
  and Palestine problem 51, 53, 54, 57, 58
  relations with Security Council 36–7, 40
  staffing 109–12, 128–9
  see also International Civil Service
UN secretary-general see secretary-general
UN Security Council 65, 109, 111
  Berlin Blockade 78–9, 82, 83
    neutral members 79, 82, 160n61
  Chinese representation conflict 92–4, 163n22
  Cold War 70–1, 89
  Committee of Experts 152n21
    Iranian crisis 1946 33, 34, 35
    Security Council rules of procedure 37, 38, 39, 40, 46
  as concert of great powers 83
  election of secretary-general 17, 18–19, 23, 26
  Greek civil war 43–5
  Iranian crisis 1946 8–9, 31–2
    Lie's legal memorandum 33–5
  Korean War 83–5
  Lie's peace plan 94, 96
  Lie's re-appointment 68, 101, 103–4
  Lie's statement on UN membership 40–3
  Palestine problem 52–3, 54, 55, 56–8, 62, 132
  permanent members (P5) 72–3, 87
    Chinese representation conflict 92, 94
    election of secretary-general 23, 25
    and Kurt Waldheim 138
    Lie's peace plan 96, 98–9
    Lie's resignation 126, 127–8
    Palestine problem 52, 53, 54
    And peacekeeping 137
    relations to secretary-general 72, 87, 92, 94, 140
    and UN membership 41
    UN Secretariat 113

veto 41, 73
voting procedures in Security Council 20
see also great powers
relationship between secretary-general and 6, 21, 29–30, 34, 36–40, 44–5, 46–7, 54, 63, 64, 65, 80, 84, 85, 89, 92, 94, 133–4, 135, 140
rules of procedure 36–40, 46
UN armed guard 59
UN membership 41–2
veto 17, 19
UN Special Committee on Palestine (UNSCOP) 51, 155–6n27, 155n24
UN truce observers 66
UN Truce Supervisory Organization (UNTSO) 59, 61
UN Trusteeship Council 40, 59
UNESCO 97
United Kingdom 85
  see also Britain
United Nations (UN)
  founding of 8, 16–20
  headquarters 117–23
  and the League of Nations 13–15
  membership 40–3, 48–9, 60–1, 95
United States
  Berlin Blockade 78, 79, 80, 81, 82–3, 132
  Chinese representation conflict 92, 93, 94
  Cold War policy 74–8
  Dumbarton Oaks conference 17–18
  founding of UN 15, 16–18, 19
  Greek civil war 44
  Iranian crisis 1946 31–2
  Korean War 83, 84–5
  Lie's election 23, 24, 25–6
  Lie's peace plan 99
  Lie's re-appointment 68, 101, 102–3, 104
  Lie's resignation 127
  McCarthyism 108, 123–6, 129
  nuclear arms race 89, 90–1
  Palestine problem 52, 53, 54–6, 57, 58, 62–3, 157n79
  Truce Commission 157n80
  UN armed guard 59, 60
  post-war cooperation 73
  role of secretary-general 27, 28, 34, 37–9, 40, 84–5
  UN headquarters 66, 117–18, 120, 122
  UN Secretariat 110, 111, 114, 116, 123–5
  view on UN membership 41–2
  see also US State Department
UPU 97
Urquhart, B. 3, 11–12, 22, 109, 113, 114, 115, 123, 131, 137, 138
Uruguay 19, 155n24
US State Department 13–14, 16–18, 27, 84, 102, 126
USSR 163n26, 164n50
  see also Soviet Union

193

V
vacuum effect 5, 6, 71, 89, 104, 135, 139
  see also institutional pull
Venezuela 19
vetoes 17, 18–19, 20, 23, 41, 44, *68*, 73, 79, 93, 101, 103
Vietnam 42, 93
Vyshinsky, A. 80, 97, 99

W
Waldheim, K. 6, 133, 136, 138, 145n18, 151n109
Ward, J. 39
Warner, E. 97

Watson, T.J. 118
White, E.W. 97
World Bank 97
World Health Organization (WHO) 97
World War 2 31, 49, 72, 130

Y
Yalta voting formula 19
Yugoslavia 44, 92, 155–6n27, 155n24, 163n26, 164n50

Z
Zeckendorf, W. 120
Zinchenko, C. 113

www.ingramcontent.com/pod-product-compliance
Lightning Source LLC
Chambersburg PA
CBHW051545020426
42333CB00016B/2112